New Financial
Instruments
and Institutions

YASUYUKI FUCHITA
ROBERT E. LITAN
Editors

New Financial Instruments and Institutions

Opportunities and Policy Challenges

NOMURA INSTITUTE OF CAPITAL MARKETS RESEARCH
Tokyo

BROOKINGS INSTITUTION PRESS
Washington, D.C.

New Financial Instruments and Institutions:
Opportunities and Policy Challenges may be ordered from:
BROOKINGS INSTITUTION PRESS, c/o HFS
P.O. Box 50370, Baltimore, MD 21211-4370
Tel.: 800/537-5487; 410/516-6956; Fax: 410/516-6998
Internet: www.brookings.edu

Library of Congress Cataloging-in-Publication data
New financial instruments and institutions : opportunities and policy challenges /
Yasuyuki Fuchita, Robert E. Litan, editors.
    p.   cm.
Includes bibliographical references and index.
ISBN-13: 978-0-8157-2983-9 (pbk. : alk. paper)
ISBN-10: 0-8157-2983-9 (pbk. : alk. paper)
1. Finance—Japan. 2. Financial institutions—Japan. 3. Finance—Japan—
Technological innovations. 4. Japan—Economic policy—1989– 5. Finance—United
States—Technological innovations. I. Fuchita, Yasuyuki, 1958– II. Litan, Robert E.,
1950–
HG187.J3N49 2007
332.10952—dc22   2007018701

9 8 7 6 5 4 3 2 1

The paper used in this publication meets minimum requirements of the
American National Standard for Information Sciences—Permanence of Paper for
Printed Library Materials: ANSI Z39.48-1992.

Typeset in Adobe Garamond

Composition by R. Lynn Rivenbark
Macon, Georgia

Printed by R. R. Donnelley
Harrisonburg, Virginia

Contents

     Jennifer E. Bethel and Allen Ferrell

7   The Development of Improved Exchange-Traded
     Funds in the United States   193
     Todd J. Broms and Gary L. Gastineau
     Comment on chapters 6 and 7 by Kenneth E. Scott   210

     Contributors   217

     Index   219

Preface

THE BROOKINGS INSTITUTION and the Nomura Institute of Capital Markets Research have joined in a collaborative project, headed by Robert Litan, Brookings senior fellow, and Yasuyuki Fuchita, director of the Nomura Institute of Capital Markets Research, to conduct research in selected topics of financial market structure and regulation.

In October 2004 an introductory seminar was held at the Brookings Institution on the subject of the financial services industry in the aftermath of the Gramm-Leach-Bliley (GLB) Financial Modernization Act. The papers and a summary of that seminar are available on the website of the Tokyo Club Foundation for Global Studies (www.tcf.or.jp/seminars/2004/20041005.html), which is underwriting this annual forum and publication of a conference volume. A first volume, *Financial Gatekeepers: Can They Protect Investors?* was published in 2006, featuring papers presented at a conference held at Brookings in the fall of 2005.

This current volume is the result of a meeting on September 12, 2006, at Brookings that focused on new financial instruments and institutions. All of the papers and discussion comments represent the views of the authors and not necessarily the views of the staff members, officers, or trustees of the Brookings Institution or the Nomura Institute.

The manuscript was edited by Anthony Nathe. Jesse Gurman provided research assistance. Eric Haven checked for factual accuracy, and Teresa Wheatley organized the conference and provided administrative assistance.

New Financial
Instruments
and Institutions

YASUYUKI FUCHITA
ROBERT E. LITAN

1

Introduction

ONE OF THE most important characteristics of financial markets and institutions is change. The industry, and the products and services it offers, is constantly evolving in response to financial innovations developed by entrepreneurs within existing and new institutions and the ever-changing needs of users and suppliers of funds.

This book is about some of the recent innovations—especially new financial instruments—and new institutions that are changing the financial sectors in the United States and Japan. It contains the papers presented, and the formal remarks of discussants, at the third annual conference of financial issues of mutual interest to the two countries held at the Brookings Institution on September 12, 2006, and cosponsored by Brookings and the Tokyo Club Foundation for Global Studies.[1]

As in the volume produced for the second annual conference, which focused on the "financial gatekeepers," the third annual conference highlighted some interesting contrasts and commonalities in finance in the two countries.[2] For one thing, it will be clear from reading the papers on Japanese finance that financial innovation in Japan has taken its cue from the United States and is proceeding more rapidly than many in America (and possibly in other countries) may realize.

---

1. The Tokyo Club Foundation for Global Studies was established by Nomura Securities Co., Ltd., in 1987 as a nonprofit organization for promoting studies in the management of the global economy.

2. Fuchita and Litan (2006).

For another, in at least one important market—the secondary market for residential mortgages—Japan shows evidence of learning from the United States, specifically what features are best to adopt and those that are best to avoid.

As for the U.S. financial market, this volume focuses on the growth of two relatively new, and in some circles controversial, financial institutions: hedge funds and private equity funds. The two main financial instruments of interest are *structured products*—investment vehicles whose performance depends on the performance of some other underlying instrument (and thus are analogous to derivatives)—and *exchange-traded funds*, or EFTs, increasingly popular means of asset diversification that are alternatives to mutual funds. All of these institutions and products illustrate the seemingly never-ending ingenuity of the financial services industry to come up with new methods for financing or hedging risks—but at the same time each raises novel legal and policy issues, or in some cases, risks. If Japan's history in adapting U.S. institutions and financial instruments continues to repeat itself, then surely at some future conference we will be considering how Japan has adapted and refined the more innovative U.S. institutions and instruments that we feature here.

Meanwhile, we believe the chapters that follow provide an excellent overview and introduction to some of the more innovative developments in finance today—for the benefit of investors, policymakers, and regulators who may not have the time to keep up with the seemingly dizzying pace of change in the financial markets.

This volume begins with two chapters analyzing recent innovations in the Japanese financial market. Chapter 2, by Yuta Seki, addresses the development and increased use of two types of financial securities first introduced in the United States: exchange-traded funds (ETFs) and real estate investment trusts (REITs). Both securities are collective investment vehicles, offered to both retail and institutional investors. Both are also relatively recent in Japan, having been introduced in that market in 2001, although each had a very different history.

In reviewing the history of investment trusts in Japan, Seki notes that collective investment vehicles of all types (beginning with mutual funds) always have accounted for a much lower share of household financial assets in Japan than in the United States (the same is true of stockholdings). Japanese consumers have been more comfortable with lower-risk investments in bank accounts, especially at the country's Postal Savings Banks. Stocks grew in popularity during the boom of the 1980s, but growth halted after the stock market bubble burst in 1989.

In an effort to boost the flagging stock market in the mid-1990s, the Japanese government eased several restrictions aiming to encourage the growth of mutual funds. In 2001 defined contribution pension plans were first introduced in the country, which also encouraged demand for mutual funds. An additional boost came in 2005, when Postal Savings Banks for the first time began selling investment trusts. By 2006 net assets in such trusts reached a record level of 60 trillion yen. Still, however, the mutual fund market in Japan remains small relative to that of the United States, composing roughly 3 percent of household financial assets compared with 13 percent in the United States.

By 2001 the stock market was still languishing, as were the fortunes of Japan's banks, which still held significant corporate shares on their balance sheets. In an effort to bolster the stock market, and thus indirectly its banks, the Japanese government borrowed an idea from Hong Kong, where the government purchased shares in companies listed on the Hong Kong exchange. Essentially, the Japanese government did something similar, authorizing an organization capitalized by the banks themselves and other parties to buy Japanese stocks, but through a new index vehicle for the Japanese market, the ETF. But unlike the United States, which allowed exchanges and entrepreneurs to innovate with new indexes to serve as benchmarks for ETFs, the Japanese government strictly limited the indexes to which Japan's ETFs could be linked, ostensibly to "maintain balance in price formation and to prevent price manipulation."

Since 2001 ETFs have grown in Japan, but not at the rapid pace seen in the United States, where by 2006 the outstanding volume of such instruments (roughly $335 billion) outstripped the volume in Japan by a factor of roughly 10 (at $35 billion). Given the greater popularity of mutual funds—the ETF's main rival—in the United States, this is not surprising. In addition, Seki points out that the first Japanese ETF was based on a relatively new index, the Nikkei 300, which was not well known to Japanese investors.

Further, after an initial increase in their number, some ETFs in Japan have been delisted in recent years, giving Japanese investors less choice than is available to American investors.

Seki is cautious in predicting the future growth of Japanese ETFs but offers several recommendations for increasing their popularity, including expansion in the number of ETF products, efforts to improve understanding and to promote the purchase of ETFs by Japanese investors, and diversification of distribution channels (primarily in defined contribution pension plans, a step he suggests is also needed in the United States).

Seki next turns his attention to another collective investment vehicle pioneered in the United States and later copied in Japan: the real estate investment trust (REIT). REITs are securities backed by estate holdings and pass through their returns (minus fees of their managers) to investors. They were first introduced in the United States in 1960 and became especially popular for investors with high fixed returns (with some prospects for capital gains) after the Tax Reform Act of 1986, which among other things also allowed REITs to manage as well as own real estate. Initially REITs were issued as initial public offerings (IPOs), but by the mid-1990s many established REITs were raising funds through secondary offerings. Over time, the investor base for U.S.-issued REITs expanded, especially as pension funds and foreign investors grew interested in the securities as a way to invest in U.S. real estate in an efficient, diversified manner.

REITs were introduced into Japan in 2001, through a vehicle popularly known as the *J-REIT*. That they were not introduced earlier was due to the absence of securitized loan and other investment products in Japan. This began to change in 1998, when the Japanese Parliament enacted legislation authorizing the issuance of corporate bonds and preferred stock backed by leasing credit receivables and revenue from commercial real estate. The legalization of the J-REIT came several years later.

The J-REIT is legally defined in Japan as an investment trust, in contrast to the corporate structure (with pass-through tax features) common in the United States. Seki describes other features of the J-REIT, concluding that it is more complicated from a legal point of view than its U.S. counterpart.

J-REITs have become relatively popular investment vehicles in Japan for several reasons according to Seki. First, they have offered higher yields than have been available on low-interest Japanese government bonds. Second, the low interest rate environment has enabled J-REITs to finance their real estate acquisitions at low cost. Third, Seki argues that the strong disclosure in the prospectuses of the J-REITs, including announcement of the expected amounts of dividends, encourages investors to buy them.

Banks and investment trusts (investment vehicles that purchase shares in as many as 10 to 15 individual REITs) have become the dominant purchasers of J-REITs, although retail investors also have been important purchasers. In the process, J-REITs have lowered the cost of capital (or capitalization rate) for real estate properties, while making the Japanese real estate market more liquid and transparent. Still, as with equity collective investment vehicles, the total REIT market in Japan is about one-tenth as large as that in the United States.

Looking ahead, Seki suggests that in the future it is likely that Japanese policymakers will have to wrestle with how to deal with conflicts and possibly other problems posed by having outside managers oversee the real estate held by J-REITs. In particular, there has been some concern about J-REITs investing in buildings that are not built according to seismic codes (and thus are technically illegal). Meanwhile, the existence and growth of both ETFs and REITs in Japan should continue to offer global investors a way of investing in Japan through diversified financial vehicles.

Yasuyuki Fuchita in chapter 3 discusses how Japan has successfully adapted, and arguably improved upon, yet another American financial innovation: the securitization of mortgages. The importance of this financial innovation cannot be overstated. The notion has been that individual mortgages can be pooled together in a trust and securities sold to the broader public representing proportionate interests in the trust. Agencies directly or loosely affiliated with the U.S. government—Fannie Mae, Freddie Mac, and Ginnie Mae, in particular—have guaranteed the interest and principal of these securities, giving comfort to a wide class of retail and institutional investors. Today, about 70 percent of all U.S. mortgages are guaranteed in this way. This securitization process has enabled global capital markets, and not just the U.S. financial institutions originating the mortgages, to finance the construction and sale of residential real estate.

Fuchita documents how Japan is in the process of catching up to the United States in the securitization of its residential mortgages. Still, however, the Japanese market in such securities—residential mortgage–backed securities (RMBS)—is small by comparison with that of the United States. But this is rapidly changing, and Fuchita documents how.

In particular, historically Japan encouraged residential ownership largely through government-provided subsidies on mortgage loans. At times, such subsidized loans, extended by the Government Housing Loan Corporation (GHLC), have accounted for over half of new mortgages. In recent years, however, the GHLC has essentially ended its subsidy program, substituting instead a system of securitizing loans originated by private lenders. For example, from roughly 0.5 trillion yen in 2001, the Japanese RMBS market increased to 5.0 trillion yen in 2005. Fuchita describes the institutional arrangements under which GHLC operated during this period, as well as the nature of the subsidies it provided in previous years.

But reform has not stopped there. Writing in late 2006, Fuchita reports that as of April 2007, the GHLC will be dissolved and will be replaced by a new independent housing agency, the Japan Housing Finance Services Agency (JHFSA). The primary task of the new JHFSA will be to provide support for the securitization of residential loans originated by private lenders. The JHFSA will be modeled on the operations of Fannie Mae in the United States—but with one notable exception. Unlike Fannie Mae, which both securitizes loans and also purchases loans and holds them in portfolio, the JHFSA will concentrate only on securitization and will not hold mortgages. Thus the JHFSA should not be subject to the "interest-rate" risk—the risk to shareholder capital arising from the difference in maturity of assets and liabilities—that has been a lightning rod for criticism of Fannie Mae. Much of Fuchita's chapter is devoted to explaining how the new JHFSA will operate and the nature of the guarantees it will provide.

Over time, the JHFSA and the new securitization process should change mortgage finance in much the same way securitization changed housing finance in the United States. Currently, about 25 percent of Japan's residential mortgages are securitized, far short of the nearly 70 percent in the United States. One can reasonably expect this differential to narrow. At the same time, given the rapid aging of the Japanese population, the demand for new housing will not grow as fast as in earlier periods. This will reduce the relative importance of housing in the Japanese economy over time.

Fuchita concludes his analysis by pondering several possible futures for the JHFSA in this environment: It may stay as a government agency, or eventually it may be privatized in some form (as has been the case in the United States with Fannie Mae and Freddie Mac). One potentially heretical possibility if the agency is privatized is that it will merge with another large, private Japanese financial institution.

In sum, Japanese financial markets continue to evolve, as have those in the United States. Japan's private institutions and its policymakers learn from developments in the United States and adapt them to their market. It is hoped that the learning process will entail fewer difficulties that seem inevitably to come with financial market leadership.

The next two chapters focus on the U.S. financial market and two financial institutions offering new opportunities for investment. One of the major financial institutions, though it has been around since the late 1940s, is the hedge fund, a limited partnership vehicle that typically holds shorter-term positions in the debt and equities of public companies. Some hedge funds invest in other financial instruments as well. We nonetheless treat the hedge fund as "new" primarily because of the rapid growth in this particular form of investment vehicle. In chapter 4, Frank Partnoy and Randall Thomas examine the rise of hedge fund "activism," which they view as a logical extension of activism by institutional investors in general.

Economists typically distinguish between two ways that shareholders can be active, that is, ways to influence corporate behavior, especially of underperforming companies: "exit" (selling shares) or "voice" (voting their shares in favor of certain directors or corporate governance rules, or more directly by negotiating with managers about ways to improve company performance). Historically, institutional investors have preferred the strategy of exit to voice; it is much easier, after all, simply to sell the stock of a company not doing well than to take the time and energy to persuade its management to change course. The authors note, however, that this began to change in the 1990s, as some institutional investors—public pension funds and labor unions, in particular—decided to exercise their relatively large voting positions to make their views known to corporate managers. In principle, this should be a welcome development, since precisely because of their relatively large share holdings, institutional investors have a stronger financial incentive than smaller investors to monitor the activities of the corporation and thus to reduce the "agency costs" arising out of the separation of ownership from control of public companies.

The authors point to some recent public policy developments that reflect this view. The Securities and Exchange Commission in 1992 made two major changes in proxy voting rules that facilitated activism by institutional investors. The following decade, in 2003, the SEC required mutual funds, the largest class of institutional investors, to disclose how they were voting the proxies of firms in which they owned shares. The objective of this rule change was to expose any potential conflicts of interests at funds that had close ties with company managements (for example, by managing the employee pension funds at those firms).

These rule changes have helped to offset the effect of other rules that have the effect of discouraging activism on the part of institutional investors. In particular, section 13(d) of the Securities Exchange Act requires any "group" holding more than 5 percent of any class of equity of public companies to disclose their ownership, a rule that has the effect of discouraging institutional investors from acquiring enough stock to trigger this disclosure requirement. In addition, insider trading rules can apply to institutional investors and thus can discourage them from acquiring large blocks of stock as well.

Despite these barriers, the authors report that some institutional investors have found various ways to exercise their voice: by announcing to the public how they have voted their shares, explicitly identifying underperforming companies, and in extreme cases, filing class action lawsuits against management misconduct (the authors discuss the pros and cons of such litigation in some detail). In addition, institutional shareholders have made use of the SEC's Rule 14a-8, the SEC's shareholder proposal rule, which allows shareholders, under certain conditions, to force corporations to include shareholder-initiative proposals in proxy materials. The authors note that, not surprisingly, such proposals have tended to be concentrated at poorly performing companies. Although shareholder proposals have met with mixed success, in recent years proposals dealing with executive compensation have attracted increasing levels of shareholder support. In some cases, institutional investors have used their bargaining power to negotiate agreements with company managers for changes in corporate policies.

In principle, the most direct way shareholders can influence corporations is through their votes on corporate directors, but state corporate laws generally give shareholders little or no ability to nominate directors for election. In 2003 the SEC proposed a rule that would have allowed large shareholders to nominate a limited number of directors, but this proposal generated such strong opposition—especially from corporate managers—that the commission withdrew it. The authors note that institutions nonetheless have found other ways to make their views about directors heard, notably by organizing "vote no" campaigns against particular directors. Such a campaign eventually forced the Disney board to remove Michael Eisner from the chairman's position. In addition, Disney agreed to another tactic employed by some institutional investors: persuading shareholders to adopt a change in the company bylaws to require that directors receive not only just a plurality of votes cast at the annual meeting but a majority of the votes cast. Still, despite the adoption of such bylaw changes at some corporations, at no public companies had shareholders actually withheld more than 50 percent of their votes from a nominated director, at least as of the time the authors wrote their chapter. And even if this occurred, the authors observe that most boards could still appoint any director not elected by the requisite shareholder percentage, even the same person that shareholders may have rejected.

Unlike other institutional investors, hedge funds typically do not buy and hold shares for long periods but instead engage in various types of short-term trading. Partnoy and Thomas distinguish between three broad trading strategies and offer their assessment of the social utility of each. Funds with informational advantages (or "information asymmetries," as the authors call them) can use their trading of shares to indirectly affect firm performance through their impacts on share prices. The authors note that this kind of trading often occurs when a hedge fund has uncovered negative information about particular companies. The sale of stock of such companies can provide a useful signal to the market, and the threat of this occurring can spur corporate managers to keep their companies from underperforming. The authors take a more cautious view, however, of the social utility of hedge fund trading aimed at inducing firms to change their capital structures, highlighting the dangers of market manipulation. They are even more skeptical of the value of merger arbitrage by hedge funds, when the funds bet that a particular merger will or will not go through. Because the interests of the funds may not be aligned with those of the firms or other shareholders, such activity can lead to mergers that reduce shareholder value.

Each of these strategies involves trading, and until recently these strategies were the only methods by which hedge funds influenced the behavior of firms whose shares they bought or sold. But some funds have begun to exercise voice in much the same way that some institutional investors have done during the past decade. However, because they are unregulated and operated by managers with strong incentives to realize returns for investors, the authors claim that hedge funds may be even better positioned to monitor corporate behavior than other institutional investors.

Is there any evidence that hedge funds are doing this? In an effort to answer this question, the authors report the results of their examination of a sample of Form 13D filings, which are required under the securities laws when any investor, including a hedge fund, acquires 5 percent or more of a company's shares. Although imperfect, the authors assert that the number of filings by hedge funds is a useful measure of corporate governance–related hedge fund activism. In their sample of filings during a randomly chosen two week period in 2005, the authors found that hedge funds indeed were the leading category among investors reporting a 13D filing, an outcome they argue is consistent with an increase in corporate governance–related hedge fund activism. In general, the authors applaud this development, although they warn of possible manipulations of corporate voting by hedge funds.

Hedge funds have their critics. As the collapse of Long-Term Capital Management (LTCM) in 1998 demonstrated, hedge funds that are permitted to engage in excessive leverage can put the entire financial system at risk. Although banks and other lenders appear to have been far more careful in their lending to hedge funds since LTCM, the authors note that concerted selling or buying by the funds of particular assets also can lead to systemic risk. The authors outline various ways hedge fund trading can destroy rather than enhance shareholder value. More recently, some hedge funds have resorted to litigation to press target companies to change their behavior, which the authors note raises some novel legal issues.

On balance, Partnoy and Thomas conclude that hedge funds are playing a constructive role by helping to align the interests of corporate managers and shareholders. At the same time, they express concern that hedge funds can act in ways that are inconsistent with this objective.

In chapter 5, Thomas Boulton, Kenneth Lehn, and Steven Segal focus on the rise of private equity funds in the United States, the other major financial institution discussed in this volume. Like the typical venture capital fund, private funds are typically organized as limited partnerships by a general partner with expertise in identifying underperforming companies with the objective, in most cases, of "taking them private"—that is, off the public exchanges. The purposes for going private are varied—to avoid the regulatory requirements and public scrutiny that are necessary parts of being a public company and to dispense with the need to satisfy Wall Street with meeting the quarterly earnings targets set by stock market analysts. But in the end, the main objective is to provide a much healthier return on investors' funds than is available in the public securities markets.

The authors present the results of their examination of a sample of 245 public companies that went private between 1995 and 2005. They offer several findings.

They confirm what anecdotal evidence would suggest, namely that the number and market value of companies going private has increased over time. Between 1995 and 1999, for example, roughly 20 public companies per year went private, with an inflation-adjusted market capitalization averaging $231 million. During the 2000–05 period, these numbers increased to 24 firms per year, with an average market value of $431 million.

Manufacturing accounted for approximately one-third of the going private transactions during the entire sample period, followed by firms in the services, retail, financial, and technology industries. Although technology came in last, the 1995–2005 period differed from earlier periods when virtually no technology firms went private.

As one would expect, the stock prices of the firms involved in these transactions typically increased when the going-private decisions were announced. During a three-day window following the announcement, the additional increase (over what would have been expected on the basis of general market movements alone), or the residual return, averaged 21 percent. A related finding is that the average residual return for management-led buyouts exceeded that for other going private transactions by almost 7 percentage points, which is inconsistent with the view (or the criticism) that management-led buyouts somehow involve or create an inherent conflict of interest that deprives shareholders of value. The very opposite is the case.

Firms taken private during the sample period performed substantially worse (measured by stock price returns or return on equity) than their industry peers, which supports the view that the prime motivation for taking firms private was to reverse prior poor returns. At the same time, firms taken private had significantly more cash, as a percentage of their assets, than their industry peers, which made them an attractive source of liquidity for those who took them private.

Finally, the authors shed light on the controversy over the costs of complying with the Sarbanes-Oxley Act of 2002, enacted to prevent the kinds of corporate financial reporting scandals that surfaced in the years before the act from happening again. Supporters of that legislation claimed it was necessary to restore confidence in the corporate sector and in the capital markets. Critics have attacked the act, and specifically the provisions in section 404 that require auditors to attest to the adequacy of a firm's internal controls, for imposing excessive costs on public firms. The data in the authors' sample lend some credence to the specific criticisms of those who have argued that the compliance costs of Sarbanes-Oxley have been especially burdensome on smaller public companies. For the entire sample of firms that went private, the compliance costs were estimated to be 1.3 percent and 2.6 percent of the firms' market capitalization in 2004 and 2005, respectively. However, for firms with market capitalization less than $100 million, these costs were estimated at 3.6 percent and 7.2 percent in the two years, respectively. The authors conclude that their compliance cost estimates are consistent with the popular view that firms are going private to avoid the costs of complying with Sarbanes-Oxley.

The next two chapters deal with new financial instruments rather than institutions or investment vehicles. Structured products are examples of such new instruments, and they are the subject of chapter 6, written by Jennifer Bethel and Allen Ferrell.

The authors begin by noting that *financial derivatives*—financial instruments whose value depends on the value of some other underlying financial instrument, such as an option or a futures contract—have been in use for some time, both by those seeking to hedge certain risks and also by speculators. A *structured product* is a new form of financial derivative that has no precise definition; the authors imply that it is simply a more complex, and often more customized, form of a derivative. Examples of these types of products include such exotic-sounding names as equity-linked or commodity-linked debt, collateralized debt obligations, reverse convertibles, and credit-default swaps, among other instruments (new examples of which are continuously developed). The market in structured products is rapidly growing, with nearly $50 billion placed in 2005 and a further 20 to 25 percent growth expected for 2006.

Structured products are sold to institutions or high net worth individual investors (or accredited investors, defined by the securities laws as individuals with at least $1 million in net worth, including the equity in their homes, and with at least $200,000 in annual income). The authors' main purpose in the chapter is to examine whether the disclosures relating to these new products provide sufficient protection, especially to these high net worth retail investors. The question is a relevant one because even for these investors the growing complexity of these products, and the structure of their payoffs or returns, can be difficult to understand, even given their income, wealth, and supposed financial sophistication. Furthermore, even privately placed structured products can be sold to the public, typically after a two-year holding period, with very little in the way of disclosure.

The authors review the various disclosure rules that do exist and find one of them wanting. In particular, while the sponsors of the asset pools that make up these investments must disclose the credit scores of the obligors whose loans are in the pools, credit scores say nothing about the risk of investing in the pooled product itself. In particular, they note, the product can be very risky (because of the way its payoffs are structured), but the assets that make up the product may have very little or no default risk.

The authors refer to two important changes that affect the registration and sale of structured products. One change is the deregulation of content of permissible communications during the offering of a structured product, although what is known as a free writing prospectus can be sent to potential investors. The authors are implicitly critical of the fact that while this material may not be misleading, there is no requirement that it provide a balanced view of the risks and benefits of the product. The other change, reflected in regulations governing the offering of structured products, is that issuers of these products are unlikely to face liability if the materials promoting the product were prepared and disseminated by third parties.

The authors observe that, while U.S. retail investors do not appear to have suffered significant losses due to disclosure failures relating to structured products, problems have surfaced in Europe. The Financial Services Authority (FSA) in the United Kingdom, for example, has penalized several companies for selling inappropriate structured products to retail investors. The authors worry that as baby boomers in the United States grow older and search for yield they too could find themselves investing in securities whose risks they do not fully comprehend.

The authors conclude by outlining several approaches for addressing this potential problem. One idea is to modify the definition of *financially sophisticated*, which would have the effect of broadening the required disclosures or perhaps even rendering some of these products unsuitable for certain investors who, by reason of their income or wealth, would qualify for them now. A second idea would be to raise the required minimum purchase amount of these products, which effectively would put more of them out of reach for some current retail investors. Third, the SEC or an industry group could maintain a web-based repository of offering memoranda for structured products; more information should lead to better investor understanding.

Each of the foregoing ideas turns on who can qualify or should be able to buy structured products. An alternative approach, being considered by the FSA as of late 2006, would tie the level of investor protection to the type of product, rather than to base it on characteristics of the investor. For example, structured products with shorter maturities (and thus presumably less risk) would be more suitable for a broader investor audience than would products with longer maturities. Whatever is done, the authors caution that too much regulation could drive structured products into the private, unregulated markets, where there is essentially no disclosure.

Chapter 7 deals with the rise of a particular new financial instrument: the exchange-traded fund, or ETF. The authors, Todd Broms and Gary Gastineau, are two individuals who have played an instrumental role in developing this product.

The authors focus their attention on the open-ended ETF, which is analogous to open-ended mutual funds, or investment vehicles that can continuously accept new investors. As distinct from a mutual fund, an ETF is a security that is itself traded. Buyers can "liquefy" their investment not by asking the issuer for a return of their money, at the latest net asset value of the fund (as is the case for mutual funds), but instead by selling the security representing the average value of the financial instruments in which the funds collected by the ETF are invested.

The ETF was first invented in Canada, in 1989, and four years later was introduced in the United States by the American Stock Exchange. Broms and Gastineau devote most of their chapter to discussing what they believe are two major advantages of ETFs relative to mutual funds: the additional shareholder protection they provide and their tax efficiency.

The essence of the shareholder protection advantage arises from the fact that ETFs do not offer what is essentially free liquidity, which is available to investors entering and leaving mutual funds. In the case of mutual funds, anyone purchasing mutual fund shares obtains a share of the securities position already held by the fund, at its latest net asset value. The new investor typically pays no transactions costs, and when he or she leaves the fund, the amount received is calculated on the basis of the net asset vale of the fund at the time. To the entering and leaving shareholder, liquidity is essentially free. But the fund itself must absorb the transactions costs associated with these activities, which acts as a drag on the fund's performance over time.

In contrast, creations and redemptions of ETF shares are typically *made in kind*: baskets of portfolio securities are deposited with the fund in exchange for fund shares when the shares are created; likewise, on redemption, shares are turned into the fund in exchange for a basket of securities. As a result, the creating or redeeming shareholder is responsible for the costs of his or her own activity. The other shareholders do not bear this cost; as a result, the performance of the fund itself is not subject to a downward drag. This is the source of the shareholder protection offered by ETFs, the authors claim.

The tax efficiency of ETFs arises from the fact that investors in an ETF realize capital gains or losses only from the sale of the ETF; they are not responsible for gains and losses on a flow-through basis, reflecting investment decisions of the fund manager. The authors assert that the ETF removes any conflict that may exist between taxable and tax-exempt investors, which is unlike the situation that may exist for mutual funds.

So far, investments made by ETFs are all based on indexes and thus are not actively managed, as is the case with many mutual funds. The authors conclude by suggesting that in the future managed ETFs also may be offered, which would offer the two advantages of the ETF structure generally to investors interested in having an alternative to currently managed mutual funds.

Reference

Fuchita, Yasuyuki, and Robert E. Litan, eds. 2006. *Financial Gatekeepers: Can They Protect Investors?* (Brookings).

YUTA SEKI

2

ETFs and REITs in Japan: Innovation and Steps for Future Growth

IN JAPAN, ALTHOUGH the markets for exchange-traded funds (ETFs) and the real estate investment trust (REIT) both emerged in 2001, each has a different story of how it came into being. The speed of growth of the two markets has also differed. However, ETFs and REITs are collective investment schemes traded in the public securities market, and both resulted from innovations in investment trusts.

Investment Trusts in Japan and the Emergence of ETF, REIT Markets

Like mutual funds in the United States, an investment trust in Japan is a collective investment scheme in which professionals manage pooled funds under a predetermined investment policy, similar to how mutual funds are managed in the United States. However, unlike U.S. mutual funds, Japanese investment trusts are not structured as corporations but as contracts (trusts). Investment trusts in Japan are mainly invested in securities. Further, because of the strict regulatory separation between commercial banks and investment banks, beneficial securities in investment trusts are sold only by broker-dealers and are usually managed by the asset management firms affiliated with the broker-dealers. As a result, investment trusts were not widely introduced to individual investors. At the same time, an environment did not exist in which the fund managers could compete and grow

15

on the merits of their investment performances and the popularity among the investors.

The Investment Trust Market in Japan: History of Regulatory Reform

Historically in Japan, the share of the investment trusts in the financial assets of individuals was not much smaller than the share of mutual funds in the financial assets of individuals in the United States. However, the gap between the two has been expanding since the 1980s. The assets of mutual funds in the United States have grown rapidly as a result of the long-term increase in equity prices, the introduction of defined contribution pension plans, and the increased participation of the baby-boom generation in the securities markets. This growth helped develop an investment management industry in the United States in which independent management firms compete on the basis of investment strategies and performances, while the growth of the investment trust market in Japan remained stagnant. The divergent trends of growth resulted in a further widening of the gap, especially since in Japan distribution was limited.

During the major restructuring effort of the financial system in Japan through deregulation (the Big Bang program), the government believed that it was crucial to expand and grow the investment trust market to revive the depressed securities market. The government realized that the concentration of household assets in bank deposits and postal savings (a deposit scheme run by the Japanese Postal Service) prevented the capital market from maturing. It was expected that investment trusts would be the driving force in the diversification of household assets as well as in the growth of capital markets.

The Japanese government undertook major restructurings of the investment trust system in 1995 and 1998. The first priority of the government during this restructuring period was to ease regulations on investment trust management companies, while maintaining securities as the main investment choice. As a result of these restructurings, many foreign management companies entered the Japanese market for the first time and helped develop a highly competitive fund management industry. At the same time, allowing the banks to sell investment trusts in their branches contributed greatly to the growth of the industry. It encouraged individual investors who had deposited a majority of their assets at the banks and who previously had not been interested in asset management to buy investment trusts.

In a complementary action, the amendment of the Investment Trust Act of 1998 introduced privately placed investment trusts and corporate-type investment trusts and bolstered requirements for disclosure. Privately placed investment trusts, whose membership can range from two to forty-nine accredited investors, have been used by corporate pensions, regional banks, and credit unions, and assets in such private trusts are increasing. Investment corporations were finally established in Japan after several attempts to introduce such company-type funds based on foreign models. Although investment corporations have a governance mechanism similar to that of other corporations (for example, operating officers, unit holders meetings, and so on), asset management companies did not use investment corporations at all until the emergence of REITs, because investment corporations were required to have independent directors and the administrative costs were high. To this day most securities investment trusts are still contract-type, and most investment corporations are REITs.

The amendment to the Investment Trust Act in 2000 was intended to form a new framework for financial services regulations. Traditionally, regulations of Japanese financial services were created on a product-by-product basis. The amendment intended to change this framework and create rules to encompass a wide variety of assets. The amendment also reorganized regulations according to function with regard to collective investment schemes, in which assets are gathered from investors and administered and managed by professionals.

The Financial Council, an advisory body to the Japanese Financial Services Agency, established a Working Group for Collective Investment Schemes in its first subcommittee to discuss issues relating to investment trusts for ten months and on December 21, 1999, issued a report outlining the government directive for amending the Investment Trust Act. The draft of the 2000 amendment, which was approved by the cabinet on March 17, 2000, largely reflected the content of the Financial Council's report.

Important sections in the 2000 amendment include expansion of investment choices; regulations concerning investment trust managers (for example, strengthening of fiduciary duties, prohibition of conflicts of interest, among others); and establishing investment trusts that trust banks, as fiduciaries of certain assets, could manage for themselves. The expansion of investment choices in particular was epochal because it completely reformed the Japanese investment trust system. Along with this amendment, the name of the act was changed from the Securities Investment Trust and Securities Investment Trust Corporation Act to the Investment Trust and Investment Corporation Act.

Impact of Institutional Reform

It is widely believed that the combined easing of regulations and expansion of sales channels contributed to increased activity in the investment trust market in Japan. Simultaneous to the approval of sales of investment trusts in bank branches, the worldwide information technology (IT) boom played a role in invigorating the equity market in Japan. As a result, investment trusts became popular among individual investors, and in June 2000 net assets of publicly offered investment trusts exceeded 60 trillion yen (or ¥60 trillion), an all-time high. Then with the end of the IT boom and prolonged loan problems of the banks, the stock market in Japan stagnated again, and the net asset of investment trusts started to decline once again as well. However, even during this period of market fluctuation, the assets of publicly offered investment trusts (including ETFs) continued to grow. Since the third quarter of 1999, net cash flow (sales minus redemptions minus exchanges) of publicly offered investment trusts increased for twenty-eight consecutive quarters. And since the second quarter of 2005, cash inflow has been particularly rapid.

Competition among asset management companies accelerated, and the sales channels continued to be diversified and more open. By May 2005 all of the regional banks and second-tier regional banks (111 in total) registered to conduct securities brokerage business, mostly to sell investment trusts. In addition, thirty-six credit unions and twenty-eight life and casualty insurance companies conduct such businesses. It is particularly noteworthy that the net assets of investment trusts sold by banks and other financial institutions were about ¥22.9 trillion, while net assets of investment trusts sold by broker-dealers were about ¥22.8 trillion in June 2006.

In October 2001 defined contribution (DC) pension plans were introduced in Japan. According to the Japanese Ministry of Health, Labour and Welfare, about 1.93 million people were enrolled in company-type defined contribution plans offered by employers (as of May 2006), and about 65,000 people were enrolled in individual-type defined contribution plans (established in April 2002) that are offered to employees whose employers do not have an employee pension plan. As of March 2006, net assets of company-type DC plans were about ¥2.2 trillion, and net assets of individual-type DC plans were ¥1.1 billion. The research by Nomura Institute of Capital Markets Research shows that about 30 percent of these assets are invested in investment trusts. At the end of 2005, net assets of DC pension plans in the United States (for example, 401(k), 403(b), 457, among others) are 3.7 trillion U.S. dollars (or $3.7 trillion), and about 48 percent (about $1.78 trillion) are invested in mutual funds. About 60 percent of the shareholders of mutual funds initially purchased them through DC plans. Currently, the DC pension plan market in Japan is much smaller than that in the United States. However, DC plans are expected to contribute to the expansion of investment trusts in Japan as they continue to grow with the additional reforms to the pension system (such as increased contribution limits, introduction of DC plans for government workers, and so on).

The entry of Japan Post into the investment trust market is expected to have a major impact. Following the enactment of the "Act Governing the Certain Businesses That Can Be Provided by Japan Post" in December 2004, Japan Post began selling investment trusts at 575 of its post offices throughout the nation in October 2005. By June 2006, net assets of investment trusts sold stood at ¥226.3 billion.[1] By our analysis, although the level of postal savings at Japan Post (scheduled to be privatized in the fall of 2007) has been declining for several years, the total savings still stood at ¥196 trillion in July 2006, rivaling the total deposit of ¥250 trillion at the top three mega banks (Mitsubishi UFJ, Mizuho, and Sumitomo Mitsui). Japan Post has 25,000 post offices, which is more than the combined number (23,000) of branches of banks, credit unions, and credit associations. Individuals with limited knowledge of investing are expected to gain exposure to investment trusts through increased education and marketing efforts of Japan Post, which until now has limited the number of post offices selling investment trusts to ensure that its customers thoroughly understand the product they are buying. Japan Post now plans to expand the sales network of investment trusts to 1,500 post offices by March 2009 through an enhanced training program for its sales staff, and this expansion is expected to contribute significantly to the growth of the investment trust market.

Introduction of the ETF and REIT

Net assets of investment trusts in Japan in 2006 exceeded ¥58 trillion, approaching the record level of ¥60 trillion (figure 2-1).[2] While there appears to be a boom in investment trusts, at the end of 2005, the size of the investment trust market in Japan was still only 5 to 6 percent of the size of the mutual fund market in the United States. The share of investment trusts in the financial assets of households in Japan was 3.4 percent compared with 13.2 percent in the United States.

The investment trust market in Japan is still a small part of the overall economy; despite a relatively strong growth in 2006, investment trusts are not yet widely accepted among individual investors. There are many factors contributing to this situation, such as the recent poor performance of the Japanese stock market, difficulty in managing bond investment trusts because of the historical low interest rates, negative returns experienced by several money market funds in 2001, complicated forms of disclosure (the prospectus, for example), and issues with the tax treatment of investment gains. In the United States various investment strategies,

1. Data from Japan Post.
2. Data from the Investment Trust Association of Japan.

Figure 2-1. *Net Assets of Publicly Offered Investment Trusts in Japan*[a]

Trillions of yen

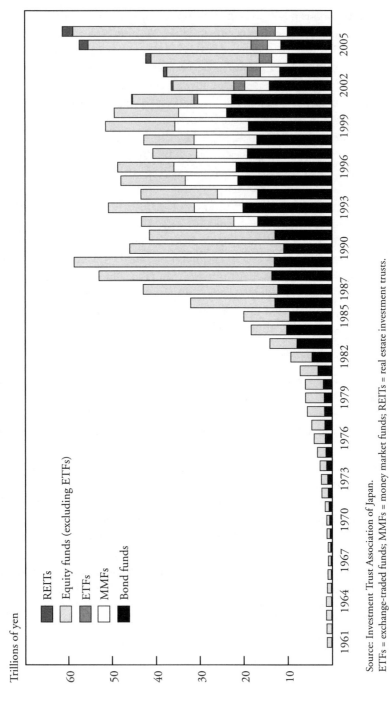

Source: Investment Trust Association of Japan.

ETFs = exchange-traded funds; MMFs = money market funds; REITs = real estate investment trusts.

a. Year 2006 ends in June.

such as indexing, as well as innovative products have been developed as the size of the mutual fund market and the asset management industry continued to grow. Japan, however, struggled to attract investors to its securities markets. The Japanese government envisioned reforming the investment trust market as a way to attract money to the securities markets and as part of the reform effort. Thus new instruments such as ETFs and REITs were created to turn investment trusts into more attractive means of asset management.

Development and Diversification of the ETF market in the United States

ETFs (exchange-traded funds) are, in general, index funds traded on securities exchanges. The first ETF in the United States was SPY (Standard & Poor's Depositary Receipts or SPDRs, called "Spiders"), which was listed on the American Stock Exchange (AMEX). Then DIAMONDS (Diamonds Trust Series I), QQQQ (NASDAQ-100 Index Tracking Stock or "Cubes," former ticker is QQQ), and others followed.

In the 1990s the ETF market in the United States developed mainly through the broad-based stock indexes that tracked funds, represented by the three mentioned above. In those days, SPDRS and QQQQ dominated the ETF market in terms of asset size and the daily trading volume. Taking advantage of the exchange-traded feature, proprietary trading departments of investment banks and institutional investors such as hedge funds frequently used ETFs for short-term trading and as hedging tools. At that time, individual investors seldom invested in ETFs.

Since 2000 the ETF market in the United States has experienced a rapid expansion, and in December 2006, there were 359 ETFs in the United States with a net asset of $422.6 billion (figure 2-2).[3] The marked expansion has been due to the continuous development of new types of ETFs that have enabled new ways to use ETFs and to attract new classes of investors.

Diversification of ETFs began in the late 1990s starting with regional and country diversification, followed by sector diversification and investment-style diversification. In 2000 alone, fifty new ETFs were launched. Barclays Global Investors (BGI), for example, aggressively developed new ETFs including those with different investment styles and set the trend for the rapid growth in the market. BGI expanded quickly and became the top provider of ETFs, rivaling State Street Global Advisers (SSgA), the manager of SPDRs.

---

3. Based on statistics by Investment Company Institute.

Figure 2-2. *Change of Net Assets of ETFs: Comparison of Japan with the United States*[a]

Billions of dollars

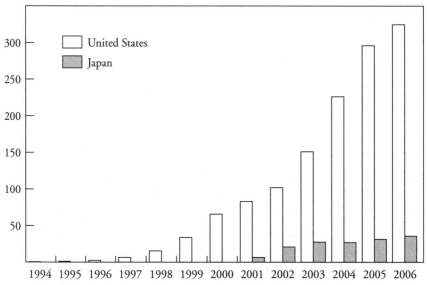

Source: Compiled by Nomura Institute of Capital Markets Research, based on data from Investment Company Institute and Investment Trust Association of Japan.

ETFs = exchange-traded funds.

a. Year 2006 ends in May. The net assets in Japanese ETFs were converted into dollars using the exchange rate at the end of each year.

BGI introduced an ETF linked to a bond price index in July 2002, thus putting an end to the notion that ETFs are linked to stock prices. The diversification in the asset class of ETFs began in the United States, and at the end of 2003, with the listing of an ETF linked to TIPS (Treasury Inflation-Protected Securities) bonds (iShares Lehman TIPS Bond) on the New York Stock Exchange (NYSE), ETFs began to be viewed as an inflation-hedging tool.

With the recent worldwide increase in energy commodity prices, there has been a race to develop commodity ETFs. The streetTRACKS Gold Shares ("Gold Shares"), which was listed on NYSE in November 2004, triggered the race. The streetTRACKS is a gold ETF linked to the portfolio of gold bullion that HSBC stores and manages in an underground vault in London. By April 2006, the net assets exceeded $700 million and gained popularity in the United States. BGI followed by listing its own gold ETF (iShares COMEX Gold Trust) in January 2005 and a silver ETF (iShares Silver Trust) in April 2006. Also in February 2006, Deutsche Bank sponsored an ETF linked to a commodity-price index, the DB Commodity Index Tracking Fund.

With the diversification of the products, market share of ETFs linked to broad-based stock indexes (the S&P 500 or the Dow Jones Industrial Average) has declined from above 80 to 70 percent, and instead the shares of ETFs linked to sector-stock indexes, foreign-stock indexes, or bond price indexes have gradually been rising. Regional and market diversification in ETFs is also becoming prominent. The ETFs linked to foreign-stock indexes (such as the MSCI EAFE Index, MSCI Japan Index, or MSCI Emerging Markets Index) set up by Morgan Stanley Capital International (MSCI) rank high in the asset size. Although the expense ratio of these ETFs that are linked to international stocks is higher than that of other ETFs, they have gained popularity. In other words, these ETFs that are dollar denominated and traded during the trading hour in the U.S. markets are being recognized as a tool for international diversification by the investors.

In the United States, ETFs were developed, in a way, as part of the competitive strategies of stock exchanges. For instance, AMEX, which once thrived with the initial public offerings of the new companies that did not meet the listing standards of NYSE, was losing listings to the Nasdaq Stock Market. As a means of reviving itself as a stock exchange, AMEX developed its own ETFs and aggressively promoted them to institutional investors.

With the ETF market growing rapidly, other stock exchanges started to list ETFs and trade existing ETFs listed on AMEX through unlisted trading privileges. NYSE has been particularly aggressive in listing ETFs; the number of ETFs listed on NYSE increased from 3 in 2002 to 135 in December 2006.[4] Further, NYSE has been the exchange for BGI since it agreed to move 61 iShares ETF listings there in July 2005. (BGI listed 40 iShares on NYSE in November 2005 and will have moved its remaining 21 iShares to NYSE by 2007.) NASDAQ lists four ETFs including QQQQ, formerly on AMEX. As a result of increased competition, AMEX is losing ground, but it continues to list newly developed ETFs by sponsors other than the big two (BGI and State Street).

Acceptance of ETFs by Individual Investors

Among the reasons for the rapid growth of the ETF market in the United States an especially notable one concerns the influx of money from individual investors. Originally, ETF investors were mostly institutional investors. Initially ETFs were mainly utilized for a transition trade by proprietary trading desks at broker-dealers or by hedge funds to hedge price risks of stocks through short-selling of ETFs.

---

4. Data from the World Federation of Exchanges.

Another reason is that there has been an effort to emphasize the benefits of ETFs. The minimum investment unit for ETFs is one share, which can be purchased at a relatively cheap price: about $120 for a SPDRS share and $35 for a QQQQ. Also ETFs can be traded throughout the day on the exchanges at market price and, therefore, have greater flexibility in trading and transparency in price than mutual funds that are priced once a day at the close of the market. Moreover, ETFs have lower management costs, even though the brokerage commissions are charged at sale. They are also tax efficient. Like index funds, ETFs seldom realize or distribute capital gains because they do not change the composition of the stocks in the portfolio frequently. Individual trades by shareholders do not affect other shareholders because ETFs trade the share of the fund and not the individual stocks in the portfolio. Finally, the dividends issued by companies in the portfolio could be an incentive for some individual investors to invest in ETFs.

In the1990s neither financial advisers in financial institutions nor independent financial planners were active in marketing ETFs. The ETF's structure had to be explained to clients, and fees were relatively low, so there was little incentive for them to recommend ETFs. When they sell actively managed mutual funds, financial advisers receive not only front-end load fees but also agent fees paid from the fund's assets in the form of a 12b-1 fee. With ETFs, however, they receive fees only once, at the time of sale.

However, there have been some changes in the environment surrounding the asset management industry in the United States. ETFs have benefited from well-publicized scandals concerning improper trading practices in mutual funds that surfaced in 2003. Certain mutual funds were accused of allowing hedge funds and other privileged investors to engage in market timing and late trading that were generally discouraged for or prohibited to regular investors. With ETFs, such impropriety could not occur. Also, no incentive compensation can be exchanged between management companies and sales companies, another issue mutual funds have had to face. The transparency and low costs of ETFs have attracted the attention of investors who lost confidence in the mutual funds.

At the same time, the players in the ETF market began emphasizing education and bolstering advertisement and marketing efforts targeting individual investors as well as financial advisers. AMEX, the central market for ETFs, and the two largest ETF management companies (BGI and SSgA) have been the most active in such efforts.

Moreover, emphasis on the assets management services for individual investors shifted from recommending individual stocks or mutual funds to portfolio management and asset allocation on the basis of each investor's attributes and risk tolerance. This shift contributed to the wider acceptance of ETFs by individual investors. Because ETFs reflect average risk and return characteristics of each asset class, they are useful for analyzing and formulating asset allocation. Further, with the diversification of products since 2000, diversification of portfolios by investment style and sector as well as by country can be achieved while continuing to benefit from low management costs. Some financial institutions began providing services to create a portfolio composed of multiple ETFs within managed accounts, which charge fees based on the asset under management.

The data indicating the ETF market share of individual investors are not available in the United States. Moreover, because of the large number of funds, it is likely that the shares of retail investors vary greatly among ETFs. However, in general, retail investors are gaining presence in the ETF market in the United States, and at the same time, the ETF market is maturing through a growth spiral created by the continuing diversification of products and the expansion of the market.

Structure of the ETF

The exchange-traded fund is a kind of index fund that is managed by linking to a specific stock index. However, while index funds are open-ended and can accept an investor's request for redemption or exchange anytime at a price based on the net asset, ETFs are basically closed-end funds whose shares are listed and traded on stock exchanges.

Although ETFs are closed-end funds, they often purchase underlying stocks in the portfolio and set up separate funds or make redemptions using the stocks. Such a process is called "in-kind creation and redemption" of an ETF. For example, management companies collect "a basket of stocks" that are linked to a specific index (for example, TOPIX [Tokyo Stock Price Index], Nikkei Stock Index 300, Nikkei Stock Average, S&P TOPIX 150) from institutional investors and broker-dealers (called "authorized participants") who hold a large number of stocks or brokerage houses, and in turn, the management firms issue beneficial securities in the stock index–linked investment trusts (ETF beneficial securities) that are traded in the markets.

It is possible to exchange beneficial securities with in-kind stock portfolios, just as it is possible to receive ETF beneficial securities by contributing in-kind stocks. In an investment-in-kind ETF, the stocks and cash are not exchanged for selling and buying of the investment trusts in the fund. Instead, ETF beneficial securities and the basket of stocks are exchanged between management companies and institutional investors or authorized participants.

Under such a management structure, ETFs may have arbitrage opportunity with the actual stocks; therefore, the net asset value of ETFs and the trading prices of ETFs seldom differ widely. Moreover, unlike traditional mutual funds, ETFs set up as in-kind investments could significantly reduce the cost of trading stock in the market, thereby keeping the compensation level of the trusts low.

Emergence of the ETF in Japan

The Nikkei 300 Index Fund, which was listed in May 1995, is characterized as the first ETF in Japan. When it was listed, the Japanese government revised rules related to the basic functions of ETFs (for example, establishing legal provisions related to the exchange of ETF beneficial securities and in-kind stock portfolios and enacting tax law provisions that treat ETF shares the same as stocks). However, these new rules could only be applied to investment trusts linked to the Nikkei 300 Index and not to ETFs linking to other indexes.

At the time, the Nikkei 300 Index, which began publication in October 1993, was a relatively new index. It was developed as an alternative to the Nikkei 225 because of criticism of the negative impact on the stock market caused by heavy trading of Nikkei 225 futures. In a sense, the Nikkei 300–linked ETF was a "political" tool to promote the popular use of the new index. The Japanese government's decision to limit which stock indexes could be linked to ETFs indirectly prevented the diversification of ETF products in Japan. In fact, a series of redemptions significantly decreased the net assets of ETFs, and new sales hovered at a low level, partly because of the lack of recognition of the Nikkei 300 Index among investors.

However, in 2000 the amendment of the Investment Trust Act had a provision stating that "an investment trust (excluding the securities investment trusts which government deems not to have the potential to harm beneficiaries) must be a money trust" (section 5-3). The Japanese government made this provision because of the concern that investors could be harmed if in-kind-type real estate investment trusts were to be formed with real estate and assets other than money. As a result of this provision, an in-kind-type ETF, which was a mainstream investment product in the United States, could not be formed.

In Japan, ETFs received much attention in 2001. At the time, the stock market was notably depressed with increasing dissolution of cross-shareholding between banks and companies. Although the Nikkei 225 Index was more than ¥20,000 as of the end of March 2000, it was below ¥14,000 at the beginning of 2001, and it was below ¥13,000 at the end of February 2001. Many people were worried that shares held by banks would bring massive capital losses, with the Japanese financial system subsequently facing a serious problem if the depression of stock prices continued. Because of this concern, in February 2001 the ruling government parties (the Liberal Democratic Party, the New Conservative Party, and the New Komeito) drew up and released a package for revitalizing the securities market. At the Economic Policy Ministerial Meeting of the Japanese government, the parties developed an emergency economic package. This package proposed the introduction of ETFs as part of a structural change in the securities markets, as well as a lifting of a ban on treasury stocks, the early establishment of the Defined Contribution Pension Act, and the reform of the securities settlement system.

The reason why ETFs were listed as part of the package for revitalizing the securities markets was that the government expected ETFs to contribute to the expansion of the investor base and the revitalization of securities markets. It was also expected that ETFs could be utilized as a means of purchasing stocks held by financial institutions, while setting a limitation on the number of shares held by banks.[5]

The Japanese government released the emergency economic package on April 6, 2001. The government expected to protect the health of banks by limiting risks of price fluctuations of the stocks held by banks to a level that the banks were capable of managing. It also expected that a reduction of cross-shareholding would promote structural changes and the revitalization of the stock market. At the same time, the government was concerned that a massive selling of stock by banks would affect the demand and supply as well as the price formation in the stock market, which in turn would cause instability in the financial system and the overall economy. Therefore, the emergency economic package proposed a framework for the stock trading scheme that would establish an organization to acquire stocks from the banks with contributions from the banks and others; purchase stocks from the banks at market prices; choose stocks for purchase with the intent of forming ETFs; and utilize ETFs, investment trusts, and defined contribution pension plans for the disposition of the stocks acquired by the purchasing organization.

5. Before Japan did, the Hong Kong government initiated a plan that consisted of two actions: using ETFs and purchasing stocks with public funds. When interest rates were rising just after the Asian currency crisis in 1997, in response to the speculators driving down stock prices by massive shorting of stock index futures, the Hong Kong government intervened by buying stocks in the open market in August 1998. In December of that year, the Exchange Investment Fund Limited (EFIL) was established to manage the stocks the government had purchased in August. EFIL initially sought to minimize the impact on the market by managing those stocks in ETFs and formed the Tracker Fund (TraHK), which was an ETF linked to the Hang-Seng Index. State Street Global Advisers (SSgA) was involved in the development, marketing, and management of TraHK, thus making management mechanisms of TraHK similar to those of the in-kind investment ETF in the United States. Although the market intervention by the Hong Kong government continues to be a topic of contention, TraHK is widely viewed as having had positive effects, such as increasing the interest of retail investors in the stock markets.

Acting on the emergency economic package, in June 2001 the Japanese government undertook a major reform of the Investment Trust Act (which triggered the expansion of the ETF market in Japan) by defining the in-kind contribution ETF as a securities investment trust that meets the requirements below and provides for the exemption of section 5-3 of the Investment Trust Act:

—The fund invests in the stocks that constitute the index so that the volatility of the underlying asset is aligned to that of the broad-based stock index.

—When accepting an invitation to invest in the trust, investors will receive beneficial securities whose composition is based on the ratio of the number of shares of each stock in the investment portfolio.

—The beneficial securities are listed on securities exchanges or in the over-the-counter market. The exchange of beneficial securities and the stocks represented in the beneficial securities is conducted according to the rules of the Cabinet.

In addition, the government amended the rules governing tax treatment of the newly formed ETFs to follow that of the shares in the Nikkei 300 ETFs.

Similar to the rules adopted when the Nikkei 300 ETF was introduced, the government limited the indexes to which an ETF can be linked.[6] The Financial Services Agency explained its reasoning for such limitation: "To maintain the balance in the price formation and to prevent price manipulation, we determined that the indexes [to] which ETFs can be linked should be composed of a considerable number of stocks, should not excessively be affected by the price movement of certain stocks, and should be widely accepted by investors (for example, the futures are traded on the stocks)."[7] These rules prevented innovations in products that are readily available in the U.S. ETF market. Unlike the ETFs in the United States that are strategically developed by a stock exchange (AMEX), ETFs in Japan are developed by management companies and are linked to the same broad-based index and listed on the stock exchanges in Japan. With the ETFs closely tracking the indexes, funds did not compete on the merit of management skills, and the existence of multiple, similar ETFs limited the asset growth potential of each ETF. Despite the surprising result of the lowering of management costs below the level of similar costs in the United States, the rules were not effective in promoting ETFs to investors. At the same time, the regulation did not encourage market players to increase investor participation in the market through innovative use of ETFs.

6. The Financial Services Agency designated, by announcement, the Nikkei Index (Nikkei 225 Index), the Tokyo Stock Exchange Stock Price Index (TOPIX), the Nikkei 300 Index, and the TOPIX S&P150 as indexes to which in-kind-contribution ETFs can be linked.

7. Financial Services Agency, "Public Comments on Amendment of Implementation Order of Investment Trust Act," press release, June 5, 2001.

Growth of the Japanese ETF Market

The ETF market in Japan in 2006 is the second largest in the world after that in the United States. However, net assets of the ETF market in Japan are about one-tenth of the market in the United States ($35 billion compared with $335 billion; converted at US$1 = JP¥115).[8]

The net assets of the Japanese ETF market were ¥1.5 trillion a year after the market was formed in July 2001, increasing to ¥2.5 trillion one and a half years later, and reaching ¥3.2 trillion in September 2003.[9] However, since then growth of net assets has slowed (figure 2-3). Although net assets increased just before 2005, the increase was mainly the result of the rise in the stock index. Also, in late 2003 redemptions of ETFs increased. The reason behind the increase is believed to be the increase of exchange transactions in which institutional investors bring their ETF shares to management companies and exchange them into baskets of underlying stocks.

In other words, when the ETF market was initially formed, the ETF was used as a means of dissolving cross-shareholding by financial institutions or as a vehicle to switch stocks in the portfolio. This drove the expansion of the ETF market for a while, but later, it is highly likely that financial institutions exchanged their ETF shares with the stocks because of the lack of diversification in the market and the investor base.

Another problem is that the number of ETF listings has been declining. Of the nineteen ETFs listed in July 2002, five delisted by September 2005; of the remaining fourteen, eleven were on the Tokyo Stock Exchange, two on the Osaka Stock Exchange, and one, the Nikkei 300 Index Fund, was on five stock exchanges.[10] The reason that the five ETFs were delisted was that the number of investors (beneficiaries) within one year of listing did not meet the minimum requirement for an ETF to continue to be listed on the Tokyo and Osaka Stock Exchanges. Thus investors were presented with a smaller number of ETFs from which to choose (table 2-1).

Considering market liquidity, the trend is that trading volume and trading values of ETFs are increasing. However, when comparing the trading values in each of the remaining funds, which are dominated by the ETFs linked to the Nikkei 225

8. The Investment Trust Association of Japan, Investment Company Institute.

9. The Investment Trust Association of Japan.

10. First, iShares S&P TOPIX 150 (former description code: 1315) delisted on January 9, 2004, and iShares TOPIX (former description code: 1307) delisted on September 10, 2004. Daiwa ETF-TOPIX Transport Machine (former description code: 1611) delisted on August 27, 2005, followed by Nomura TOPIX Transport Machine ETF (former description code: 1614) on September 3, 2005. At the Osaka Stock Exchange, FTSE Japan Index Fund (former description code: 1616) delisted on August 31, 2004.

Figure 2-3. *Change of Net Assets and Number of ETFs in Japan*[a]

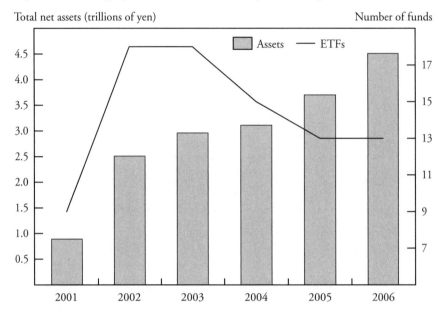

Total net assets (trillions of yen)   Number of funds

Source: Compiled by Nomura Institute of Capital Markets Research, based on data from the Investment Trust Association of Japan.
ETFs = exchange-traded funds.
a. Year 2006 ends in June. These data do not include Nikkei 300 Stock Index–linked ETFs.

Index or TOPIX, both of which are broad-based indexes, the trading volume and value of ETFs linked to sector indexes (such as banks or electronics) or the TOPIX Core 30 Index are small. Moreover, there is a difference in the trading value among ETFs linked to identical stock indexes. Further, according to the analysis based on the average bid–offer spread or average depth (sales volume per minute of trading hours) by Nomura Securities Quantitative Research Center, there is also a difference in the liquidity among ETFs linked to identical stock indexes.

Although the ETF market in Japan seems to have been steadily growing for the last five years, product innovation, diversification of the investor base, and liquidity in the market have not been sufficiently developed. Therefore, the explosive growth and expansion seen in the ETF market in the United States after 2000 has yet to occur in the Japanese market.

Yet the investor in Japan has an advantage—that is, the expense ratio of ETFs is lower. Ironically, the existence of multiple ETFs linked to identical indexes brought on the price competition among management companies. In the composition of trading volume of ETFs by investor type, the share of individual investors started to increase around October 2005 and now is nearly equal to the share of ETFs in the portfolios of foreign investors (figure 2-4). The recovery of the stock market contributed to this trend. Further, there is a possibility that individual investors have finally begun to appreciate the benefits of ETFs five years after the market was formed. At the same time, broker-dealers, especially Internet-based brokers, are aggressively promoting ETFs.

There is a possibility that the influx of individual investors mentioned above will lead to an explosive expansion of the ETF market in Japan. However, considering differences in attitudes toward asset management between Japanese individual investors and investors in the United States as well as the differences of market environments, there is a possibility that the United States–style rapid expansion of the ETF market will not be seen in the near future in Japan. By analyzing the experiences of the United States, several measures could be taken to accelerate the growth of the ETF market in Japan.

The first is to list diversified ETFs and to continue diversifying products. If the variety of sector ETFs (currently only two are listed), the ETFs linked to total market value, and ETFs based on investment style and regions are listed, then different ETFs could be combined as an investment strategy (such as a diversified international investment, long and short trades, or core and satellite management). Expanding the use of ETFs and the number of asset classes (for example, a bond ETF, an inflation-protected bond ETF, or a commodity ETF) as well as listing enhanced-index-linked ETFs (such as an ETF linked to a stock index composed of stocks of companies whose dividends are continually increasing) and fundamentals-index-linked ETFs will contribute to the increase in the popularity of ETFs among hedge funds as well as individual investors.

In Japan, increased recognition among the investors of ETFs through the listing of various foreign ETFs may stimulate product innovation. Currently, when ETFs listed abroad are sold in Japan, the foreign management companies issuing the ETFs must comply with the filing requirements in Japan, which impose a heavy cost. However, it is reported that the Financial Services Agency recently decided to abolish the filing requirement in 2007. In December 2005 the Japanese government eased regulations to allow disclosure in English of the financial statements and prospectuses of foreign ETFs. Further relaxation of the regulations is expected, including a new rule that will make it easy for Japanese individual investors to buy foreign ETFs.

A second possible measure to accelerate the growth of the Japanese ETF market is to promote diversified ETFs to individual investors. Securities exchanges, broker-dealers, management companies along with the Institute for Securities

Table 2-1. *Summary of ETFs in Japan*[a]

ETFs	Market	Index	Net assets (Millions of yen)	Manager	Inception
Daiwa ETF-TOPIX	TSE	TOPIX	356,603	Daiwa Asset Management	July 11, 2001
Nomura ETF-TOPIX			987,568	Nomura Asset Management	July 11, 2001
Nikko ETF-TOPIX			717,186	Nikko Asset Management	December 20, 2001
Daiwa ETF-TOPIX Core 30	TSE	TOPIX Core 30	8,364	Daiwa Asset Management	March 28, 2002
Nomura TOPIX Core 30 ETF			4,972	Nomura Asset Management	April 2, 2002
iShares Nikkei 225	TSE	Nikkei 225	4,845	BGI	September 4, 2001
Nikko ETF 225			719,459	Nikko Asset Management	July 9, 2001
Daiwa ETF-TOPIX Electric Appliances	TSE	Electric Appliances	2,181	Daiwa Asset Management	March 28, 2002
Nomura TOPIX Electric Appliances ETF			19,280	Nomura Asset Management	April 2, 2002
Daiwa ETF-TOPIX Banks	TSE	TOPIX Banks	4,652	Daiwa Asset Management	March 28, 2002
Nomura TOPIX Banks ETF			108,699	Nomura Asset Management	April 2, 2002
Daiwa ETF-Nikkei 225	OSE	Nikkei 225	440,021	Daiwa Asset Management	July 9, 2001
Nomura Nikkei 225 ETF			1,134,833	Nomura Asset Management	July 9, 2001
Nomura Nikkei 300 Index Fund	TSE, OSE, Nagoya, Fukuoka, Sapporo	Nikkei 300	22,573	Nomura Asset Management	April 12, 1995

Source: Nomura Securities Company, Inc. based on data from Bloomberg.

BGI = Barclays Global Investors; OSE = Osaka Stock Exchange; TOPIX = Tokyo Stock Exchange Price Index; TSE = Tokyo Stock Exchange.

a. As of the end of June 2006.

Figure 2-4. *ETFs in Japan: Change of Trading Value by Investor Type*[a]

Percent

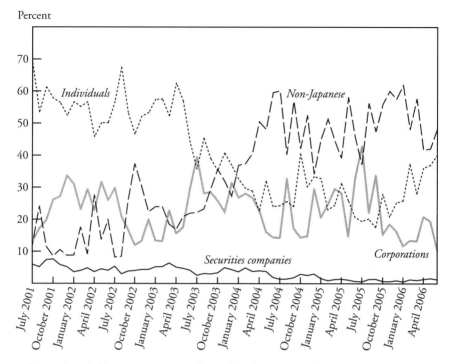

Source: Compiled by Nomura Institute of Capital Markets Research, based on data from the Tokyo Stock Exchange and Osaka Stock Exchange.
a. Trading values of each investor type are a percentage of the total. Aggregated values in Tokyo Stock Exchange and Osaka Stock Exchange.

Education and Public Relations are making efforts to promote ETFs in Japan.[11] However, they seem to emphasize only the basic elements of ETFs—that ETFs are investment trusts linked to indexes representing broad markets or specific industries and are traded on the exchanges like stocks. Few people understand the differences among index funds, investment trusts, and ETFs. Unlike in the United States where Barclays Global Investors, for example, publishes educational materials for individual investors as well as for financial advisers through its website, iShares.com., no organization plays a similar role in Japan.

11. The Institute for Securities Education and Public Relations is part of the Japan Securities Dealers Association.

Another possible measure is to diversify distribution channels. In 2005 broker-dealers started to offer separately managed accounts (SMAs) to retail investors in Japan. In SMAs and wrap accounts, which offer asset allocation, ETFs can be an effective tool to diversify assets in the portfolio with low liquidity, for example. While investors in the United States are familiar with such benefits of ETFs, they are seldom used in defined contribution pension plans. The main reason for this is that plan administrators are hesitant to make changes to the current investment trust platform or investment choices that largely consist of mutual funds. Japan could learn from this experience in the United States and aggressively promote the use of ETFs in defined contribution pension plans, for example.

Development of REITs in the United States

In the United States, a REIT (real estate investment trust) means a legal body that fulfills the requirements prescribed in the Internal Revenue Code. A REIT that fulfills the requirements can deduct dividends from annual corporate income, if it distributes more than 90 percent of annual taxable income that does not include capital gains. Therefore, investors can avoid double taxation. However, the reality of the REIT is that it represents more than a mere passive securitization vehicle. Most REITs are corporations founded under the corporate laws of the states where they were incorporated. As a result of an amendment to the law in 1986, REITs do not need to outsource management. Therefore, as an organization, a REIT in the United States is a "company" while a J-REIT is a "fund." REIT shares listed on exchanges are simply listed securities. Publicly traded REITs are regulated by federal securities regulations and all the other regulations governing the trades of securities.

The literal Japanese translation of *investment trust* is a securities investment fund that is similar to a mutual fund in the United States; therefore, Japanese market participants as well as government officials may have understood a REIT to be a type of mutual fund. Such perception may have contributed to the Japanese government's efforts to amend the Investment Trust Act to allow the creation of J-REIT, although it is difficult to ascertain. It should be noted that a REIT in the United States is not a mutual fund established under the Investment Company Act of 1940 and does not have the same structure as a J-REIT, which was established under the Investment Trust Act in Japan.

From Foundation to 1986

In the United States, the REIT was established in 1960 with the purpose of giving small investors opportunities to invest in large-scale, profit-earning real estate. At that time, Congress believed that the best way for retail investors to invest in commercial real estate was through pooling of funds. Therefore, it adopted a corporation-type investment trust that avoided double taxation on the dividends.

Initially, although REITs were allowed to "own" real estate, they were not allowed to operate or manage actual properties. In that sense, REITs were passive investment vehicles. The REITs were operated by outside management companies that received compensation but did not necessarily have an incentive to maximize shareholder values of the REITs. Therefore, the REITs were not highly regarded by investors.

Moreover, the property tax system of the time had a negative effect on the development of the REIT market. In the early days of REITs, investors were allowed to aggregate the losses from real estate investments with income from other sources. Thus investors had an incentive to raise debt leverage and to realize losses on the books by recording interest costs and capital depreciation. During the real estate boom of the 1980s, limited partnerships were frequently used because of their tax advantages. However, REITs were not allowed to aggregate profit and loss, and because of this, investors did not consider them to be advantageous as an investment tool.

The Tax Reform in 1986

The Tax Reform Act of 1986 included two important reforms that greatly changed both the real estate and the REIT markets. One reform was to limit, in a significant way, the aggregation of profit and loss between real estate income and other income. This reform raised the competitive advantages of REITs for investment in real estate. Another important reform was to enhance the function of the REITs by letting them operate and manage real estate. As a result, the self-managed REIT or internally managed REIT was created, and investors and managers came to share a mutual interest.

The effect of the tax reform gradually surfaced around 1990 when the U.S. real estate boom came to a turning point. The investments in and loans to the real estate market rapidly declined as the crisis of the savings and loan corporations (S&Ls), which surfaced around 1982, deepened and the quality of real estate loans continued to deteriorate as a result of excessive lending by commercial banks.

IPO Boom in REITs (1990–94)

When credit was tight, the U.S. REIT market underwent three major changes. The first was the growth of initial public offerings (IPOs) of REITs. The IPO boom in the REIT market was not brought on by a flood of new ventures going public. Rather many of the unlisted real estate companies, financed by partnerships and facing the need to raise capital in the stock markets, became REITs so that they could go public. During the commercial real estate boom at the end of the 1980s, mini–permanent loans with five- to seven-year terms were popular, reflecting an optimistic forecast for the real estate market and the loose standards of the lenders. When the loans became due in 1990 to 1993, property values had declined contrary to initial expectations. However, financial institutions did not allow refinancing, and as a result, many realty investment firms and developers faced cash flow problems. For such investors, going public with the existing portfolio was an alternative to refinancing. Another factor in the move to offer IPOs was related to investors who had purchased a large number of commercial real estate properties at a bargain price from life insurance companies or Resolution Trust Corporations (formed by the government to handle the assets of the failed S&Ls) and who now wished to liquidate their holdings by listing stocks on the markets. For those investors, IPOs of REITs were a way to raise capital for further growth or to realize returns on their investments.

The second change was the emergence of retail investors' buying of publicly traded REITs, in response to investment firms and developers looking for refinancing and exit strategies. Investors, trying to take advantage of the cyclical movement of real estate prices and hunting for bargains, began to appreciate REITs for their high liquidity and their quality of governance. The number of investors, which included individual investors, mutual funds, and pension funds, gradually increased as the listings and the market value increased, providing higher liquidity.

The third change was the development of UPREIT (Umbrella Partnership REIT). Under this scheme, REITs, operating as "parent companies," do not directly own real estate but acquire general partnerships or operating partnerships (OPs), which are "subsidiaries." Limited partners, who are owners of a partnership or other interests, usually include former owners and managers of the real estate. In other words, those who own the real estate through partnerships exchange their interest in the partnership with the shares in OP or the stocks of REIT. Because of the capital gains tax deferral in such exchanges, transforming a partnership into a REIT and acquiring a limited partnership through a REIT became easier.

Public Offerings and Mergers and Acquisitions (1995–97)

After 1995 the main method of financing for REITs changed from IPOs to secondary public offerings. In 1997, $263.8 billion (292 financing cases) was raised exclusively through secondary offerings. A stable economy and low inflation and low interest rates contributed to the stable revenue, and mergers and acquisitions in the REIT industry occurred at a brisk pace.

One of the contributing factors for the increased activity of mergers and acquisitions in REITs was the segmentation of the REIT market. After the IPO boom in 1993–94, the market was dominated by small and medium-sized REITs with a market value of around $150 million whose financing abilities are not so strong. Another was that investors improved their understanding and investment analysis of the REITs. Moreover, the gaps in performance among REIT stocks became more prevalent, and smaller REITs, which had questioned the costs and benefits of listing their stocks, sought mergers and acquisitions. The benefits of mergers and acquisitions included cost reduction and realization of economies of scale that resulted in a significant increase in cash flow at some REITs that in turn attracted investors. These REITs that acquired management skills through the process of mergers and acquisitions then challenged those real estate operating companies whose management style was outdated and solidified their place in the real estate market.

The Maturing and Expanding of the Investor Base (1998 to Present)

The Equity REIT Index declined 17.5 percent in 1998 after peaking at 3,020.11 in December 1997 and declined a further 4.6 percent in 1999.[12] Various factors contributed to the bear market. By 1997 the price of REIT stocks escalated, and there was a move to raise taxes on REITs. The securitized real estate market (for example, commercial mortgage–backed securities) was regarded pessimistically as a result of the Russian financial crisis and the collapse of Long-Term Capital Management, a hedge fund. The divergence of stock price movements of the IT sector (the new economy) and other sectors (the old economy) most likely was another factor.

From 2000 to 2005, in contrast, the NAREIT Equity REIT Index exceeded the S&P 500 index for six consecutive years. In addition to the booming real estate market in the United States, there was an expansion of the investor base. For example, pension funds, which mainly had invested through direct purchases of real estate, increased their real estate investments through REITs. Currently, the GM pension plan, the New York State Teachers Retirement Fund, CalPERS (California Public Employees' Retirement System), the Florida State Board, and others are believed to have invested over several hundred million dollars to a billion dollars in REITs. REIT investments enable big pension plans to diversify their real estate holdings. Some small and middle-sized pension plans have started to invest in real estate but only through REITs, instead of trying to diversify real estate holdings through direct investment.

12. The Equity REIT Index is compiled by the National Association of Real Estate Investment Trusts (NAREIT), the industry trade organization, and is calculated by a weighted average total market price of all publicly traded equity REITs.

Moreover, foreign investors are increasing investments in U.S. REITs. For example, ABP, a Dutch pension plan, has about $2.5 billion in REIT shares, composed solely of the top five REITs in market value as of the end of September 2005.[13] At the same time, after the amendment to the rules of the Investment Trust Association in 2004, Japanese investment trusts started to invest in U.S. REITs or in Australian Listed Property Trusts (LPTs), similar real estate investment vehicles in Australia, to meet the needs of investors looking for steady dividend income. At the end of 2005, the total net assets of Japanese investment trusts bearing such names as Global REIT or U.S. REIT reached ¥1.1 trillion, more than a half of which is believed to be invested in U.S. REITs.[14] Such inflow of capital from domestic and international investors supported the long period of rising REIT stock prices in the United States. The pace of growth in the aggregate market capitalization in the U.S. REIT market from 2002 to 2005 rivals that of the REIT boom from 1993 to 1997 (figure 2-5).

The J-REIT in Japan

The emergence of the J-REIT in 2001 seems to have reflected two major trends in the Japanese financial market. One was the financial reform including reform of the investment trust system. Another was the securitization of real estate.

Stimulating growth of the asset management industry and product innovation were two major goals for reforming the investment trust system. The belief was that easing the regulatory barrier of entry by new asset managers and expanding sales channels would encourage competition in management and sales, and the introduction of private-offering investment trusts would spur product innovation. The J-REIT emerged with the expectation that it would lead product innovation. In J-REITs, many Japanese investors experienced for the first time investment trusts that invested in assets other than stocks and bonds or closed-end exchange-traded funds.

It should be noted that the J-REIT market was created against the backdrop of the trend toward *securitization of finance* and *securitization of real estate*. The securitization of financial assets and real estate can be defined as a shift from indirect financing to direct financing in the broad sense and, in the narrow sense, as a shift toward pooling and packaging of the loans and real estate business revenues into securities. However, in the United States, the trend was first seen in the

13. Estimate by Nomura Institute of Capital Markets Research, based on the list of largest institutional shareholders.

14. Estimate by Nomura Institute of Capital Markets Research, based on Bloomberg data.

Figure 2-5. *Growth of the U.S. REIT Market*[a]

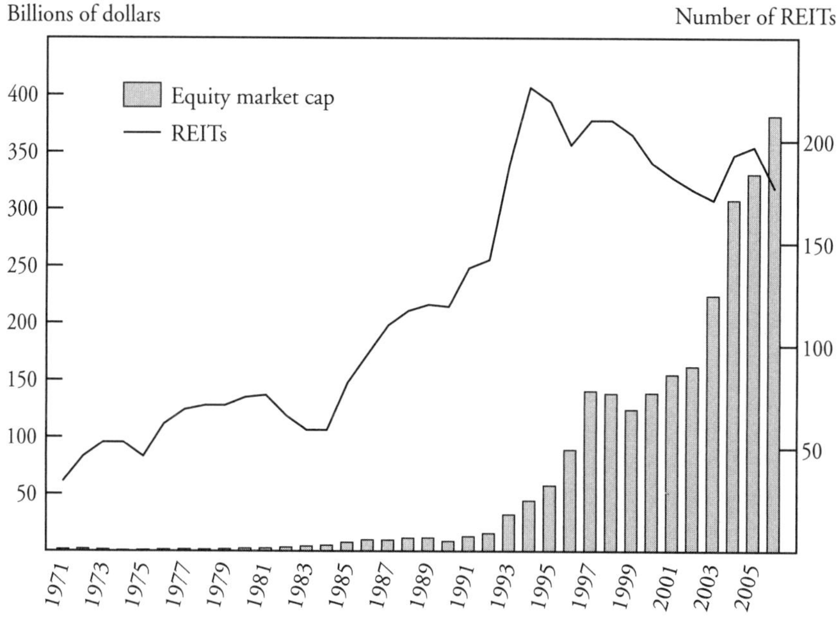

Source: National Association of Real Estate Investment Trusts (NAREIT).
REIT = real estate investment trust.
a. Year 2006 ends in July.

expansion of the residential mortgage–backed securities market that began in the mid-1970s.

In Japan, until the early 1990s, securitization of real estate was only a concept for feasibility studies, because of the aggressive real estate lending by commercial banks and because the price appreciation of land, which continued to rise, was not necessarily based on cash flow income. For example, when securitization was considered as a means of disposing of the land of the former Japan Railways, it had as its special purpose the concealment of the real estate transaction to prevent a hike in land prices in downtown Tokyo. Further, concerning property investment products, Japan did not have any laws that established any qualifications for fund-raisers or that provided protection measures for investors, given that the products were sold to retail investors at large. In addition, although small-lot real estate products were sold through certain legal schemes (such as trust accounts in trust banks or stakes in foreign real estate) in the late 1980s, values in many of them later collapsed because of sharp declines in land prices after the real estate bubble burst or because of other liquidity issues. As a result, investors and financial institutions distrusted property-related investments. Although under normal circumstances Japan should have prepared for a fair and transparent market for property investment products sooner, institutional reform was likely delayed because of adverse reactions to even the mere discussion of the property investment market.

The idea of securitization or liquidation of real estate to restructure corporate balance sheets came into discussion because of the experiences in Europe and the United States, and in particular the establishment of the Resolution Trust Corporation as a response to the loan problems in the 1990s. In open and mature markets, securities markets could be leveraged to promote the revitalization of the market and restructuring of the companies in the event that the liquidity crisis and loan problems arise in reaction to the real estate boom. Also in Japan, it was proposed that the opportunity to invest in real estate to help revitalize the economy should be as freely available as it was in Europe and in the United States. Japanese tax rules, however, prevented the creation of investment vehicles with securitized assets that could avoid double taxation.

The enactment of the Liquidation of Specified Assets by Special Purpose Company Act (so-called SPC Act, now called the "Law Concerning Asset Liquidation") in September 1998 provided for the creation and issuance of such investment vehicles as corporate bonds and preferred securities backed by leasing credit receivables or revenue from commercial real estate through special purpose companies (SPCs). However, most securitized real estate products were privately offered to institutional investors, and thus the secondary market for such products did not form.

J-REITs emerged as a securitization product and, like SPC corporate bonds, had the same legal recognition as securities under the U.S. Securities Exchange Act. J-REITs can buy real estate from companies in financial restructuring, thereby promoting asset liquidation to the same extent as SPCs. Both REITs and SPCs were expected to promote the securitization of real estate and to end the dependency on land-collateral loans.

Structure of the J-REIT and Differences from the U.S REIT

As mentioned above, U.S. REIT refers to the status of a corporation with regard to tax laws. Japanese tax laws do not have any eligibility requirements for REITs as do those of the United States; therefore, corporations cannot choose the REIT status in their tax treatment. J-REIT is an investment trust in which the main investment asset is real estate. Although the Investment Trust Act of Japan provided for the creation of investment trusts (contract-type investment trusts) and investment corporations (company-type investment trusts), currently all of the listed J-REITs are structured as investment corporations. An investment corporation is formed for the purpose of managing assets by investing in specified assets.[15] An investment corporation entrusts its asset management to an investment trust management company. If the investment trust management company manages mainly real estate, it has to acquire a license as a real estate brokerage agent and get an authorization of discretionary transactions before it can be approved as an investment trust management company.[16]

Also, currently all listed J-REITs are closed-end investment corporations. If funds that invest mainly in real estate are formed as open-end types, they could have trouble meeting investors' requests for redemptions because of the low liquidity of real estate. Therefore, all listed J-REITs are closed-end investment corporations, and they ensure liquidity of the investment securities by trading on the market instead of making redemptions.

An investment corporation issues investment securities, like a corporation issues stocks. An investor in investment securities can attend a unit holders' meeting, similar to a shareholders' meeting. A closed-end investment corporation can issue investment corporation bonds, which are similar to corporate bonds, under issuance limits laid out in its constitution.[17] In reality, the Investment Trust Act does not include definitions for a property investment trust or a property investment corporation but allows an investment trust to include real estate into its specific assets. Instead, eligibility requirements for operating as a J-REIT are provided in the listing standards of real estate investment trust markets (for example, the Tokyo Stock Exchange among others).

As explained above, the current J-REIT system is much more complicated than the U.S. REIT system. In the United States, the Revenue Act provides a clear

15. See art. 2, sec. 19, of the Investment Trust Act. "Specific assets" mean assets in which investment trusts can invest under a government order. Major examples include security; right in security index futures trades; right in security option; right in foreign security future trades; over-the-counter security index trades and other forward trades; right in over-the-counter security option trades; right in over-the-counter index trades and other swap trades; real estate, leasehold right of real estate, surface right; monetary claim; promissory note; right in financial future and so on; right in financial derivatives transactions; beneficial interest in trust of money, security, monetary bond, real estate, surface right, or leasehold right or real estate; and share of investment in silent partnership (art. 3 of the enforcement order of Investment Trust Act).

16. Although the prime minister of the Financial Services Agency approves investment trust management companies, the minister of land, infrastructure, and transportation issues the license for a real estate brokerage agent and approves discretionary transactions under the Real Estate Transaction Act (art. 6 and 9 of the Investment Trust Act). Actually "a discretionary transaction" business by a real estate agent was allowed when the J-REIT market started, through the amendment of a related law of the Investment Trust Act, to allow companies to operate under full discretionary capability (blind fund management) at the stage when specific real estate is not decided.

17. See art. 139-2 of the Investment Trust Act. This clause was added by the amendment of 2000.

definition of a real estate investment trust, its content of funds, and conditions for certain tax treatments. In comparison the J-REIT system is not unified under a single law: The Investment Trust Act provides the structure of the vehicle; tax law provides requirements for getting certain tax treatment; listing standards of securities exchanges provide asset requirements for treatment as a J-REIT. Given its multilayered oversight, J-REITS are difficult for investors to understand and also cause practical problems. For example, a person planning to start a J-REIT must get prior authorization or submit prior notification to various institutions.

Further, as mentioned above, the main difference between the J-REIT and the U.S. REIT is whether the REIT utilizes outside management or inside management. J-REIT is a fund; therefore, it must entrust real estate registers, registration certificates, and bank books, as well as business judgment regarding sales and management of real estate to investment trust managers. J-REIT is an investment trust; therefore, it can only engage in asset management as its business. Additionally, the standards for listing a J-REIT on the Tokyo Stock Exchange require that more than 50 percent of the assets must be real estate currently yielding (or expected to yield) rental income. None of the J-REITs has thus far invested in development projects. J-REITs are, in fact, very passive investment schemes.

In the past, U.S. REITs were also passive property investment schemes. However, the amendment of the tax law in 1986 allowed internal management of REITs. Although differences between REITs and real estate operating companies (REOCs) were nearly eliminated by the amendment, subsequent amendments took into account the status of REITs as active property investment corporations. For example, the REIT Modernization Act, enacted in 2001, allows a REIT to establish a taxable REIT subsidiary (TRS) in which the REIT can hold up to 100 percent of ownership. The act allows a REIT to supply a variety of services to tenants through a TRS governed by the REIT, while maintaining the exempt status from corporate tax. In addition, the act reduced the dividend restriction from more than 95 percent of taxable income to 90 percent, which was the standard from the time the REIT system was established until 1980. This reduction allows a REIT to accumulate more earning retention than before. It can be said that the U.S. REIT came closer to the REOC. In Japan, listed REOCs (such as Mitsubishi Estate, Mitsui Fudosan, Sumitomo Realty & Development, and so forth) have traditionally formed a main sector of the stock market. It is highly likely, therefore, that differences between J-REIT and REOC were factored into the law and tax law when the J-REIT market was formed. It remains a topic of discussion of how the differences in structure between the J-REIT and the U.S. REIT will affect the development of the market.

Figure 2-6. *J-REIT: Change in Total Market Value and Number of Listed Funds*[a]

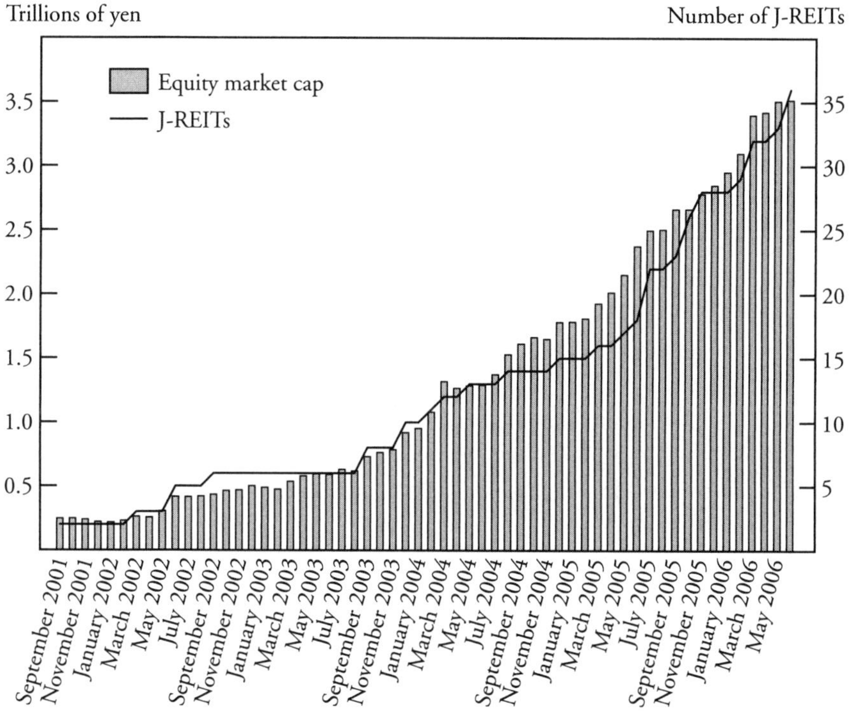

Trillions of yen   Number of J-REITs

Source: Nomura Institute of Capital Markets Research, based on data from Bloomberg.
J-REIT = Japanese real estate investment trust.
a. Year 2006 ends in June.

Expansion of the J-REIT Market and Contributing Factors

The J-REIT market was started when the Nippon Building Fund and Japan Real Estate, both of which are investment corporations, listed J-REITs on the Tokyo Stock Exchange in September 2001. At the time, the total market capitalization was about ¥260 billion, but as of August 2006, it reached ¥3.7 trillion with 37 listings (figure 2-6).[18]

The following factors have contributed to the expansion of the J-REIT market.

DIVIDEND YIELDS AND YIELD SPREADS. Corporate taxes are not imposed on an investment corporation if it distributes over 90 percent of divisible profit (including profit on the sale of real estate) in each fiscal period. This requirement

18. Based on data from Nomura Securities.

brings high dividend yields of J-REITs, which have attracted investors because the Japanese government maintained its low interest rate policy and because the stock market slump continued through the summer of 2005. In fact, financial institutions and financial planners actively promoted J-REITs as suitable for the asset management needs of elderly investors because investors received dividends every month through investment in several J-REITs with different fiscal terms.

Nevertheless, just after J-REITs began to be listed on the Tokyo Stock Exchange, the spread between the dividend yield of J-REITs and the yield of a ten-year government bond reached about 400 basis points. The reason for such a high premium was that investors were afraid of the credit risk and were concerned about the marketability of J-REITs. The terrorist attacks in the United States on September 11 and the bankruptcy filing by a major Japanese retailer, Mycal, three days later were also believed to have contributed to the high premium. However, investors' confidence in J-REITs has increased gradually since then, and the corporations initially listing J-REITs began to release financial statements and steadily distribute dividends. Although the yield spread between J-REITs and the long-term interest is still 170 to 180 basis points, the average dividend yield in the J-REIT sector has declined with the increase in the price of each investment unit (figure 2-7).

CONSERVATIVE DEBT LEVERAGE. The average cost of the debt for J-REITs has been about 1 percent, benefiting from the low interest rates. However, the average loan-to-value ratio is 30 to 50 percent, a sign that most funds have maintained conservative financial policies.[19] The reason for their stance is probably due to the lower risk of rising interest rates and to maintaining borrowing capacity for future real estate acquisitions. Another reason is that management companies of J-REITs recognized that the investors preferred to keep the debt leverage low. As a result, the relative financial stability of J-REITs in comparison with privately offered real estate funds was emphasized.

Yet when a J-REIT acquires additional real estate and expands its size, the J-REIT has to raise capital. Fortunately, J-REITs were successful in raising capital and expanding through additional acquisitions of real estate as their recognition in the market increased with the price of the investment units.

CONFIDENCE IN TRANSPARENCY AND PROFITABILITY. Strong disclosure is one of the characteristics of J-REITs. The prospectuses provided to the investors explain in detail the investment policies of the investment corporations, so that investors can learn the J-REIT's financial management policy; for example, "the corporation principally invests in existing real estate and not in development projects"; or "the corporation borrows only from accredited institutional investors

---

19. Analysis by Nomura Securities Financial Research Center.

Figure 2-7. *Dividend Yield of J-REIT and Yield Spread*

Percent

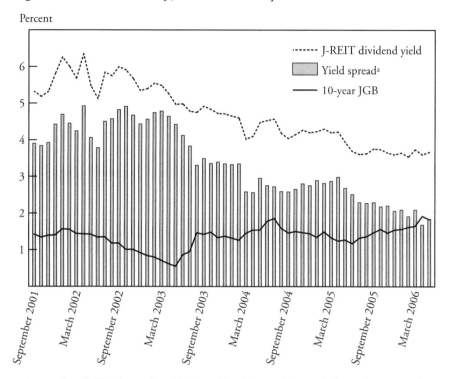

Source: Compiled by Nomura Securities Financial and Economic Research Center, from various data sources.
a. Yield spread = dividend yield of J-REIT − interest rate of 10-year Japanese government bond (JGB).

and only up to one trillion yen." Management reports and other related documents disclose address, dimensions of rental property, book value, term-end valuation, operating rates, number of tenants, rent income for each fiscal period, and other information for each real estate owned by the J-REIT. Planned and completed acquisitions of additional real estate are disclosed on a timely basis to analysts, rating agencies, and other related parties. The information on the earthquake damages to the real estate owned by J-REITs and the changes in the level of debt are also disclosed periodically. Considering traditional real estate deals in which only a limited number of players had access to information, such disclosure practices of J-REITs are significantly open to the investors.

In addition, management companies of J-REITs announce expected amounts of dividends. So far, actual dividends have almost always exceeded expected amounts, although this has been partly due to conservative announcements at each company. The transparency and profitability explained above gave investors a sense of security in the J-REIT market where dividends are one of the major factors attracting investors.

INSTITUTIONAL REFORM AND EXPANSION OF THE INVESTOR BASE. Looking at the past trading behaviors by investor segment, banks and investment trusts emerge as the most aggressive buyers of J-REITs and have led the market. It is believed that there were two system reforms behind this result.

First, in December 2002, the Japanese Bankers Association issued an instruction that allowed bankers to allocate gain sales of J-REIT investment units into gross income, which is income from the main business. This change in the accounting system as well as the relatively high dividend yield of J-REITs attracted banks. In particular, regional banks, which had sluggish loan growth and difficulties in managing their funds, started to invest in J-REITs actively. Also, because two of the J-REITs were added to the MSCI (Morgan Stanley Capital International) stock index in May 2005, institutional investors also started to recognize J-REITs as a valid investment choice.

Second, the Investment Trust Association of Japan classified the J-REIT as a type of investment trust, in which the association had a voluntary regulation preventing each investment trust fund from investing more than 5 percent of its net assets in other investment trusts. At the same time, the association limited the scope of investment by "fund of funds" only to securities. Then Japanese investment trusts were not allowed to hold J-REIT units over a certain amount. In July 2003 the association amended the regulation to treat a REIT as an eligible investment scope of a fund of funds. This amendment made it possible to form a REIT-specific investment trust in which the portfolio was composed of a minimum of 10 to 15 REIT securities. As a result, financial institutions started to form investment trusts for individual investors and distributed monthly dividends as a result of investing in multiple REITs with different fiscal terms.[20]

The Significance and Effect of the Expansion of the J-REIT Market

Reviewing the history of real estate deals in Japan, there was a tendency to not attach importance to "the ability to create a lasting and stable cash flow," which was a major feature of real estate as a financial asset because it was strongly believed that real estate did not depreciate and was a scarce resource. As a result, commercial real estate was seldom traded as a financial asset. It continued to be

---

20. This amendment of the voluntary regulation had effect not only on J-REITs, as mentioned above, but also on investments in the U.S. REIT or other similar foreign public real estate securities.

owned even if the owners did not need it anymore. Commercial real estate was traded only to acquire capital gains through development or resale. Each transaction amount in such trades is big. Further, because limited investors or limited market participants possess detailed information in such strongly closed trades, transaction costs are high. Therefore, there is little opportunity for retail investors to be involved in such trades. Because of the inefficient real estate market, the creation of a huge amount of credit was accomplished through land-collateral loans in the late 1980s. It seems that the emergence of the bubble was largely influenced by the fact that land appraisal methods relied not on the discount cash flow model but on comparisons with similar properties. In the market environment where there were strong expectations for increases in land prices, oversized financing of land increased the price of surrounding land and enabled the owner of the land to borrow more, and as a result, the pace of credit creation accelerated.

When the cycle reversed in the 1990s and land prices rapidly declined, the quality of bank loans deteriorated to a point that caused a crisis in the financial system. At the same time, real estate ownership was heavily concentrated among corporations and real estate developers, and there was no system for securitizing real estate. Therefore, when the loan problem emerged, it was not widely recognized how pervasive it was, and it remained largely unnoticed for many years.

Although the J-REIT market has not solved all the problems mentioned above, it can be said that the J-REIT market has had some significant impacts.

OPENING OPPORTUNITIES TO INVEST IN REAL ESTATE AND EXPANSION OF THE INVESTOR BASE. The first significant impact of the emergence of the J-REIT is that it opened the door to investment in real estate for retail investors. The J-REIT enabled diversified methods of asset management to become available for individual investors and for domestic financial institutions, which were puzzled over finding reasonable investment choices (figure 2-8). Foreign investors also aggressively invested in J-REITs. The expansion of the market was also supported by the 4 to 6 percent dividend yields of J-REITs, while the Japanese government continued the zero-interest-rate policy. Furthermore, many investors invested in J-REITs because they thought that the Japanese economic recovery would put upward pressure on real estate values. Expansion of the investor class in J-REITs indirectly activates trades of actual real estate. At the end of September 2006, the total value of real estate that J-REITs have acquired is more than ¥5 trillion.[21] It can be said that the liquidity and efficiency of the real estate market has been strengthened by the market participation of today's investors who have different ideas from those of traditional investors.

---

21. Data from Nomura Securities.

Figure 2-8. *Share Distribution of J-REIT Market, by Investor Type*[a]

Trillions of yen

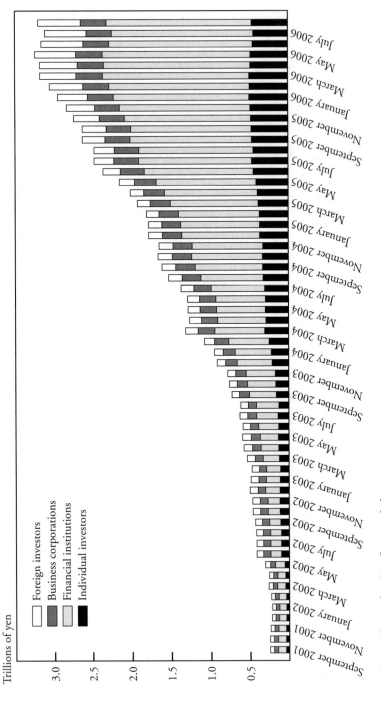

Source: Nomura Securities Company, Ltd.
a. Equity market capitalization.

CHANGES IN REAL ESTATE VALUATION METHODS. The J-REIT has influenced changes in real estate appraisal methods. Because a REIT is a financial product backed by operating real estate, its valuation methods are based on cash flow or earnings yield. It is likely that an extravagant appraisal will be adjusted by the market. Further, the expected returns that investors seek in the J-REIT market had an effect on the entire real estate investment market, and the appraisal methods for commercial real estate were changed to put greater importance on the cash flow and earnings yield.

In fact, dividend yields have been the most important factor in determining the price of J-REIT investment units so far. Study results show that dividend announcements cause fluctuations in the stock prices of J-REITs, drawing attention to how changes in the interest rate environment and other changes affect J-REITs.[22] However, given the experiences in the U.S. REIT market, substantial positive yield spreads are not needed for the growth of the REIT market; rather, total return is an important contributing factor for the growth of the REIT market.

CHANGES IN THE BEHAVIORS OF BANKS AND REAL ESTATE OPERATING COMPANIES. It is possible that the expansion of the REIT market has influenced the behaviors of the banks and existing real estate development companies, triggering the real estate bubble in Japan. Now, banks focus on project-based finances that are easily securitized, because it is highly risky for banks to increase commercial loans collateralized by low-liquidity real estate or vacant land properties, which are not suitable for securitization. REOCs are also avoiding exposure to the risk of asset price movement and instead are altering their business model to one in which they do not own assets and concentrate only on the management of the assets owned by others.

FORMING AN INSTITUTIONAL REAL ESTATE INVESTMENT MARKET. Because a J-REIT is a fund that distributes income gain from portfolios of operating real estate under a conservative financial strategy, it is possible to formulate the concept of an investment fund designed to exit through the J-REIT market. To be more precise, the fund invests in development projects, properties with a high rate of vacancy, and real estate collateralized for bad loans and sells these assets to the J-REIT after the completion of construction, acquisition of tenants, and adjustment of rights and obligations. Because such funds have a relatively high risk, the funds should raise capital through a private offering to a small number of investors and should set its debt leverage high.

In Japan, private real estate investment funds were actively formed as the trend of expansion of the J-REIT market became apparent. Foreign players (Morgan

---

22. Kawagushi and Hisatake (2005).

Stanley, Goldman Sachs, Secured Capital, and CB Richard Ellis, among others) and investment firms founded in Japan (for example, Pacific Management, daVinci Advisors, Creed) became fund managers of private funds. Many of the funds sell real estate that they own to J-REITs. At the same time, there are examples in which a fund looking to unwind its real estate holdings succeeded by appointing the fund manager as the sponsor of the J-REIT. It is important that funds operate with the mandate to increase the cash flow of operating properties and add value, instead of profiting from real estate development and rising land prices as happened in the late 1980s.

The market size of private real estate funds has rapidly grown in Japan and is estimated to be about ¥5.5 trillion at the end of June 2006, which is bigger than the J-REIT market capitalization.[23] As mentioned above, a cash flow crunch in private funds triggered the growth of the REIT market in the United States. However, it can be said that the private real estate investment market in Japan is maturing, using the formation of a public real estate market as a trigger.

REDUCTION OF RISK PREMIUM FOR REAL ESTATE INVESTMENT. To estimate the real estate investment yields that investors require of J-REITs, the implied capitalization rate is useful, which is calculated by dividing net operating income (NOI) by the REIT's enterprise value (total market values of equities plus securities deposits plus net debt obligation).[24] The gradual decrease in the capitalization rate shows the surge in popularity of J-REITs among investors and encourages J-REITs to acquire real estate more aggressively (figure 2-9).

The capitalization rate in the overall commercial real estate market has decreased as the J-REIT market has expanded. Because there was no circumstance in which real estate was traded on the basis of investment yields, it is very difficult to scrutinize the capitalization rate in real estate deals. Therefore, adequate objective and quantitative analyses regarding the influence of the J-REIT market on the capitalization rate after 2001 or the comparisons with the bubble period do not exist. However, according to recent research, the gradual expansion of investment choices by investment funds that included J-REITs has had an impact on the capitalization rate of studio apartments and suburban shopping centers, which decreased after the capitalization rate of office buildings in big cities

23. STB Research Institute, "Field Survey about Real Estate Private Fund" (July 26, 2006). According to this survey, the market size of private offering real estate funds had exceeded that of its counterpart the J-REIT at the end of 2004. Further, in 2006 the Association of Real Estate Securitization also issued its first field survey about private offering funds, reporting that the total number of the funds managed by its members (194 companies) was 430 with total investment assets about ¥6.1 trillion (May 31, 2006).

24. Net debt with interest is calculated by deducting cash equivalent from total debt with interest.

Figure 2-9. *Implied Cap Rate of J-REIT and Market Cap Rate*

Percent

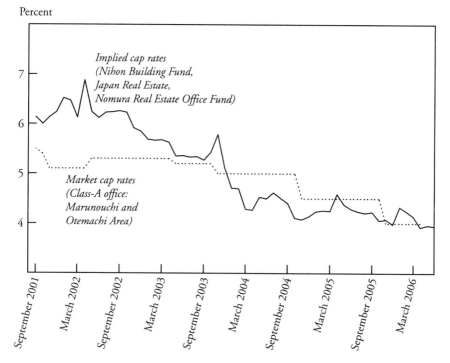

Source: Compiled by Nomura Securities Financial and Economic Research Center, from Japan Real Estate Institute survey "Research about Real Estate Investors" and CB Richard Ellis, "Office Market Report," among others.

decreased; the capitalization rate in Osaka, Nagoya, and Fukuoka showed a downward tendency following Tokyo's.

As explained above, the emergence of the J-REIT improved transparency in Japanese real estate deals, and the inflow of ample money into real estate funds (including J-REITs) gradually reduced the risk premium for real estate investment in Japan.

REAL ESTATE MARKET LINKED TO THE CAPITAL MARKET. In the past in Japan, the price of real estate was almost always determined by expectations of price increase unrelated to revenue from the real estate. Beyond the fact that real estate appraisals based on income or earning yields did not take root in general, there was a tradition of corporations having many pieces of real estate for their own use.

Securitization has progressed, and as a result, discount cash flow and other appraisals methods based on income are now becoming a mainstream.

Moreover, because of the appearance of the J-REIT market, the capital market has an influence on the physical real estate market. More specifically, investors in J-REITs require expected earning yields that include a certain risk premium over other financial assets. The implied capitalization rate is an index that shows one standard of the market participants. The managers of J-REITs recognize the need to ensure the earning yield of invested assets so that they can distribute dividends according to the expected earning yields in the market. Therefore, it is natural for them to question the acquisition of real estate at a price that excessively lowers earning yields.

Investment behaviors of J-REITs, which have already become key players in the real estate market, influence behaviors of private real estate funds and other real estate investors. Thus the J-REIT market can prevent price formations from differing excessively from fundamentals, and it can prevent speculation from overheating if the J-REIT market, which is a capital market, exercises healthy market mechanisms.

ISSUES IN THE FUTURE. The J-REIT market steadily continues to expand and mature in both asset size and the investor base. Its influence on the overall real estate investment market is more prevalent, and one can conclude that the initial political intention of creating the REIT market has largely succeeded.

Concerning issues in the future, the first is to figure out how to cope with potential problems created by using outside management. Considering the structure of J-REITs, it is possible that managers' behaviors will conflict with investors' interests. For example, the management company (or its employee manager) of a J-REIT fund may be motivated to make investment decisions without enough due diligence, when the management fee is based on the size of the outstanding asset. It is a common occurrence that management companies hired to manage the real estate portfolios by J-REITs are at the same time the subsidiaries of the asset management companies that manage assets and facilities. In such cases, there are potential conflicts of interests. Although such conflicts have not yet surfaced, because management companies operate under strict internal rules for trading and management, the rapid expansion of the J-REIT market is fueling such concerns.

Recently, some have pointed out that there is a risk that investment funds could rush to acquire assets and then invest in illegal buildings (that is, buildings for which seismic assessments were forged). In one case, the Financial Services Agency prohibited J. P. Morgan Trust Bank and Shinsei Trust and Banking from accepting new contracts for six months (for the former) and for one year (for the latter) because they lacked a system to review the appraisals of the real estate that they manage and securitize.[25] Further, on July 21, 2006, the Financial Services Agency prohibited Orix Asset Management, which is a management company and a subsidiary of Orix, from executing new management contracts for three months. The reason for the penalty was that Orix Asset Management improperly managed assets entrusted by Orix Real Estate Investment, which was a J-REIT (it omitted examinations at the acquisition of real estate, among other actions). Although there was a recent scandal behind the tightening of regulations in Japan involving forged seismic assessments, the government has a growing interest in the compliance of J-REIT management as well as in the disclosure of real estate–specific risks. For a J-REIT to become a financial product backed by the full confidence of investors, further discussions from various angles may be required.

Conclusion

ETF and REIT are new collective investment schemes in which amateurs pool money and professionals manage it. There are other common features to both schemes. Both are instruments in which investors can invest not solely in securities or real estate but in a diversified portfolio, and both are listed on exchanges. In Japan, the ETF and REIT, the concepts of which were imported from the U.S. market, were both introduced with specific political purposes from the end of the 1990s to 2001, when the demand for reform of the securities market was becoming strong. However, both are actually different from their counterparts in the United States. The Japanese ETF is technically different in that an in-kind creation of ETF shares can be formed only when the ETF links to stock indexes specified by rules of the Financial Services Agency. The J-REIT is rather fundamentally different in that the J-REIT has the outside management system, which the U.S. REIT no longer uses. However, in another respect, it is inevitable that the Japanese ETF and the J-REIT are different from their U.S. counterparts because both were instruments created on the basis of laws related to Japanese investment trusts that had developed independently from similar laws in other countries. Nevertheless, when comparing them with each other on the points of style of corporation, public offering, listing, existence or nonexistence of outside management, and so forth, each collective investment scheme in Japan or in the United States has features that are subtly different from those of its counterpart (table 2-2).

In Japan both the ETF market and the J-REIT market have grown to have about ¥3 trillion to ¥4 trillion in total market value in five years since their actual

25. The Financial Services Agency announced the penalty on J. P. Morgan Trust Bank on April 5, 2006, and announced the penalty on Shinsei Trust and Banking on April 26, 2006.

Table 2-2. *Financial Instruments: Japan and the United States*
$U.S. 1 = ¥115

	Market size (billions of dollars)[a]	vs. Japanese market (times larger)	Corporate-type	Publicly offered	Exchange-traded	Externally managed	Tax transparency
Japan							
Investment trust	510.0			○		○	○
Privately placed investment trust	250.4					○	○
ETF	35.3			○	○	○	○
J-REIT	30.6		○	○	○	○	○
REOC	109.2		○	○	○		
United States							
Mutual fund	9,328.5	18.3	○	○		○	○
Closed-end fund	280.7	n.a.	○	○	○	○	○
ETF	335.1	9.5	△	○	○	○	○
REIT	381.9	12.5	○	○	○		
REOC	n.a.	n.a.	○	○	○		

Source: Investment Trust Association of Japan, Bloomberg, Investment Company Institute, and National Association of Real Estate Investment Trusts (NAREIT).
a. Market size: Data of investment trust, private placed investment trust, Japanese ETF, Japanese REOC, and the U.S. REIT are as of July 2006; Data of J-REIT, U.S. mutual funds, U.S. closed-end funds, and the U.S. ETF are as of June 2006.
n.a. Not available.
△ = About half of U.S. ETFs are corporate-type funds.
ETF = exchange-traded fund; REIT = real estate investment trust; REOC = real estate operating company.

inception. Although they have grown rapidly and their market sizes are not small when compared internationally, their market sizes are about one-tenth of the ETF market and the REIT market in the United States. Moreover, the ratio of the size of the Japanese investment trust market to that of the U.S. mutual fund market is even wider (1:18). When one views the U.S. securities market during the past ten to twenty years, the mutual fund market, which steadily increased assets, kept stride with the expansion of innovative products (for example, the syndicated loan) and contributed to the growth of the market for such products. In Japan also, the further growth of the investment trust, which can be regarded as a representative of collective investment schemes, will likely encourage investors to increase their understanding of the benefits of the ETF and J-REIT, which in turn will lead to the widening of the investor base for such products. With the J-REIT, one can already see the expansion of investment trusts promoting the growth of the markets for other innovative products. Since Japan Post started to sell investment trusts in the autumn of 2005, funds allocating resources among the three major asset classes in a balanced manner (equity, fixed income, real estate) have been gaining popularity. The real estate allocations in such funds are composed of portfolios of J-REITs or foreign REITs. There has been a movement in which J-REITs are used as one asset class in a diversified portfolio. This trend will probably lead to the increase in investment in J-REITs by the retail investors.

It should be pointed out that the ETF and REIT are used by many investors and financial institutions as investment tools for global diversification. For example, U.S. ETFs linked to an international stock market index and several global REIT funds, which are sold in Japan, opened up opportunities to invest in global stocks and real estate at relatively low cost even if the investment unit was small. Given that the movements to introduce the REIT system are brisk in countries in Asia and Europe, the significance of the ETF and the REIT are globally acknowledged. The global recognition of ETFs and REITs and the expansion of the investor base will possibly have an impact on the ETF and the REIT markets in Japan and the United States. How the globalization of ETFs and REITs will affect local markets and price formation of the underlying individual assets will be the topic of future study.

References

Investment Trusts
Hayashi, Kohji. 2003. "Prospect of Investment Trust Market in Japan." *Shouken Analyst Journal* (July).
Kanda, Hideki. 1995. "Legal Aspects of Security Investment Trust." *Financial Review*. (November).

Nomura, Akiko. 2006. "Prospect of Defined-Contribution Pension Market in Japan." *Shihon Shijyou Quarterly* (Summer).

Ohsaki, Sadakazu. 2003. *Miscalculations in the Financial Structural Reforms*. Tokyo: Toyo Keizai.

Seki, Yuta. 2000. "The Draft of the Amendment of Investment Trust Act Which Will Expand Investment Choices." *Shihon Shijyou Quarterly* (Spring).

————. 2001. "Collective Investment Schemes in Asia: The Current Situation." *Capital Research Journal* 4, no. 2 (Summer): 32–41.

Taki, Toshio. 2006. "Start of Selling Investment Trust at Postal Offices." *Shihon Shijyou Quarterly* (Winter).

Exchange-Traded Funds

Ariga, Juinichirou, and Yukihiro Asano. 2003. "Asset Management of Individual Investors and Evolution of Index Funds—Appearance of ETF and Possibility of Self Indexing Fund." *Shouken Analyst Journal* (July).

Gastineau, Gary. 2006. *The Exchange-Traded Funds Manual*. Hoboken, N.J.: John Wiley & Sons.

Ishikawa, Yasushi. 2006. *Japanese ETF Monitor*. London: Nomura International (July 26).

Ohsaki, Sadakazu. 2001. "Movement of Promoting Exchange-Trading Fund (ETF) Market in Japan." *Shihon Shijyou Quarterly* (Summer).

Poterba, James, and John Shoven. 2002. "Exchange Traded Funds: A New Investment Option for Taxable Investors." Working Paper 02-07. MIT Department of Economics (January).

Seki, Yuta 2005. "Development of Commodity ETF and Diversification of the U.S. ETF Markets." *Shihon Shijyou Quarterly* (Summer).

————. 2006. "The U.S. ETF Market Where Innovations Continues to Be Made." *Shihon Shijyou Quarterly* (Summer).

————. 2005. "The U.S. ETFs Which Are Increasingly Utilized for Asset Management of Individual Investors." *Shihon Shijyou Quarterly* (Summer).

Suzuki, Kiyoshi, and Asami Ohde. 2006. *Global ETF Monitor*. Tokyo: Nomura Securities Quantitative Research (April 4).

Watanabe, Shiichi. 2003. "ETF Market and Liquidity—Analysis by Tick Data." *Annual Review of Japan Society for the Economic Studies* 38 (May).

Zeniya, Kaoru. 2001. "Foundation of Exchange-Trading Fund (ETF) by Hong Kong Government." *Shihon Shijyou Quarterly* (Autumn).

Real Estate Investment Trusts

Araki, Tomohiro. 2006. "Steadiness of J-REIT Index Which Is Distinct on the Decline Phase in Stock Market Prices." Nomura Securities Japanese Equity Research 06-244. Tokyo: Nomura Securities (June 14).

————. 2005. "J-REIT Market at a Crossroad." Nomura Securities Japanese Equity Research 05-751 (December 29).

Block, Ralph L. *Investing in REITS: Real Estate Investment Trusts*. New York: Bloomberg Press.

Fukushima, Daisuke, and Tomohiro Araki. 2006. "The Deflation Has Ended: Should Emphasize Selection and Resorting of Descriptions with the Change of Financial Policy." Nomura Securities Japanese Equity Research 06-178. Tokyo: Nomura Securities (May 10).

Japan Association for Real Estate Securitization. 2006. *Handbook of Real Estate Securitization 2006–2007*. Tokyo (July).

Kawaguchi, Yuhichirou, and Masato Hisatake. 2005. "Japanese Real Estate Investment Trust (J-REIT)—Adequacy of Price Formation and Future Issues." Paper presented at the RIETI Policy Symposium, Tokyo, March 18, 2005.

Kawai, Nobuaki. 2006. "Review of J-REIT: Retrospect of 2005 and Prospective for the Future." Tokyo: STB Research Institute (January).

Sasaki, Koichi, Yoshitaka Ichinose, and Noriko Shimizu. 2005. "Expansion of J-REIT Market and Price Formation." *Bank of Japan Review* (June).

Seki, Yuta. 2001. "The Emerge of J-REITs and Viewpoints for Valuation." *Shihon Shijyou Quarterly* (Winter).

———. 2002. "Institutional Investment and J-REITs." *Shihon Shijyou Quarterly* (Summer).

YASUYUKI FUCHITA

3

Securitization of Residential Mortgages: Can Japan Create a "Good" GSE?

SECURITIZATION OF RESIDENTIAL mortgages, like derivatives, is a financial innovation that has seen explosive growth over the past two decades or so. In the United States, securitization of home loans got its start as a response to the regional partitioning of the housing finance market caused by state banking regulations. In other words, securitization of residential mortgages in the United States arose from structural problems within the U.S. financial market rather than the advanced state of the market.

Although structural problems in the financial market were the catalyst, the financial technology of converting illiquid assets into a liquid product became the core element of U.S. government housing policy. Thus a financial innovation wound up sparking a policy revolution in a sector completely separate from finance. A different package of government housing policies was chosen in other countries, where mortgage securitization was undeveloped. The use of securitization in Japan not only revolutionized housing policy, it also promoted a power shift within the Japanese economic system from the bureaucracy to the private sector.

In the United States, where it all began, home loan securitization gave birth to giant, quasi-governmental entities called government-sponsored enterprises (GSEs), and the new structural problems created by the GSEs are now the subject of hot debate. In this chapter, I examine whether there is reason to be concerned that this financial innovation, which was designed to resolve one type of structural problem, may lead to new structural problems.

The Current State of Home Loan Securitization
in Japan and the United States

Total issuance of residential mortgage-backed securities (RMBS) in Japan was
approximately ¥5 trillion in fiscal year 2005. With roughly ¥20 trillion in home
loans underwritten annually, a straightforward calculation indicates that 25 percent of those loans are securitized. Annual issuance of Japanese government bonds
(JGBs) is more than ¥30 trillion, making Japan's RMBS issuance market look
rather small in comparison.[1]

In the United States, 64.9 percent of all home loans were securitized in 2004.[2]
Issuance of mortgage-backed securities (MBS) by GNMA, FNMA, and FHLMC
alone totaled $966.1 billion in 2005, more than the $746.2 billion in bonds
issued by the U.S. Treasury.[3]

These numbers show Japan's RMBS market to be rather small compared with
that of the United States, a fact that can be attributed to the way that the Japanese government has intervened in the housing finance market. Rather than promote securitization, as was done in the United States, the government created the
Government Housing Loan Corporation (GHLC), a financial institution whose
main policy objective is to provide home loans at below-market rates.

In recent years, however, Japan has radically overhauled its housing finance
policy, moving away from providing low-interest public loans and toward promoting the securitization of home loans. As shown in figure 3-1, at times public
loans written by the GHLC have accounted for more than 50 percent of all home
loans in Japan, but in the few years since the beginning of this decade, when the
GHLC decided to reduce its direct lending and provide more support for securitization, the number of GHLC loans has declined to nearly zero. The resulting
gap has been filled by growth in home loans made by private sector financial
institutions, which have seen rapid growth in their share of the market. Some of
the home loans made by private sector lenders have been purchased and then
securitized by the GHLC.

Although the GHLC has been purchasing and securitizing home loans originating in the private sector since October 2003, there was a rapid increase in
RMBS issued by the GHLC beginning in 2005. As shown in figure 3-2, it was

---

1. Estimates of residential mortgage-backed securities in Japan are from Nomura Securities; estimates
of home loans underwritten annually come from the Bank of Japan, and estimates of annual issuance of
Japanese government bonds are from the Ministry of Finance.

2. Inside Mortgage Finance Publications (2005).

3. GNMA, "Ginnie Mae" (Government National Mortgage Association); FNMA, "Fannie Mae" (Federal National Mortgage Association); FHLMC, "Freddie Mac" (Federal Home Loan Mortgage Corporation).

that increase that made it possible for total RMBS issuance to reach ¥5 trillion in 2005; before that, Japan's RMBS market was considerably smaller. The GHLC therefore has already greatly transformed its role; however, the government has decided to dissolve the GHLC in March 2007 and replace it with the Japan Housing Finance Services Agency (JHFSA), a new independent administrative agency with the primary task of securitizing home loans originated by private sector financial institutions.

The basic idea behind the creation of the agency is to eventually make the RMBS market as critical a segment within the securities market in Japan as it is in the United States, and operation of the new agency will be modeled on that of FNMA (Fannie Mae). There is, however, a great deal of debate right now over how to best reform Fannie Mae and other housing-related government-sponsored enterprises (GSEs), raising concern that Japan may simply repeat the problems already experienced in the United States.

This chapter looks at the developments that led to the change in Japan's housing finance policies, the characteristics that define Japan's RMBS market, and the outlook for the new agency.

Traditional Public Support of Housing Finance in Japan

Much of the industrialized world has implemented policies to provide assistance to those who are purchasing or renting of a home, but the policy package varies widely among countries. For example, in the United Kingdom the emphasis is on supplying government-run rental housing. Sometimes these housing units are sold off cheaply as a way to promote home ownership, but there is no assistance with home financing specifically.

In contrast, the governments of the United States, Germany, France, and Japan, although they also maintain publicly owned rental housing, provide assistance to the home buyer through their involvement in home financing. The U.S. government plays a key role in the securitization of loans originated by private sector financial institutions, while Germany, France, and Japan have implemented government-sponsored housing finance mechanisms. Nevertheless, in Germany and France the government provides assistance with home loans originated by private sector financial institutions, while Japan stands apart in that in 1950 it established a government-affiliated financial institution that specialized in housing finance. Prospective home buyers who meet certain conditions can take out a GHLC mortgage, up to a limited amount, under more favorable terms than are available in the private sector. The GHLC signs an agreement with a private sector financial institution to do the actual processing and servicing of the loan.

Figure 3-1. *Japan's Home Loans*[a]

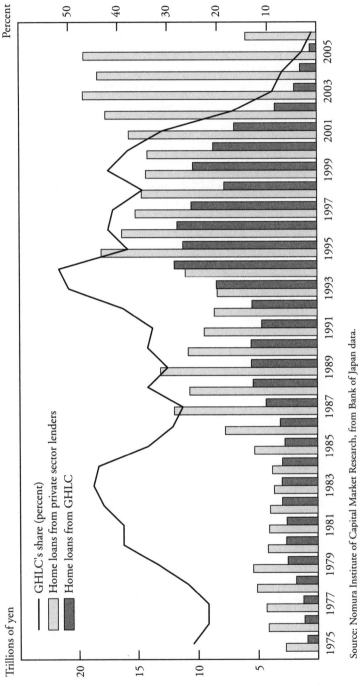

Trillions of yen

Percent

GHLC's share (percent)

Home loans from private sector lenders

Home loans from GHLC

Source: Nomura Institute of Capital Market Research, from Bank of Japan data.

GHLC = Government Housing Loan Corporation.

a. Private sector share is the total for domestic banks, Shinkin banks, and the Shinkin Central Bank. Year 2006 ends in March.

Figure 3-2. *RMBS Issuance Amount*

Trillions of yen

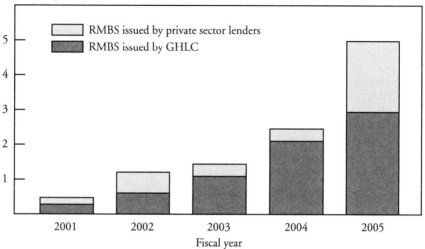

Source: Nomura Securities.
GHLC = Government Housing Loan Corporation; RMBS = residential mortgage-backed securities.

As shown in figure 3-1, until the rapid decline at the beginning of this decade, the GHLC typically accounted for 20 to 50 percent of the home loans written in Japan. Until the early 1980s, private sector lenders focused on meeting the demand for loans to large corporations and took a dim view of home loans and other high-maintenance loans to individuals. When loans to large corporations later became less profitable, private sector lenders began to focus their efforts on the home loan market. However, because the economic stimulus packages aimed at battling Japan's post-bubble economic slump included measures to increase lending through the GHLC, the GHLC's share of that market still rose to record-high levels in the mid-1990s.

Like other government-affiliated financial institutions, the GHLC operates under the framework of the Fiscal Investment and Loan Program (FILP), which is also referred to as the "second budget." The FILP was a mechanism to make investments and loans for public purposes, including loans through government-affiliated financial institutions and investments in road construction through public corporations, using as a primary funding source deposits made by the public to postal savings accounts, the public pension program, and other means, apart from taxes and government bonds.

Figure 3-3. *GHLC's Flow of Funds, Fiscal Year 1994 (Actual)*

Billions of yen

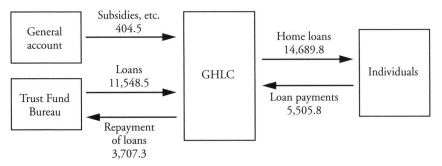

Source: Nomura Institute of Capital Markets Research.
GHLC = Government Housing Loan Corporation.

The GHLC came to be the most important institution within the FILP for making investments and loans for public purposes. The GHLC primarily borrowed from the Trust Fund Bureau, which managed FILP funds, to make home loans to individuals. Figure 3-3 shows the main flow of funds for the GHLC in 1994, the year that GHLC loans hit an all-time high. Basically, the GHLC borrowed ¥11.5 trillion from the Trust Fund Bureau, combined those funds with money collected from previous loans, and then originated home loans worth ¥14.7 trillion. As explained below, since the GHLC would often run a deficit if it had to depend on loan interest income alone to cover its expenses, it also received funds from the general budget.

When interest rates at private sector financial institutions, including the rates paid on deposits, were regulated, the interest rate at which the GHLC borrowed from the FILP was set low, unrelated to the market rate, and its mortgage rate was capped at 5.5 percent by the Government Housing Loan Corporation Law. As a matter of housing policy, the rate on home loans that met certain conditions was set at a favorable rate, lower than the rate paid to borrow from FILP. Consequently, GHLC's mortgage rates often were lower than the normal FILP rate and, of course, lower than mortgage rates offered by private sector lenders. As a public institution, the GHLC did not need to earn a profit, and it would even be reimbursed from the general budget for its negative spreads, making its core mission the subsidization of residential mortgage interest payments.

In addition, as noted earlier, private sector lenders were able for a long period following World War II to earn profits from their corporate lending businesses and therefore were not fully geared to handle the home loan business. Consequently, it was only natural that individuals thought first of the GHLC when it was time to finance the purchase of a home.

The government began liberalizing interest rates at private sector financial institutions in the 1980s, and the interest rate on loans from the Trust Fund Bureau has been tied to yields in the JGB issuance market since March 1987. That has made it more difficult for the GHLC to offer home loans at more favorable interest rates than those offered by private sector lenders.

Beginning in the 1990s, a long period of low interest rates took hold in response to the economic slump following the bubble's burst, leading to an increase in GHLC mortgage prepayments. Faced with declining demand for corporate lending, private sector lenders became much more aggressive in their home loan business, encouraging prospective clients to prepay their existing GHLC mortgages and refinance using private sector loans. Also, as evident from figure 3-1, there was an increase in low-rate GHLC mortgages after stimulus packages were offered to promote GHLC loans in order to invigorate housing construction. The result was an increase in subsidies from the general budget (figure 3-4).

The GHLC procures funds for a twenty-three-year term at a fixed rate tied to long-term yields, and because it could not prepay its loans to the Trust Fund Bureau, it was unable to rapidly lower its mortgage rates. In fact, with fixed-rate lending increasing in the face of interest rates that were at historic lows, from 1997 GHLC set a floor rate of 4 percent for all loans with a maturity of eleven years or longer in order to constrain growth in interest rate subsidies from the government. Meanwhile, by using interest rate swaps, private sector lenders were able to offer conventional mortgages at lower rates than the GHLC's for the first ten years, and after that they began offering adjustable-rate mortgages as well as thirty-year fixed mortgages using securitization. (As with the GHLC, rates on home loans of eleven years and longer did not increase, and thus its rates on those loans were also lower than the GHLC's.) Thus, depending on the length of the mortgage, the private sector could offer more favorable terms. During these changes in the business environment, the FILP went through a major transformation, as did the housing loan policy implemented through the GHLC and under the FILP.

The Debate over Reform of Housing Loan Policy

The dramatic systemic reform described in the preceding discussion was based on the fundamental guidelines contained in the Basic Law on the Reform of Central Government Ministries and Agencies, a law passed in June 1998 to promote greater overall government efficiency. The trend toward smaller government

Figure 3-4. *Subsidies and Other Assistance to the GHLC*[a]

Billions of yen

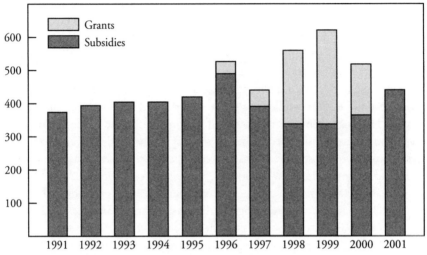

Source: Business documents from the Ministry of Land, Infrastructure and Transportation.
GHLC = Government Housing Loan Corporation.
a. Treasury grants to cover required subsidies partially slipped to the following year.

began gaining momentum in the 1990s, even in Japan, and when the growing fiscal deficits during the recessions of the 1990s were identified as a problem, the government became committed to reform. Reform of the FILP was also seen as a necessary part of the process.

Although GHLC reform was only a part of FILP reform, which in turn was only part of broader administrative reform, it was in the housing finance sector that the problems in Japan's economic system that were caused by overreliance on the bureaucracy became most obvious. That put GHLC reform at the forefront of the overall wave of government reform that arose in the late 1990s. One conceivable reason that the overhaul of the FILP became a core goal of the administrative reform movement was that the FILP had been putting pressure on private sector companies and had created an environment that encouraged the special corporations (agencies) like the GHLC and the four highway authorities to finance inefficient projects. Reform of this system was thought to be very important, since a huge amount of money flowed through this system. For example, postal savings, one source of FILP funds, accounted for 20 percent of all financial assets held by individuals, while the GHLC owned a 50 percent share of the home loan market.

The system under which management of postal savings and other funds was concentrated in the Trust Fund Bureau was dismantled. The special corporations, which had been able to borrow funds from the Trust Fund Bureau to engage in investment and financing activity, were forced to procure funds by issuing government-guaranteed bonds, borrowing from a special account, or issuing their own bonds without a government guarantee. Serious consideration of special corporation reform pursuant to the basic guidelines gained traction once the cabinet issued its broad outlines for administrative reform in December 2000, although after debate over the specifics began it became clear that there was an ongoing conflict between two sides. On one side stood the government agencies with jurisdiction over the GHLC and the four highway authorities, as well as politicians involved in housing and highway administration, all of whom did their best to minimize the scope of reform; and on the other side stood those arguing for radical reform by placing the priority on more efficient government and market mechanisms as well as on the reduction of fiscal deficits.

After Junichiro Koizumi became prime minister in April 2001, however, the proponents of reform gained the upper hand, and in December 2001, a plan to streamline the special corporations was approved by the cabinet. The plan called for dismantling the GHLC within five years; meanwhile, it was to gradually shrink its financing activities and to begin supporting the securitization of private sector mortgages. Once the GHLC closes shop, the securitization function is to be turned over to an independent administrative agency (IAA) created specifically for that task.

The decision was made to shrink the number of direct loans made through the GHLC and start supporting the securitization of private sector home loans for several reasons. First, although the GHLC, which was funded by postal savings and other funds concentrated in the Trust Fund Bureau, had previously originated its own loans, the decision to take away that stable source of funds made direct financing more difficult. Second, supporting the securitization of private sector home loans solved the problem of competition between private sector lenders and a public institution for the home loan business. Third, Japan was striving to move away from a financial structure that was excessively dependent on banks and toward a structure in which securities markets play a larger role. Therefore, it was considered desirable to achieve growth in the RMBS market as a path to a larger and more diverse securities market. Fourth, although there probably is a need to think through the impact that simply eliminating the GHLC's function will have on the citizens who benefit from low-interest loans and on the agency's more than 1,000 employees, the example of Fannie Mae in the United States suggests that the organization may be able to continue its role as a promoter of housing finance by becoming an agency for supporting securitization as well by remaking itself as a pillar of support for a key securities market.

In a roundtable on housing finance held from October 2001 into 2002 that was sponsored by the Ministry of Land, Infrastructure, and Transport (MLIT), which is in charge of housing policy, there was no notable opposition to the idea of the GHLC supporting securitization. In the United States, however, it took about twenty-five years for efforts to securitize home loans through the GSEs to attain critical mass, and some observers in Japan saw no need to reduce the GHLC's direct lending role. Furthermore, some have argued that if the scope of home loans purchased by public institutions is not limited to what is appropriate for public purposes, securitization by the private sector could be unfairly hindered.

In line with the reform guidelines mentioned above, the GHLC began cutting back its loan business in fiscal year 2002. It had already begun securitizing the home loan assets in its own portfolio in March 2001 in order to get accustomed to the securitization process, and in October 2003 it began supporting the securitization of home loans originated by the private sector. The GHLC's funds flow for the fiscal year 2005 budget, shown in figure 3-5, has changed dramatically from what it used to be, depicted in figure 3-3. Both funds borrowed from FILP and home loans declined substantially, and some of the home loans that the GHLC originated were securitized. In addition, it has been buying home loan assets from private sector lenders for securitization.

The dismantling of the GHLC and its replacement with a new IAA was mandated by law. According to the law, the primary activity of the new agency is to purchase home loans from ordinary financial institutions and to support securitization of those loans by providing loan guarantees for bonds backed by the loans.[4] The agency's other services include insuring private sector home loans, providing consumers with information related to home loans and housing, making direct loans limited to the purposes of disaster recovery and urban residential renewal, and servicing loans originated by the GHLC. In performing those services, the agency is expected to strive for a suitable division of roles with ordinary financial institutions.

The new agency, in the form of an IAA, was created to make government smaller and more efficient. The specifics of how IAAs are to be operated is spelled out in Basic Law on the Reform of Central Government Ministries and Agencies, as follows:

---

4. Law Concerning Independent Administrative Agency for the Provision of Support for Housing Finance.

Figure 3-5. *GHLC's Flow of Funds, Fiscal Year 2005 (Plan)*

Billions of yen

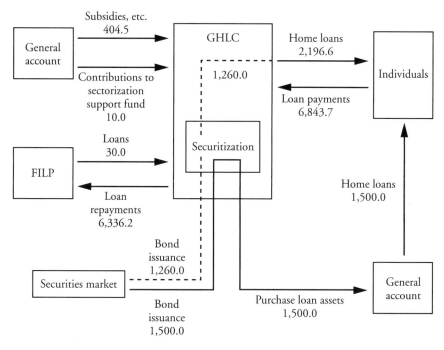

Source: Nomura Institute of Capital Markets Research.
FILP = Fiscal Investment and Loan Program; GHLC = Government Housing Loan Corporation.

[IAAs] are established pursuant to this law and other specific laws for the purpose of performing, both efficiently and effectively, those tasks and projects: that are necessary from the public perspective for ensuring lifestyle and socioeconomic stability; that do not need to be directly performed by the state itself; and either entail the risk of not being performed if left up to the private sector or need to be performed by a single monopolistic entity.[5]

IAAs are similar to private sector corporations in that they must compile financial statements in accordance with corporate accounting principles and undergo

5. Basic Law for the Reform of Central Government Ministries and Agencies (Law no. 103 in 1988): chapter 1, section 1, article 2.

audits and disclose the results. They differ from private sector corporations, however, in a number of respects. For example, the head of an agency is appointed by its governing minister. The agency also must compile business and service documents to be approved by the minister; create for the minister's approval a medium-term business plan based on business goals established by the minister that must be achieved within a three- to five-year period; and submit to evaluation by an independent administrative agency established by the governing ministry to assess the degree to which the agency has achieved its medium-term goals. Also, if provided for under a separate law, the state may take an ownership stake in the agency. Unlike those of a government institution, however, the details of an IAA's operations are not subject to intervention as long as the agency is on track to meet its medium-term goals.

The new agency to be created when the GHLC is dismantled will be started on funds invested by the government, and if necessary it may also receive additional government funds within limits set forth in the budget. The new agency's long-term loans and bond issues also are eligible for government guarantees, up to the amounts set forth by Diet resolution. The new agency is thus modeled after Fannie Mae, although the format in which it is being launched is substantially different from that of a housing-related GSE listed on the stock market. In actual operation, however, the agency is not in principle expected to seek government guarantees on its loans and bond issues. That is because the objectives of system reform include making the financial system more efficient and reducing the government's fiscal burden by lowering its involvement in financial activity.

The process of transforming the GHLC into an IAA has already begun. A private sector individual was hired to head the GHLC beginning in August 2005, the objective being to move away from bureaucratic management and toward a more efficient, flexible, customer-oriented operation.

The Securitization of Residential Mortgages by the GHLC

Under the current setup, GHLC's securitization of its own home loans is different from securitization through Fannie Mae and Freddie Mac. The big difference is that the GHLC's credit does not necessarily have a very high ranking. Although securities (not RMBS) issued by the GHLC have been rated AAA by R&I, a credit rating agency in Japan, they are rated only AA– by S&P. That is the same rating that S&P has given to Japanese government bonds, and in that respect it suggests recognition of the GHLC as a public institution.

An objective look at the GHLC's balance sheet and the ongoing losses it has generated suggests that the agency would have a hard time getting an AA– rating

Figure 3-6. *Securitization Support Business (Purchase)*[a]

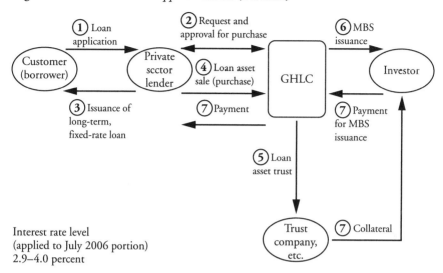

Interest rate level
(applied to July 2006 portion)
2.9–4.0 percent

Source: Government Housing Loan Corporation (GHLC).
MBS = mortgage-backed securities; SPC = special purpose corporation.
a. Graph shows example when using a trust and an SPC.

as a private sector lender, although since the RMBS have credit enhancements based on overcollateralization, discussed below, the securities may receive a rating that exceeds the creditworthiness of the GHLC itself.

That is, the pool of purchased loans to be securitized is assessed by the rating agency to determine the appropriate credit enhancement level (expressed as a ratio); home loan assets already held by the GHLC (past loans) of an amount equal to that ratio (which in the past has been around 0.1) are added as overcollateralization; and then the entire package (referred to as the collateral asset pool) is entrusted to an outside trustee. Also, apart from that process, existing loan assets amounting to approximately 30 percent of the collateral asset pool are maintained, and if loan assets within the pool fall into arrears by four months or more, they can be replaced if desired.

The credit enhancement mechanism for the GHLC's securitization of the home loan assets of private sector lenders is the same as that for its own home loan assets. First, there is securitization based on outright purchase, wherein the GHLC purchases the home loans of private sector lenders that meet certain standards and then uses those loans to back GHLC bond issues (figure 3-6). An AAA rating is not going to be obtained in this case, even when the GHLC issues securities backed by loans purchased from a private sector lender; thus the GHLC's existing loans are used as both overcollateralization and a substitute for delinquent loan assets.

The GHLC conducts its securitization support services under the securitization support account, which is kept separate from the existing loan asset servicing account. Thus, when existing loan assets are used to support securitization, funds must be transferred from the securitization support account to the existing loan asset servicing account, while paying into a reserve account to cover collateral usage fees and compensate for losses associated with the repossession of collateral.

With securitization based on guarantee, an RMBS issued by a private sector lender is guaranteed through a payment by GHLC (figure 3-7), but this type of securitization has yet to be used. Under both types of securitization, purchase and guarantee, the private sector lender receives the loan applications and originates and services the loan. With a traditional GHLC home loan, the interest rate was the same for the same type of loan, regardless of which financial institution took the application. However, with loans predicated on securitization, the loans themselves are products of various lenders, and each lender can determine the terms it wants to offer the user. Some private sector lenders are offering the new loans at interest rates lower than those on the existing GHLC loans.

The business of supporting purchase-type securitization moved quite slowly during the first year following its launch in October 2003, primarily because during that year there was little awareness of the program, interest rates were at zero, and there was a lack of demand for securitization from private sector lenders. However, the business grew rapidly after that because the GHLC started discounting the business operating charge (0.9 percent) that it collected from private sector lenders when it purchased their loan assets and increased the discount as the volume of business grew. The agency also introduced measures that expanded the home loans available for purchase and stepped up its PR activity—all while the economic recovery was beginning to fuel concerns over rising interest rates.[6] Securitization by the GHLC thus is growing, and the business will be taken over by the new IAA when the GHLC is dismantled in March 2007. This organizational change has also necessitated change in the securitization mechanism.

Securitization through the New Agency

The MLIT's Housing Bureau launched an MBS market working team at its spring 2006 roundtable on housing finance to look at ways to ensure that the securitization of home loans continues to go smoothly during the transition to

6. See Inoue (2005).

Figure 3-7. *Securitization Support Business (Guarantee)*[a]

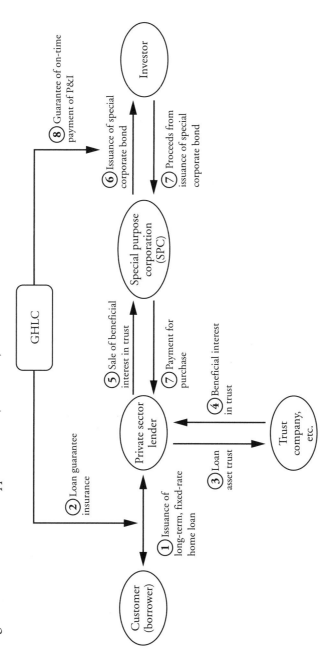

Source: Government Housing Loan Corporation (GHLC).
P&I = principal and interest.
a. Graph shows example when using trust and SPC.

the new agency. An especially important change is the need for a new credit enhancement facility.

As already noted, although it is possible for the agency to secure government guarantees on the bonds that it issues, it is not expected to do so under normal conditions. Also, because the government will be an investor in the agency, the agency will not be subject to the Corporate Reorganization Act, although the commitment from the government will be no greater than with the GHLC. The agency is expected to generate operating losses initially; accordingly, its standing in the credit market should be the same as the GHLC's, and like its predecessor, it will need a credit enhancement facility in order to issue AAA-rated RMBS.

As discussed, in order to raise credit quality, purchase-type RMBS from the GHLC used loan assets originated by GHLC as overcollateralization. It was also possible to replace nonperforming loan assets with performing GHLC loans to maintain the quality of collateral (figure 3-8). Under the new agency, however, direct lending will be quite limited, while securitization support activity will continue to grow; therefore the amount of existing loan assets is expected to gradually decline, first falling below the amount required to cover newly issued RMBS and finally becoming fully exhausted in either fiscal 2007 or fiscal year 2008.

Because of the decreasing amount of existing loan assets to be used as collaterals, the following three options have been proposed as new credit enhancement facilities for the new agency:

—First, instead of using existing loan assets as overcollateralization, use funds procured by the agency through bond issues and loans to purchase additional home loans from private sector lenders, then use the additional loan assets as overcollateralization.

—Second, use funds procured by the agency through bond issues and loans to purchase JGBs and other highly rated assets, then use those assets as overcollateralization.

—Third, rather than using overcollateralization as in the first two options, issue both subordinated RMBS and preferred RMBS with priority redemption.

Under the first option, there is asset/liability management (ALM) risk because the funds are procured normally, with debt that matures in a lump sum (a bullet bond), but the loan assets purchased with those funds are home loans, which return both interest and a portion of the principal each period and can be prepaid. Under the third option, the sale of subordinated RMBS on the market is difficult, giving rise to the possibility that the agency would have to procure new funds and hold its own RMBS or, if it does sell them, pay a high rate of interest.

Because of the risks, the second option, known as the structured capital method (see figure 3-9), is considered the best. By matching the maturities of the

Figure 3-8. *Conventional Credit Enhancement*

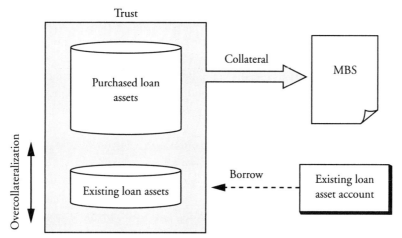

Source: Government Housing Loan Corporation (GHLC).
MBS = mortgage-backed securities.

Figure 3-9. *Proposed New Credit Enhancement*

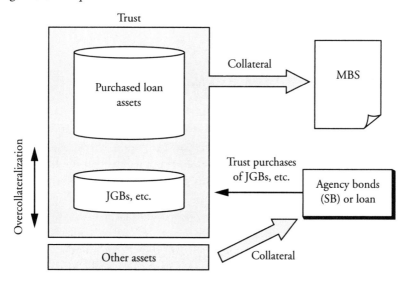

Source: Government Housing Loan Corporation (GHLC).
JGBs = Japanese government bonds; MBS = mortgage-backed securities; SB = straight bond.

bonds issued with the JGBs purchased, ALM is simplified. Of course, the agency's bonds will carry a higher yield than the JGBs, resulting in a negative spread, but that is the cost of the credit enhancement. Even the current method of credit enhancement, through overcollateralization by using existing bonds, requires payment of a collateral usage fee into the existing bond servicing account; thus the traditional arrangement also incurs costs. Because the structured capital method requires the use of a master trust and recognition of a self trust, it appears that the first option will be used until the system can be modified to accommodate those requirements.

In the opinion of some observers, when the agency becomes sufficiently capitalized it should aim for securing an AAA rating on its RMBS issues based on its own credit instead of relying on overcollateralization. Under the current GHLC format, about ¥200 billion in capital is allocated to the securitization support account, but considering that outstanding RMBS issues should easily surpass ¥20 trillion in the future, that amount probably is not enough to offset future credit risk.

That explains why the MBS working team recommended increasing the capital in the securitization support account by several hundred billion yen upon launching the new agency. It will take time, however, before capital can be built up to a level sufficient to handle the growing credit risk; there also should be careful debate over the question of whether the need to bear such risk even exists. For the time being, efforts must be made to minimize the risks by, in principle, procuring the funds needed for the securitization business with pass-through bonds.

Measures to Improve the RMBS Market

The change in credit enhancement facilities is the most important reform as the GHLC is dismantled and the new agency takes over its securitization support duties. However, a variety of measures aimed at facilitating securitization support and expanding the RMBS market have been proposed at the roundtable mentioned above. The main proposals directly concerned with the structure of the RMBS market are the following:

—*Change from separate trusts to a master trust.* Under the current RMBS structure, the loan assets purchased each month are pooled and overcollateralized and then a separate trust is established for the MBS issued that month. It has been proposed that the agency instead use a master trust to cover the loan assets purchased from private sector lenders, thus providing credit enhancement that takes full advantage of diversification across the entire pool. Analysis has shown that putting diversification to work by consolidating collateral assets with a variety of characteristics into a single pool can bring the credit enhancement level down dramatically, eventually into the low single digits, particularly when the number of collateral assets reaches 20,000 or more. Accordingly, it is preferable that the agency maximize the benefits of diversification for the huge number of wide-ranging loan assets that it purchases from various lenders nationwide. In the case of separate trusts, ratings agencies must calculate the credit enhancement level every month, thus driving up ratings costs and taking more time.

—*Introduce a swap program.* Securitization support at the GHLC is a program in which the loan assets are purchased with cash. Fannie Mae, on the other hand, also has a swap program in which RMBS issued by Fannie Mae are used instead of cash to purchase the assets, and swaps actually are used more often than cash. The lender is able to watch market trends and choose between converting its loan assets into cash or into RMBS. Because in an increasing number of cases these RMBS wind up being sold on the market (at a more favorable timing for the lender), the introduction of a swap program also appears to be contributing to growth in the secondary RMBS market. This program also makes it possible for the issuing agency to reduce the pipeline risk and underwriting fees associated with the cash program.

—*Introduce collateralized mortgage obligations (CMOs).* The CMO is an issuance method in which MBS are pooled and their cash flows (principal and interest payments) are separated into different tranches and then converted into bonds of differing maturities. In Japan, the weighted average term to maturity is about ten to twelve years for normal RMBS backed by newly purchased loan assets and about seven to eight years for RMBS backed by existing loans; accordingly, the primary investors in RMBS are life insurance companies and other long-term investors.

If bonds with shorter-term cash flows than MBS can be produced using CMOs, they should widen the investor base and result in a deeper and more efficient market. If the agency itself were to issue the CMO, it would need to acquire considerable structuring expertise and manage the risk of being stuck with residual securities; therefore the main approach envisioned here is the resecuritization business, in which the agency supports the process whereby a securities company purchases MBS and issues CMOs in an arbitrage trade.

Structuring a CMO requires separating the cash flow from the RMBS into two products, principal only (PO) and interest only (IO), which are used in the United States as hedging tools for RMBS investments. The accounting treatment and tax implications for these products in Japan, particularly for IOs, need to be addressed.

—Standardize RMBS. To invigorate the secondary market and hedge transactions, it would be preferable to push for more standardization in the market, for example, by limiting RMBS to certain maturities—say, thirty-five years and twenty years—and by changing the coupon increment, currently at 0.01 percent, to a wider increment, such as 0.5 percent.

—Introduce TBA transactions. TBAs ("to be announced") are a type of RMBS futures trading in the United States in which the price is determined ahead of time based on certain basic terms of the RMBS such as maturity and coupon, even when the underlying pool of assets is not specified. That makes it easier to set the terms of a home loan and also for short-term investors to participate. TBAs also can be used to hedge pipeline risk.

—Introduce repurchase agreements and dollar rolls. A repurchase agreement is a transaction lasting for a set period between a party that needs bonds and a party that needs funds. From the perspective of the lender of the bond (the receiver of funds), the repurchase enables it to procure funds at a lower interest rate by offering its bonds as collateral, while from the perspective of the borrower of the bond it is either a way to invest funds or a means of temporarily procuring a bond backed by cash. After a certain period has elapsed, the same bond that was borrowed is returned to its owner. If a bond of the same type is returned instead of the same bond, the transaction is termed a dollar roll.

Repurchase agreements are also common in government bonds markets, and they provide an important submarket within short-term money markets for meeting both the short-term funding needs of investors in long-term bonds and the short-term investing needs of asset managers. The existence of such a market facilitates the procurement of long-term funds and makes the financial market more efficient.

—Revise guarantee-type securitization. As noted earlier, there has not yet been any guarantee-based securitization support. One reason is that as the scale increases, securitization based on purchase becomes more advantageous to the originator and the cost of the guarantee becomes more expensive. Another reason is that most of the residential mortgage securitization currently handled by private sector lenders is based on selling home loans directly to investors in the form of a trust, without using a special purpose corporation (SPC) to convert the beneficial interest in trust acquired by the private sector lender into a bond. The Government Housing Loan Corporation Law allows for guaranteeing a bond but not for guaranteeing a beneficial interest in trust.

A reduction in loan insurance premiums and guarantee fees has been proposed, but there is currently a debate over whether guarantee-based securitization should be supported, since it involves providing guarantees for beneficial interests in trust that themselves are not very liquid and because the real purpose of establishing the agency is to improve the housing finance market by expanding and increasing the efficiency of the RMBS market, including the secondary market.

Growth in Japan's RMBS Market

The securitization of GHLC home loans has grown rapidly in only a few years, but even with a new agency taking over the task of supporting securitization, it seems likely that the rate of growth can be sustained over the medium term. First, demand for home loans is expected to remain firm for the time being. It is possible that the lifting of zero interest rates in July 2006 may dampen demand from borrowers somewhat, but interest rates still remain at historically low levels. In addition, although Japan's population continues both to decline and to age, after the baby boomers begin to retire en masse from April 2007 on, demand for funds to improve the quality of housing is expected to remain firm for a while. That demand is based on expenses associated with moving to a new home, remodeling an existing home, and otherwise accommodating lifestyle changes.

Second, in Japan only 25 percent of home loans currently are securitized, counting both existing GHLC loans and home loans originated by private sector lenders, while more than 60 percent are in the United States. With the end of the zero interest rate policy, financial institutions have to get better at handling interest rate risk, and securitization is likely to be viewed as a more important option than before. Also, the new agency will continue with the securitization of existing loans begun by the GHLC, and early redemption of funds to the FILP is planned.

Third, as noted above, the introduction of various types of improvement plans aimed at expanding securitization through the new agency is planned. Although it is true that private sector lenders can securitize home loans on their own, it is also true that if the agency takes the initiative, it will be better positioned, as a public institution, to push reforms aimed at facilitating securitization and providing the infrastructure for educating borrowers and investors alike, since it can more easily gain the understanding and cooperation of market participants. It can also benefit from economies of scale. Although criticism that expansion of the securitization business involves expansion of the bureaucracy is unlikely to go away, the GHLC's nearly complete exit from the home loan market has already effected a fairly substantial contraction in the bureaucracy from the perspective of private sector lenders. From the taxpayers' perspective, the establishment of the agency should herald a substantial improvement in organizational efficiency, and the move from a direct lending business that consistently generated losses to a securitization business that can actually generate income should lead to a welcome reduction in subsidies from the general budget. Accordingly, so far there has been little opposition to expansion of the agency's securitization business.

The agency will complete its first intermediate target period as an independent administrative agency at the end of fiscal year 2011, by which time many of the improvement measures noted above are expected to have been implemented. The annual securitization of the approximately ¥2 trillion required to erase the agency's deficit also is expected to be well on track by then. Consequently, by the end of fiscal year 2016, when the second intermediate target period comes to an end, the amount of agency-issued RMBS outstanding in the market is expected to exceed ¥20 trillion, making it an alternative within the securities market that investors cannot afford to ignore.

It is possible that the recent growth in the RMBS market will accelerate further because of increased economies of scale, improved market efficiency, and the growing importance of RMBS to investors as the securities account for a greater share of market indexes and become increasingly important components of portfolios. Investors include private sector financial institutions. In a growing number of instances, lenders will determine that investing in RMBS is more efficient—and provides more liquidity—than writing residential mortgages and holding them as loans on their books. In step with growth in the market has been the expansion of the market for RMBS-specific investment analysis and risk management software as well as various other types of analysis-related information and infrastructure, which has accelerated the market's growth even further.

The scenario above might not be realized, if lenders prefer to hold their own home loans and mortgage lending predicated on purchase by the agency does not increase. The home loans purchased by the agency are long-term, fixed-rate mortgages, but private sector lenders are aggressively going after mortgages with shorter terms. Competition among private sector lenders is fierce, and it appears that in some instances they are making loans at interest rates that are so low as to be difficult to justify economically. Accordingly, it is conceivable that consumers who take out home loans will prefer the private sector's proprietary mortgage deals over the type meant for purchase by the agency.

Although such concerns cannot be dismissed, there is still a strong possibility that home loans predicated on securitization will become more attractive than they are now as a result of agency-led efforts to reform the system and make the RMBS market even more efficient. The leadership of public institutions in forming and developing the market has been a catalyst for Japan's RMBS market, which is likely to become very large. Once the market becomes sufficiently large and the agency has fully exploited its role, maybe around 2020, it may be time to seriously question the need for such a public institution.

Growth in the Securitization Market: The U.S. Experience

Before the long-term prospects of the agency and Japan's RMBS market are considered, it is a good idea to look at what happened in the United States as its market for securitization of residential mortgages developed.

The first aspect worth noting is the structural change in the financial industry caused by expansion of the securitization market.[7] Stated briefly, securitization encouraged both the trend toward fewer and larger financial institutions and specialization by function. In the United States, the S&Ls used to have a dominant share of the home loan origination business, but that share is now considerably lower, as shown in figure 3-10. Meanwhile, although companies specializing in residential mortgages have emerged, they are largely subsidiaries of large financial institutions, because the increase in securitization and commoditization of loans that has occurred since the 1980s has made the origination of home loans a high-volume, low-margin business. The pooling and securitization of small home loans has necessitated greater standardization of loans, which makes it more difficult for lenders to differentiate their products and promotes price competition, thereby giving an advantage to the larger businesses.

The increased use of securitization also creates the need for new risk management expertise. When a lender securitizes home loans it is able to transfer risk to investors, but when it continues to service the loans, it bears the risk of the future cash flow from servicing fees disappearing as a result of prepayment. In the United States, mortgage servicing rights (MSRs) must be fairly valued when recorded as an asset, but it has become increasingly difficult to ignore the impact on the earnings of U.S. lenders from changes in that asset's value caused by interest rate fluctuations. This growing concern over the risk of MSRs is related not only to the strength of the home loan business for U.S. financial institutions in recent years but also to the ease with which information technology allows borrowers to obtain information on refinancing and interest rates. Because of the high degree of skill needed to manage MSR risk, home loan–related business has tended to gravitate to the home loan specialists affiliated with the major banks who have that skill (figure 3-11).

Securitization also has promoted specialization within the financial industry. The sale of a home loan to a potential borrower used to be handled by an employee of the lender, but increasingly in recent years mortgage brokers have emerged to handle the task. It also is common for the smaller lenders to sell their home loans to the leading lenders as is, in the form of a loan. The major lenders focus their resources on segments that allow them to leverage economies of scale, thereby allowing specialized

7. See Inoue (2005).

Figure 3-10. *Lender Share of Home Loan Originations in the United States*[a]

Percent

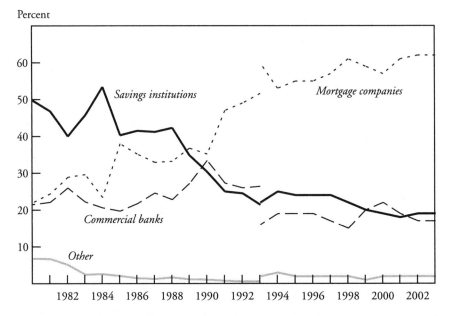

Source: Nomura Institute of Capital Markets Research, based on data from the U.S. Department of Housing and Urban Development and the *Federal Reserve Bulletin* of September 2004.

a. Some line graphs are not continuous because of changes in the survey population.

financial institutions and smaller lenders to play a more important role in the sale of mortgages that require contact with individual borrowers.

While the trend has been for smaller lenders to own less of the loan assets that they originate themselves, their ownership of RMBS is increasing. In other words, financial institutions are transforming themselves into institutional investors. In any case, the owning and securitizing of home loan assets increasingly are becoming the province of the leading financial institutions.

Another interesting development in the United States is the growing criticism of the GSEs, which can be attributed both to changes in the environment surrounding the GSEs and to changes in the nature of the GSEs themselves. Criticism has long been leveled at the existence of a tacit government guarantee on the bonds issued by GSEs as well as at incentives such as exemption from state and local corporate income taxes that subvert fair competition with purely private sector lenders. There also has been criticism of the risks associated with the market treating bonds issued by the GSEs as having a government guarantee, even though they are not in fact guaranteed by the government.

Figure 3-11. *Transaction Share of Ten Lending Servicers in the United States*

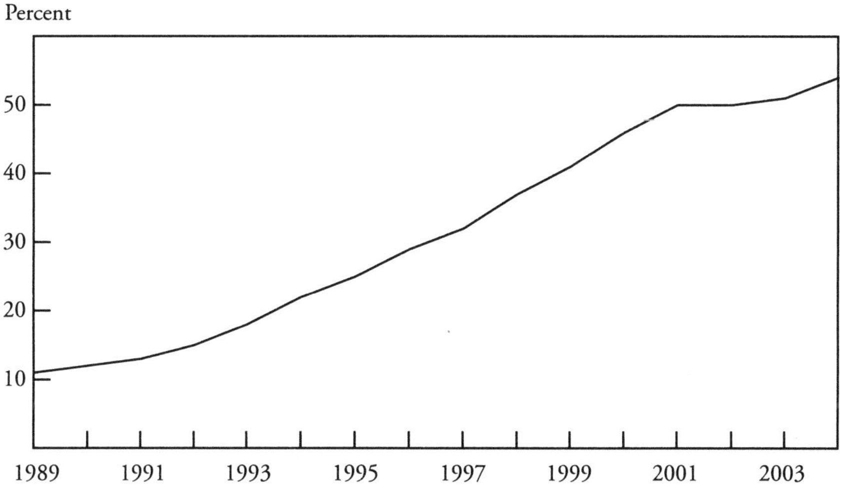

Percent

Source: Inside Mortgage Finance Publications, *The Mortgage Market Statistical Annual* (2005).

Since the end of the 1990s, however, criticism has been especially strong of the fact that Fannie Mae and Freddie Mac not only have been handling the securitization of conventional mortgages but also have begun securitizing in other mortgage segments, purchased existing RMBS and issued CMOs, and expanded their assets, both on- and off-balance sheet, as a result of their increased use of derivatives to manage risk. Such activities have heightened the GSEs' influence and increased their issuance of securities. Meanwhile the U.S. Treasury Department has reduced its issuance of securities, resulting in GSE bonds—a large portion of which are held by private sector lenders—accounting for a rising share of the market. That in turn has raised concerns over systemic risk.[8]

There also was debate in the House of Representatives around 2000, and a bill was proposed by Representative Richard Baker and others to improve regulation of financing in the housing sector.[9] Broad-ranging accounting irregularities subsequently came to light, at Freddie Mac in 2003 and at Fannie Mae in 2004, further fueling criticism of the GSEs. One of the irregularities was the accounting treatment given derivatives used in hedging transactions, even though there is really no need to use derivatives in a straight securitization. Nevertheless, such aggressive use of derivatives and other advanced transactions is a natural outcome

8. These issues were summarized by Wallison and Ely (2000).
9. Housing Finance Regulatory Improvement Act.

of the two GSEs' pursuit of profits as private sector corporations, as well as part of the process of making the RMBS market more user friendly and efficient. The questions are whether the organizations had the expertise and internal controls required, whether the outside supervision was sufficient, and whether the current status of the GSEs is suitable for those types of transactions.

The two GSEs grew further in size from 2000 until 2005, coinciding with the time when concerns over systemic risk became a bigger issue and when critics were calling for limits on the GSEs' assets.[10] Nevertheless, despite the critical problems that have been pointed out, it is clear from the large number of reform proposals since 2000 that Congress has failed to pass that the housing-related GSEs enjoy very strong political support.

The Future of Japan's GSE

It is instructive to look at the situation in the United States as described above when contemplating the future of Japan's new agency after the RMBS market has developed, but it also is important to keep in mind three relevant factors that distinguish Japan from the United States:

—the decline and aging of Japan's population

—the serious nature of Japan's fiscal deficits even when viewed from a long-term perspective

—the fact that private sector lenders have already been quite active in securitizing their own home loan portfolios

It would be difficult to argue that Japan's declining and aging population has had no direct impact on housing issues. The decline in population should reduce demand for housing in absolute terms and therefore reduce the importance of home loans. Japan's population had already begun to decline in 2005, and the more pessimistic forecasts call for the population to decline from the current level by more than 5 million by 2020 and by another 8 million between 2020 and 2030.[11] Furthermore, the aging of the population should result in a relative decline in the number of homeowners who elect to finance their homes with a long-term mortgage. The percentage of the population aged sixty-five and over was 19.9 percent in 2005, the second highest in the world behind Italy (20.0 percent), but Japan is expected to overtake Italy very soon, with seniors on track to constitute

10. Wallison, Stanton, and Ely (2004) provides a summary of the recently cited problems with the GSEs and proposes reforms.

11. Forecast by the National Institute of Population and Social Security Research, Ministry of Health, Labour and Welfare, Tokyo. That said, until now the decline in both the birth rate and the population has been proceeding at a faster pace than the Institute's pessimistic forecast.

27.8 percent of Japan's population by 2020.[12] The baby boomers who drove the robust demand for housing finance in the 1980s will begin retiring in large numbers from April 2007 onward, and they will be in their seventies in 2020.[13]

The indirect impact on public policy from a declining and aging population will be a reduction in the importance of housing finance policies as well as housing policies in general. Meanwhile, improvements in the health care system and in nursing care facilities will become increasingly important elements of public policy. Accordingly, there seem to be natural constraints on demand for the new agency's services. Because of the relative decline in the status of housing policy, it is expected to become increasingly difficult to obtain political support for attempts to expand the agency's role.

Figure 3-12 shows the five categories in which there was a major change between 1999 and 2005 in the percentage of positive responses to a Cabinet Office survey asking citizens what they wanted from their government.[14] As the figure shows, demand for measures to deal with the declining birth rate and to pursue structural reform in health care, pensions, and other components of social insurance has grown rapidly, while the citizenry has become relatively less interested in land and housing issues as well as economic packages and reform of the financial system.

Although the lack of continuous data makes accurate comparisons impossible, in response to the question "What single issue would you like to see the government focus its efforts on?" in a 1967 survey, the leading answer was inflation, followed by taxes and then, in third place, housing and land issues.[15] In contrast, the top three issues for 2005 were structural reform in health care, pensions, and other components of social insurance, economic packages, and measures to cope with the aging population. The importance of housing and land issues dropped all the way down to twenty-second on the list.

The second factor, the problem of fiscal deficits, now has Japan debating whether it can achieve primary balance by fiscal year 2011. Even if it does meet that goal, toward the middle of the 2010s it will have to start reducing its outstanding public debt as a percentage of GDP (it stood at 158.9 percent at the end of 2005).[16] Although the aging of society tends to promote bigger government,

12. "White Paper on Aging Society 2006," Cabinet Office, government of Japan, Tokyo.
13. In Japan, the baby boomers are the generation born between April 1947 and March 1949.
14. Public opinion surveys on the life of the people, Cabinet Office.
15. Public opinion survey on the life of the people, Cabinet Office, 1967.
16. Council on Economic and Fiscal Policy, "Basic Policies for Economic and Fiscal Management and Structural Reform 2006" (Cabinet Office, July 7, 2006) (www.keizai-shimon.go.jp/english/publication/pdf/060802_basic_policies_summary.pdf).

Figure 3-12. *What Japanese Citizens Want from Government, 1999–2005*

Percent

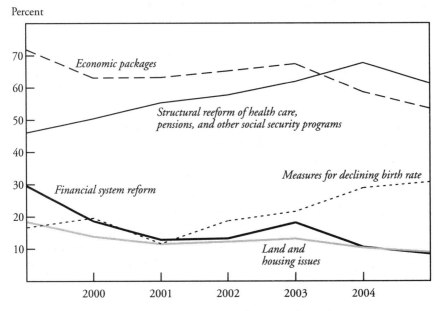

Source: Cabinet Office, government of Japan, public opinion polls of lifestyle issues.

the problem of fiscal deficits should continue to provide a counterweight to that tendency. In such an environment, it probably will be difficult to increase public support for expanding the agency's role.

The third factor distinguishing Japan from the United States is that the securitization of home loans by the private sector already is quite active in Japan. Further bolstering of the securitization infrastructure by the agency will reduce the need for the private sector's securitization efforts, but the agency's efforts to improve the infrastructure, which include improving investors' understanding of the securitization market, should also have a positive impact on private sector securitization. Private sector lenders have had a head start on the agency in acquiring securitization expertise, and thus it seems likely that they will continue to be active in the securitization arena.

In trying to form a long-term outlook for the agency, one must keep in mind the differences noted above. One lesson that the U.S. experience has taught is that if the agency is allowed to self-regulate, as the private sector is, its efforts to improve the RMBS market and increase earnings will inevitably lead to an expanded balance sheet, greater use of derivatives, and increased leverage. Moreover, if the agency continues to receive GSE-like tacit government guarantees and special treatment, the size and scope of the agency's business may increase to the point that systemic risk becomes a concern.

The agency's goal at this point is to expand its securitization business and eliminate its deficits, but an interim goal should be to obtain high ratings on the RMBS that it issues on the strength of its own credit, without resort to overcollateralization. Nevertheless, facilitating the agency's activities by increasing the government's equity in the agency and expanding the scope of the business while leaving the government's commitment unchanged is unlikely to lead to the same results as with the U.S. GSEs, given the expected decline in the importance of housing policy and the inherent fiscal constraints in Japan. It seems more likely, in fact, that there will be an increase in calls to reduce the government's involvement in the agency to the maximum extent possible.

In that case, it is conceivable that the agency, rather than rely on government funding and commitment, will opt to achieve substantial growth as an institution specializing in securitization through privatization and to increase its private sector funding sources. Some observers apparently think that that scenario describes the agency's future. Some also think that in the natural course of evolution, the agency will become a listed company like Fannie Mae.

Only time will tell what direction the agency will take. First, as time goes by, Japan's population will include fewer children and a greater number of elderly people, a shift that is likely to cast doubt on the future of a private sector corporation that specializes in supporting residential mortgage securitization. It may also present a barrier to such a corporation's status as a private company and stock market listing.

Second, it is conceivable that home loan assets eventually will gravitate to the major financial institutions, as has occurred in the United States. The result would be that the now larger private sector financial institutions would be expected to handle securitization more efficiently on their own than they had previously. As noted above, in Japan it was the GHLC that took the lead in securitizing the home loans of private sector lenders. The leading financial institutions also have accumulated substantial expertise in the management of risk related to securitization, and they face few constraints in the use of derivatives and other advanced financial transactions. For those reasons, private sector securitization should be able to grow even more easily in Japan than in the United States.

As long as the agency benefits from strong credit as a government agency receiving government funding, gets favorable treatment for its RMBS under Basel II (in current capital adequacy requirements, credit instruments issued by government-affiliated financial institutions carry a risk weight of 10 percent), and enjoys favorable information disclosure terms, private sector lenders are still likely to find some advantages in having their securitization done through the agency. If the agency becomes a private sector corporation, however, the special incentives will disappear, and the agency may become nothing more than a competitor of the leading financial institutions. Accordingly, demand for the agency's support of home loan securitization is likely to decline.

Given the issues discussed above, if the agency opts for complete privatization, it needs to do so as soon as possible in order to maintain its position as an institution specializing in providing securitization that is more efficient and more advanced than the securitization done through the major financial institutions. The key to the agency's success is to develop a business strategy that can adequately cope with the expected decline in demand over the long term. If that does not go well—that is, if the agency privatizes completely and finds it difficult to operate as a completely private concern, as does Fannie Mae—there are probably only two possible outcomes with regard to the agency's future.

The first is one in which the nature of the agency does not change much and it continues to perform its function of supplementing the private sector. Although additional capital injections from the government are unlikely, the company should be able to enhance its capital base endogenously through growth of its securitization business, which should allow for a certain degree of growth in the size and scope of its operations. By remaining a government agency, it can continue taking advantage of the government's credit strength and special treatments unavailable to the private sector. Without the need to pursue earnings growth as a private sector company, it should be able to maintain a low-cost operation. Accordingly, even if the major private sector financial institutions invigorate their own securitization business, securitization through the agency should always remain a viable option. With limits placed on its growth and a commitment to supplementing the private sector, the agency should not become a giant enterprise in which systemic risk and fair competition become issues; it should instead become a "good" GSE.

The second possible outcome is that instead of being privatized as a whole, the agency can be merged with and become a division of a private sector bank. If home loans gravitate to the major financial institutions and those institutions are able to handle the securitization business, the whole idea of the government continuing to fund the agency and grant it special status will be increasingly called into question. The agency's future viability would be suspect if it remained an entity specializing in securitization, but it should have room to survive and grow if it operates as the securitization arm of a major financial institution. In that case, acquisition of the agency may not be very attractive to a financial institution that already has its own securitization business. It probably would be attractive, however, to a second-tier lender without an adequate securitization business of its own.

One potential candidate for such a merger is Yucho Bank. Under the provisions of the postal savings system reforms, Yucho Bank will be established in October 2007 to take over the postal savings business, which historically has been operated by the government. Initially, Yucho Bank is to be a wholly owned subsidiary of the holding company Japan Post (which itself started out as wholly owned by the government), but Japan Post will sell its shares until Yucho Bank is completely privatized by September 30, 2017.

As explained earlier, the country's postal savings business used to play a critical role in procuring funds for the FILP by absorbing personal savings and then distributing those funds to the GHLC and other government-affiliated financial institutions; thus it did not have its own lending function. The idea behind converting Yucho Bank into a private sector bank, however, is to leverage its legacy as a vast presence among the general public by developing it into a family bank. It is only natural for residential mortgages to become a critical business segment at a family bank. Although it is unacceptable for a wholly public owned institution to pursue business growth that competes with growth in the private sector, starting such a business is conceivable if the government's share in the institution is sold.[17] If Yucho Bank increases its home loan portfolio, the next step probably would be an attempt to increase its ability to handle securitization on its own. At that point, a merger between the two former FILP agencies, the GHLC and the Postal Saving System, probably is a strong possibility.

If the second outcome is realized, Japan's housing finance GSE will, after ably demonstrating its capabilities in a transitional role, pass its assets on to a private sector bank. Under either of the two potential outcomes, the agency, by taking full advantage of the fundamental discipline imposed by Japan's fiscal deficits and its shrinking and aging population, should be able to avoid the major problems surrounding the U.S. GSEs while contributing to growth in the securitization market for residential mortgages. Home loan securitization could then wind up playing a historic role in normalizing Japan's economic system, in which public institutions in the finance arena have occupied important ground.

---

17. Japan Post, a company created to orchestrate postal privatization and set to serve as the holding company for Yucho Bank for a certain period following privatization, submitted an outline of its plan to implement the succession of its services to the prime minister and the minister of internal affairs and communications on July 31, 2006. According to the plan, Yucho Bank will list its shares no later than during the fourth year following its privatization, which is during fiscal year 2011, and Japan Post will sell all of its holdings during the five years following that. The residential mortgage business is listed as a new business scheduled to be introduced following privatization.

References

Inoue, Takeshi. 2005. "Securitization and the Mortgage Business in Japan." *Capital Research Journal* 8, no. 1 (Spring): 32–46 (Nomura Institute of Capital Markets Research).

Inside Mortgage Finance Publications. 2005. *The Mortgage Market Statistical Annual*. Vol. 2: "The Secondary Market." Bethesda, Maryland.

Wallison, Peter J., and Bert Ely. 2000. *Nationalizing Mortgage Risk: The Growth of Fannie Mae and Freddie Mac*. Washington: AEI Press.

Wallison, Peter J., Thomas H. Stanton, and Bert Ely. 2004. *Privatizing Fannie Mae, Freddie Mac, and the Federal Home Loan Banks*. Washington: AEI Press.

COMMENT ON CHAPTERS 2 AND 3 BY

Adam S. Posen

THE PAPERS BY Yasuyuki Fuchita and Yuta Seki are of extraordinary detail and include some very useful information in their figures and tables. Upon their publication in the latest volume by the Brookings Institution and the Nomura Institute of Capital Markets Research, I am confident that they will become references for all financial market observers. At the same time, it is worth calling attention to the very phenomena that the authors themselves carefully establish in regard to exchange-traded funds (ETFs), real estate investment trusts (REITs), and mortgage securitization: the ongoing innovation in Japanese financial markets and the ever wider adoption and use of sophisticated financial instruments by Japanese investors and issuers.

This is a particularly good time to call attention in the United States and elsewhere in the English-speaking world to such healthy developments. With the leadership transition in Japan from Junichiro Koizumi to the current prime minister Shinzo Abe, many western observers have wondered out loud and in print whether the deregulation thrust that Koizumi supposedly began would continue. Such questions show how underappreciated the financial transformation in Japan to date has been. Although it is true that Koizumi and his then financial services minister Heizo Takenaka bravely cleaned up the banking crisis left to them by

I am grateful to Robert Litan for the invitation to participate in this seminar.

their predecessors' willful neglect, financial deregulation had been under way in Japan for twenty years.[1] The "Big Bang" financial liberalization begun by Ryutaro Hashimoto in 1996 was largely completed by the time Koizumi took office in 2001, even though the full benefits could not be seen until the banking system had been recapitalized by Koizumi and Takenaka (and the Bank of Japan had supported the country's recovery from deflation).

This sustained period of liberalization and consolidation has completely transformed corporate finance in Japan as well as the structure and behavior of the Japanese financial system. This transformation has gone much too far to be reversed, and it has vastly narrowed the difference between the types of financial products offered and corporate financing behavior in Tokyo and such products and behavior in New York or London. Household investment behavior and corporate governance in Japan may still leave a lot to be desired from the point of view of the market or the economist, but that should not obscure what has taken place. So the excellent expositions of the long and steady progress of the new financial instruments outlined by Fuchita and Seki are important simply as documentation of this ongoing trend.

There is still plenty of room for political economy questions of what caused this broader trend of financial reform and how the rise of ETFs and mortgage securitization fits with standard models of reform politics. Some will immediately attribute both the trend and the introduction and advancement of these particular instruments to the competitive pressure experienced by Japanese financial firms. While that has certainly played a role, we all know that the existence of alternatives in financial markets does not immediately translate into convergence of financial behaviors across borders—otherwise Japan would have been here before the 1990s, and continental European financial markets would look very different today (and more like Japanese, U.S., and U.K. markets). Others might cite that the broader Japanese crisis provoked a response, but that explanation strikes me as disregarding the facts that, at the same time this deregulation trend was going on, Japanese bank supervisors and politicians were making the banking problems worse and that these advances in financial depth and liberalization only became evident and widespread *after* the crisis had passed. Questions about what brought about financial reforms in Japan go beyond the remit of these papers, but they do provide interesting material for future research into determinants of reform and their outcomes.

---

1. Most would argue that it was partial but real deregulation in the 1980s that sowed the seeds of the 1990s banking crisis in Japan, much as did mismanaged partial deregulation of the savings and loan institutions in the United States in the early 1980s. See Ryoichi Mikitani and Adam S. Posen, eds., *Japan's Financial Crisis and Its Parallels to U.S. Experience* (Washington: Peterson Institute of International Economics, 2000).

What is probably more relevant for this audience is to treat the adoption and spread of these financial instruments in Japan as the independent variable, rather than trying to explain where it came from. I would therefore like to address five topics on the kinds of changes that the development of these instruments may cause in Japan, three of which are raised directly in the papers and two of which arise out of my own focus in these matters: the impact of change in the financial market on macroeconomic outcomes.

First, will the supply of new financial instruments automatically create its own demand in Japan? While most economists are skeptical in the abstract about Say's Law, in practice one sometimes gets the sense that they are believers. If one reads about ETFs in Seki's paper or the development of ETFs in the United States in Broms and Gastineau's complementary paper in this volume, one finds that there is a strong case made that ETFs are an obviously better mousetrap and that it is only a matter of time before households and other savers wake up and start buying more of them. There certainly is some precedent for such responses to financial innovations, but there are also counterexamples.

All of the $1.5 trillion plus (dollars not yen) in low-yielding CDs held with the Japanese postal savings system, and rolled over into similar but still lower-yielding instruments upon expiration from 1999 to 2001—and that was the overwhelming majority of those funds, as various U.S. retail firms found to their regret—represented a decision by Japanese investors to pass up on some new savings instruments that were available to Japanese savers at that time. Let us remember that in the United States, when savers shifted into REITs and ETFs in recent years, and homeowners took out the mortgages that securitization made available, they were largely shifting out of one class of risk assets into another. For Japanese savers, large-scale adoption of such instruments would require shifting from cash and deposits into risk assets, which is something else.[2]

The shift to securitization of mortgages discussed by Fuchita is much larger, and is more persuasively inevitable, than the rise of REITs and ETFs, perhaps because it is being done by the financial firms themselves, as intermediaries trying to shift their risk. Put another way, the numbers on the growth of REITs given by Seki do not come close to the massive growth in securitized mortgages presented by Fuchita. It is not households that are buying even repackagings of these securities, at least not in large numbers.

It would be even better to build on what the authors have done and try to estimate some demand functions for these securities in a more formal manner. For

---

2. Whether U.S. small investors and mortgage borrowers fully understand the risks they are assuming, and had assumed in the past, is a matter open for discussion, but their situation and choices are not comparable with those of Japanese grandmothers with savings accounts at the local postal savings branch.

example, how much has the demand for REITs been influenced by movements in the dividend yield in Japanese equities or by equity and real estate prices, or how well have the institutional investors packaging the mortgages evaluated credit risk after years of the ZIRP (zero-interest rate policy) and declining real estate prices? The point is not that these instruments are unimportant or unlikely to last; the movement of even a few percentage points of Japanese household savings is sufficient to ensure their importance and continued existence (and it already has). The point is that it may not be enough to forecast their growth and then discuss their impact without some consideration of what drives their growth.

Second, what effect will these new instruments, particularly the ETFs, have on Japanese corporate governance? Seki as well as others have raised the issue of the governance of these funds themselves, and certainly the contemporaneous spread of ETFs in the U.S. market has accompanied concerns about the behavior of mutual funds here. Fuchita raises the same point, by another means, when he discusses the difficulties everyone has had understanding, let alone tracking, the balance sheets of Fannie Mae and Freddie Mac, as an example of how not to design a government-sponsored enterprise (GSE). We can offer this wonderful product of securitized mortgages, but there is some limit to their acceptance (or what should be their acceptance) if the behavior of their main issuer (or issuers) is suspect.[3]

Undoubtedly, compared with the various investment vehicles previously available in Japan, these new instruments have many admirable attributes. As amply demonstrated in the 1980s and 1990s, even the management of insured savings account deposits at Japanese banks could well have used greater scrutiny, both from account holders and regulators. Yet, if ETFs (and for that matter REITs and mortgage-backed securities) are inherently to display their putative benefits, the underlying corporate or real estate investments they are tied to must offer some transparency as well. Otherwise, the point of the governance of these instruments and their issuers is moot.

In other words, it is still the corporate governance of Japanese companies (and real estate developers) that is at issue, just as it has been for a long time. And the financial liberalization of the 1980s and 1990s has had insufficient impact on Japanese corporate transparency in my assessment. Japan is still a place where formal and informal interlocking of companies, insider deals, smoothing of earnings, and managerial entrenchment prevail, and shareholder rights are far

---

3. Something similar has been seen in 2005–06 with the sudden closures of REIT-like funds offered to German investors after sharp falls in their net asset values (NAVs). Whereas malfeasance is probably not at issue, the poor handling of how retail customers were informed about interruptions in access to their money has probably had lasting negative effects on the demand for these instruments in Germany.

from protected.[4] There is still only a negligible number of contests for corporate control or turnovers of management for poor performance, and the environment remains hostile to such contests. The real estate sector is in many ways worse, beset by extensive underworld involvement (far beyond that of the kind seen during the construction cycle in New York City, for example) and offering little of the information about properties that is necessary to create a liquid market outside of the one for class A office space in Tokyo. In addition, accounting in both the corporate and real estate sectors is often literally not worth the paper it is printed upon.

So will the rise of these new financial instruments in Japan be limited by the failures of the underlying assets to be well governed? Or will these new instruments themselves lead to some improvements in Japanese corporate governance? So far, the demand for these instruments has been strong, and one can well understand why under such conditions mortgage-backed securities, used as a means to get real estate loans off of their balance sheets, could be an attractive defensive strategy, at least for the lending banks. Frankly, I am of two minds and would be interested in the authors' thoughts on this issue. On the one hand, I fear that a scandal arising from conflicts over ownership of properties or from buildings whose mortgages are securitized that do not meet earthquake or other codes could erode confidence in REITs and securitized mortgages—and one can easily come up with something similar in the corporate sector that would sour the Japanese savers on equities, and thus ETFs, just as they are starting to get back into that class of assets. On the other, depending upon how voting rights of ETF shareholders and the attraction of global real estate investors to repackaged mortgages proceed to develop, one could imagine institutional investors exercising greater scrutiny and discipline on Japanese companies and developers.

Third, is it possible to design a "good" GSE to securitize mortgages? Fuchita rightly identifies this theme as perhaps the critical issue in the future development of the mortgage-backed securities market in Japan. He also correctly points out that U.S. "agencies" do not present an ideal model, while recognizing their strengths. Fuchita balances nicely the discussion of the ideal with the politically realistic, given historical and current conditions, something all of us writing to influence the public policy debate have to try to do. I expect that this paper (or

4. This is not to say that there is still (or even was) a "Japan, Inc.," the fantastic keiretsu monster of some Americans' nightmares. The more accurate statement is that larger publicly listed companies, and banks in particular, have been subjected to greater market discipline, and some of the ties to smaller suppliers and to bank loans have loosened, but the vast majority of Japanese businesses (particularly those in domestic service sectors) retain unaccountable management that tends to overinvest.

its Japanese language equivalent) will have a significant influence on the discussion of these policies in Japan.

I would, however, encourage Fuchita to more explicitly address two aspects of the issue of designing a "good" GSE that are troubling in the current U.S. situation and are relevant for this institution-building exercise in Japan. The first is such GSEs' balance sheets in general, and whether they should be allowed to keep mortgages and securities on them for investment purposes. Fannie and Freddie have been both great profit makers and great sources of concern largely because they have retained holdings of mortgage assets, rather than simply getting off of their balance sheets everything that they securitize (except whatever mortgages are necessary to retain while the assembly, securitization, and sale are in process). Whatever was the original intent of providing a legal capacity for these two agencies to engage in such for-profit activities, it is clear that such speculative holdings of mortgages are unnecessary for them to fulfill their legislated function and provide benefits to American homeowners. Moreover, it is evident that the scale of these holdings is far too great and, partly as a result, far too opaquely reported to be justified and that such a combination makes them a source of systemic risk.[5] In short, Japan would probably suffer from allowing this kind of behavior by its GSE, as I fear the United States may in the not-too-distant future.

The second aspect for Fuchita to address more directly is the question of what should be the nature of the government guarantee, if any, for a Japanese GSE securitizing mortgages. Right now, with respect to Freddie and Fannie, the United States is living with what all financial economists know to be the worst of all worlds: an implicit, open-ended, but widely believed to exist guarantee. This partly arises out of the way these agencies are seen as "too big to fail," which in turn, of course, feeds their speculative behavior, which then increases their size and systemic risk, and so on (a dynamic with which Japanese policymakers are all too familiar). And one can easily imagine that in the present declining U.S. real estate market, few members of Congress would be brave enough to suggest that the federal government not step in if Fannie and Freddie had to start selling off assets in their portfolios during a down market—even though we know from Japanese experience in the 1990s among other examples that allowing such sales

5. I am oversimplifying here to some extent. Such issues as the smoothing of earnings and executive compensation at the agencies, the use of derivatives (not limited to Fannie and Freddie), and uncertain regulatory supervision all play roles in this situation. Yet the bottom line for Japan and other countries adopting some GSE-like institutional framework to enable the securitization of mortgages probably remains simply to preclude their counterparts to Fannie and Freddie from holding such assets on their balance sheets for the sole purpose of making profit.

would be the right thing to do.[6] It is unclear, however, why a government guarantee is necessary for a securitizing GSE to do its job, and why the expectations
of investors would be all that different if such a guarantee were explicitly pre-
cluded from the start in Japan. Either the assets are worth buying, or they are not,
and the new instrument (so to speak) of mortgage securitization should make
these assets more attractive—and the market for them more liquid—irrespective
of the creditworthiness of the intermediary.

This leads directly into my one real criticism of the Fuchita paper. Fuchita discusses at length the issue of how the GSE in Japan would establish a AAA bond
rating for itself and assesses three proposals for how to do it. I wonder why this is
necessary at all. Again, the virtue of the new financial instrument is in the securitization itself, not in the agency. Although there might be some risk at any given
time for mortgages and deals in process at the agency, why is that any different
from the risks of bookbuilding for an investment bank with a new offering or
buying a derivative from a trading house? I do not mean to be disingenuous; of
course, an agency seen as unlikely to make its payments or at risk of insolvency is
not one from which an investor wants to purchase securities. Thus it would fail
in its mission. But the risk specific to the GSE is surely only during the period of
intermediation, with the asset's value and risk characteristics determined by the
mortgages underlying it and the structure of the security.

Fourth, what difference would widespread adoption of these new instruments
and practices make to the transmission of financial shocks in Japan? Underlying
this question are two ideas: first, some of the miseries of the Japanese economy
following the bursting of the asset price bubbles over the course of 1990 to 1992
were compounded, if not created, by the structure of the financial sector. Second,
financial innovation in recent years has increased the volatility of particular assets
globally but arguably has diminished the volatility of the real economy by reducing the costs of reallocating risk. One way of considering this issue of financial
structure and shock transmission is to compare the responses of the U.S. and
Japanese economies to similar equity price rises and collapses a decade apart.
Around 1990, the transmission was far greater in Japan's bank-based and highly
relationship-based (rather than securitized) financial system.[7]

6. In fact, this may well explain why efforts a few years ago to better regulate the U.S. GSEs and clarify their nonguaranteed status have dried up in Congress of late.

7. See the U.S.-Japan comparison in Adam S. Posen, "It Takes More than a Bubble to Become Japan,"
in *Asset Prices and Monetary Policy*, edited by Anthony Richards and Tim Robinson (Sydney: Reserve Bank
of Australia, Economic Group, 2003) pp. 203–49. The Federal Reserve Bank's response to the asset price
bust was far more aggressive than that of the Bank of Japan and also played a key role, along with the structural differences.

The diminished transmission and persistence of financial shocks will be seen and felt much more in real estate assets than in equities, naturally. Even in Japan, equities inherently were far more liquid than properties with collateralized mortgages, which were held by individual banks and required specialized assessment of worth relative to local markets. Although REITs and securitization cannot make the entire difference between equities and real estate assets go away, they certainly can narrow it significantly.

In particular, just as theory would predict, U.S. experience demonstrates that if real estate lenders manage to off-load properties from their balance sheets, and real estate investors buy into diversified portfolios, both the overhang of unsold properties and the impairment of bank capital following a real estate bust are lower. Thus there is a public policy interest from a macroeconomic stability point of view, as well as from those of financial stability and efficiency, in the healthy development of REITs and real estate securitization in Japan. The authors might do well to at least acknowledge the prior work done on the macroeconomic aspect of this topic as a way of buttressing their case for the virtues of recent developments.

Every responsible public policy analysis comes with the caveat that "X is not a panacea," with X being the policy change in question, and that holds as well here where X is securitization and REITs. A great deal of the benefits of securitization depend upon there being sufficient but not excessive consolidation in the mortgage market, particularly regionally, such that the major lenders and real estate investors are diversified across geographic markets. Such diversification reduces if not rules out local capital crunches for banks, of the sort that hit banks in New England from 1989 to 1992 or in Texas and California in the mid-1980s. Another key condition is that the bank supervisors do not allow the legitimate easing of some of their concerns and duties, resulting from the existence of securitization, to absolve them and the banks they supervise from properly provisioning for loan losses. Yet, more than in most cases, one can make the case that the securitization of real estate lending (including both creating a GSE to promote securitization and allowing for the creation of REITs) is a clear improvement in public welfare without apparent costs.[8]

Finally, what effect might the widespread adoption of these new financial instruments in Japan have on the growth of productivity? It has become increasingly well established in recent research that development of the financial sector is crucial to the reallocation of capital between sectors and between specific firms

---

8. One could go so far as to suggest that some dire predictions of a negative impact on the U.S. economy from the fall of real estate prices at present are likely exaggerated, beyond the direct or "first-round" effects of such declines on consumption, given the combination of securitization, diversification of lenders across regions, ample capitalization, and strong supervision.

within sectors, both of which are necessary for sustained productivity growth. From a Schumpeterian perspective, where entrepreneurial activity and innovation of all kinds are intertwined, financial firms have to be ready to support new entrants and new technologies. It is therefore worth going beyond the assessment of asking how, and by how much, new financial instruments might improve the efficiency of financial markets in Japan, which would raise growth temporarily through the productivity gain within the financial sector, to asking whether such changes might enhance the productivity growth of the entire economy in a sustained manner, by improving the allocation of capital.

As I have discovered in recent research, a large proportion of the differences in (productivity and GDP) growth rates among the OECD economies can be explained by differences in corporate governance that depend upon the ability of banks and markets to reallocate capital between firms and sectors.[9] While the general consensus has emerged among researchers that there is no significant difference between financial systems that are bank based or securities based per se in their impact on productivity growth, I find that the closer that banks come to the classic model of relationship banking (for example, Japan's former main bank system, the still extant *Hausbank* system in Germany, and so on), the less reallocation of capital and employment takes place between sectors. When banks pursue more national(ist) goals in more consolidated banking systems, along the lines of France's traditional model of *Credit Mobilier* and increasingly in the Japanese system in recent years, and thus are less captured by local interests and companies, the more willing they are to make the necessary reallocations for productivity growth. And it appears that these more consolidated banking systems are also more willing to innovate than the more fragmented and politically influenced, and partially publicly held, systems as those in Germany and Italy.

In other words, the readiness of a financial system to make its main contribution to growth in advanced countries—shifting the allocation of capital between businesses and sectors—depends primarily on the financial system's structure and political independence.[10] Those products that increase the throughput of the financial system may contribute to stability and certainly will offer some cost savings to household investors, but they will not have a first-order effect on allocative efficiency. They do not directly change the incentives of the financial system to be less rent-seeking or less tolerant of relationship clients yielding low returns. This can be seen in the continued problems of the U.S. financial system related

9. Adam Posen, *Reform and Growth in a Rich Country: Germany* (Washington: Peterson Institute for International Economics, forthcoming).

10. Classically, the other main function of financial systems is to safely mobilize savings from households, but in advanced economies that may be taken for granted today.

to fraud, looting by corporate insiders in various forms, misstatements of earnings, and so on that persist despite the existence of a wealth of financial products available to households.

So it may be for Japan, too. That is why we should welcome these new instruments in Japan as being consistent with the overall development of the Japanese financial system, but we should also recognize that the already completed significant changes on the corporate financing side are the true source for ongoing productivity gains. It is a sign of the renewed health of the Japanese financial system, and of the economy more broadly, that we are able now to focus on these matters and that such innovations can take place.

FRANK PARTNOY
RANDALL THOMAS

4

Gap Filling, Hedge Funds, and Financial Innovation

D URING THE EARLY 1980s, corporate raiders represented a potentially important monitoring mechanism of corporate management in the United States. They bought large stakes in target companies and caused significant restructuring of U.S. businesses. Many companies responded to this hostile takeover wave by adopting stronger defenses; others implemented management-sponsored leveraged buyouts. The bulk of financial innovation during this period was defensive in nature.

During the 1990s, institutional investors moved to the forefront and accumulated increasing shares of U.S. equity securities. Much ink was spilled over how this shift in ownership structure would lead managers to adopt more shareholder-friendly corporate governance structures. Yet, after twenty-five years, institutional shareholder activism appears to have had relatively little impact on U.S. corporate governance.

Instead, a new player has emerged: the activist hedge fund. Hedge funds recently have shaken up boardrooms and forced radical changes at many publicly traded firms by leveraging their large pools of capital to push successfully for restructurings, sales, increased dividend payments, and other corporate actions that have directly benefited hedge funds and other shareholders. This hedge fund "activism," while in evidence for several years, reached a crescendo in the period 2005–06 with an unprecedented flood of funds directed at a broad spectrum of corporate targets. At the same time, financial innovation shifted from defense to offense. Today's hedge funds use novel financial techniques that were unknown to corporate raiders in the 1980s.

In this paper, we begin by documenting the successes and failures of "institutional shareholder activism" in recent years. In the first section, we focus on those areas in which shareholders are most able to exert influence: voting, litigation, and change-of-control transactions. We find that on balance institutional activism has been of marginal importance at targeted firms and that many institutions, such as mutual funds and pension funds, have not been as successful as some commentators initially had predicted.

The second section contrasts institutional shareholder activism with the more aggressive recent activism of the hedge fund managers. We cover a range of issues related to the recent growth of hedge funds and discuss the costs and benefits of hedge fund activism for each of four broad strategies that these funds have pursued: information asymmetry and convergence trades; capital structure–motivated trades; merger and risk arbitrage; and, most controversially, governance and strategy. Our analysis shows that, although there are major benefits derived from hedge fund activism, there are clear costs as well.

In the third section, we turn to the challenges presented by hedge funds and their innovative financial strategies in the areas of voting, litigation, and change-of-control transactions. We conclude that, although hedge funds have better incentives than do other institutions to play an activist role in these areas, their activism also raises novel challenges for regulators.

The Traditional Institutional Investor Role

In the early 1990s, shareholder activism by large institutional investors was praised as a promising means of reducing the agency costs arising out of the separation of ownership and control at American public corporations.[1] The theory was straightforward: Shareholder monitoring was an important method of limiting managers' divergence from the goal of maximization of shareholder wealth, and institutional shareholders were well positioned to act as effective monitors. Institutions held larger blocks of stock than most other investors and collectively held well over 50 percent of the stock of most large public companies. Acting collectively, these shareholders would have the power and the incentives to push for good corporate governance and to nudge managers to pursue wealth-maximizing strategies.

The idea captured the attention of federal regulators. To facilitate shareholder collective action, the SEC made two major changes to the proxy voting system

1. Black (1990); Roe (1991).

that favored efforts of institutional investor voting. First, in 1992 the SEC adopted several rule changes that had the effect of making it easier for institutional investors to act collectively in opposition to management proposals or in favor of shareholder proposals.[2] Later, in January 2003, the SEC mandated that mutual funds disclose how they were voting their proxies at firms in which they held shares. This change was meant to lead mutual funds to be more even handed in their voting practices by exposing potential conflicts of interest of funds that had closer ties to management.[3]

Along the way, however, criticisms of institutional activism emerged. Most institutions were reluctant to incur significant monitoring costs that would depress portfolio returns, while benefiting not just themselves but also their competitors. Collective action problems proved more difficult than was first thought because the costs of communication and coordination were higher than what had been hoped. Free riding by other institutional shareholders on the efforts of the activists persisted, while other institutions had significant conflicts of interest in engaging in activism at companies with which they had commercial relationships.[4] Furthermore, critics claimed that institutional activism created its own set of agency costs because public pension and labor union funds were pursuing self-interested agendas in conflict with those of other shareholders.[5]

Although not necessarily in response to these criticisms, existing legal rules place some barriers to collective action by institutions. For example, the Securities Exchange Act of 1934, §13(d) and the accompanying rules, requires any "group" holding more than 5 percent of any class of equity securities to file a disclosure document. This obligation can discourage institutional investors who wish to keep hidden the size of their stakes from accumulating large positions in any one company. Such concerns are increased by the short swing trading rules in §16(b) of the Securities Exchange Act of 1934, which limit the ability of large block holders to trade in and out of the stock of a portfolio company. Similarly, the insider trading laws embodied in the federal securities laws affect the ability of institutions to trade in a company's stock if they are in possession of material nonpublic information. These rules inhibit institutions from designating candidates to serve on boards of directors or from getting too involved in the business of their portfolio companies.[6]

Many legal barriers apply to change-of-control transactions as well, including the insider trading rules. In addition, an institutional investor that launches a

2. Black (1992).
3. Davis and Kim (2005).
4. Rock (1991).
5. Romano (1993).
6. Black (1998).

control contest, such as a proxy fight, would have to bear the substantial expenses associated with that effort without a guarantee of reimbursement, especially if it were unsuccessful. Further, if an institution were to obtain a control block of stock in a portfolio company, state law would impose fiduciary responsibilities on it in favor of the other shareholders in the company.[7] It is not surprising that institutional investors have rarely become involved in control contests.

Despite all of these difficulties, some activist institutions engage in shareholder monitoring. Institutional shareholder activists have focused their efforts on a number of well-defined fronts, ranging from using their voting power to push for corporate governance changes to filing class action lawsuits on securities fraud to punish and deter corporate wrongdoing. Some investors have been quite vocal about their activism, publishing and distributing detailed descriptions of their objectives and policies, while others have been quiet and operated behind the scenes. For example, CalPERS, one of the largest state pension funds, has published "focus" lists of underperforming firms since 1992. It has targeted these firms for corporate governance reform and by some estimates has generated substantial shareholder wealth through its efforts.[8] In the remainder of this section, we discuss voting, suing, and selling, the main areas for institutional shareholder activism.

Voting

Shareholders are the only corporate stakeholders that are routinely given the power to vote. They must be allowed to vote to elect directors to their offices, to approve or to reject proposed extraordinary business transactions, and to recommend certain types of corporate actions. They may also have the power to remove directors from office, to call special meetings, to cumulate their votes in favor of directorial candidates, to amend the corporate bylaws, and to act in a variety of more unusual matters. Institutions are the largest stockholders in most large American corporations, and they control well over the majority of the voting stock. Are they using their voting power to bring about corporate governance changes?

SHAREHOLDER PROPOSALS AND NEGOTIATED CHANGES IN CORPORATE GOVERNANCE. For the past twenty years, Rule 14a-8, the SEC's shareholder proposal rule, has been one of the main vehicles by which institutional investors have pushed for corporate governance changes at public companies in the United States. Using this rule, subject to certain limitations, shareholders can force corporations to place in their proxy materials a proposal for shareholder

7. Bainbridge (2005).
8. Barber (2006).

approval and a short, accompanying statement of support. These proposals are not binding on the corporation, however, even if approved by a majority of the shareholders.

Beginning in the 1980s, institutions proposed a broad variety of different actions, including the removal of corporate antitakeover defenses, reductions of executive pay, and changes in board composition. Overall, such proposals were targeted at poorly performing companies.[9] Although shareholder support for many of these proposals has been low, external corporate governance measures, such as the removal of the classified board and redemption of the company's rights plan, have long enjoyed substantial shareholder support. Many of these types of proposals garner a majority of the votes cast on the proposal, thereby passing an important threshold of shareholder support and creating more pressure on corporate boards to take action on the proposal.[10]

More recent data show that levels of shareholder support for external corporate governance proposals remains high, while executive compensation proposals have attracted increasingly high levels of shareholder support.[11] However, the public pension funds that offered many such proposals in the past have largely been supplanted by private individuals and labor unions as the most frequent sponsors of shareholder proposals of this type. Although shareholder proposals on corporate governance issues have had no statistically significant impact on stock prices, there is evidence that boards of directors have become increasingly responsive to corporate governance proposals to remove takeover defenses that are supported by a majority of the shareholders.[12]

Shareholder proposals appear to have a discernable impact on corporate policies if they achieve unexpectedly high levels of shareholder support.[13] In addition, some institutional investors, such as TIAA-CREF, have been able to negotiate agreements for corporate action to achieve their objectives even without a shareholder vote on their proposals.[14] These negotiated proposals rely on quiet diplomacy, backed by the threat of more vocal opposition if the proponents are unsatisfied with the target company's response.

Overall, optimistic assessments of shareholder activism using Rule 14a-8 claim that it has had a very limited positive impact, while more pessimistic observers believe

9. Romano (2001).
10. Bizjak and Marquette (1998).
11. Cotter and Thomas (2005).
12. Cotter and Thomas (2005).
13. Thomas and Martin (1998).
14. Carleton, Nelson, and Weisbach (1998).

it is actually harmful to shareholder interests.[15] Although there is some evidence that shareholder proposals have had more impact on boards in recent years, they are still having only a limited effect on the corporate governance structures of targeted firms.

DIRECTORIAL ELECTIONS: THE PROPOSED SHAREHOLDER NOMINATION RULE, "VOTE NO" CAMPAIGNS, AND MAJORITY VOTING INITIATIVES. The most direct way for institutional investors to influence corporate policy is to elect corporate directors they believe will support their interests. Under state corporate law, however, shareholders generally have little or no ability to nominate candidates for election to the board. In 2003 the SEC proposed a rule that would have permitted large shareholders to place on the corporate ballot a small number of director candidates in a limited set of circumstances. The idea was to give shareholders a way to bring about change in unresponsive corporate boards.

This proposed shareholder nomination rule provoked a firestorm of strong reactions, ranging from wholehearted support from many institutional investors to outraged denunciations from corporate management and its supporters. After extending the comment period for several months, the SEC ultimately did not take action on the proposed rule, much to the disappointment of many institutional shareholders.

Deprived of the shareholder nomination rule, institutions have continued to use alternative mechanisms to try to force directorial change at unresponsive firms. One popular technique has been to organize a "Vote No" campaign at companies that are unpopular with activist shareholders. These campaigns attempt to communicate shareholder dissatisfaction by having shareholders mark their ballots to withhold authority for particular director nominees.[16] For example, at the Disney Corporation annual meeting in 2004, institutional investors organized a strong "vote no" campaign against CEO Michael Eisner, with over 43 percent of a the company's shareholders withholding their votes to reelect Eisner to signal their objections to his stewardship of that company and its corporate governance structure. Eisner still won reelection, although the Disney board subsequently took away his title as chairman of the board.[17]

These campaigns have had some impact. Del Guerico, Wallis, and Woidtke found that "vote no" campaigns are correlated with unusually high turnover of CEOs and directors at targeted companies and that such CEO turnover is accom-

15. Concerning optimistice assessments of shareholder activism, see Karpoff (2001); for pessimistic observations, see Romano (2001).

16. Del Guerico, Wallis, and Woidtke (2006).

17. Barry B. Burr, "Institutional Investors Are Roaring at the Mouse," *Pensions & Investments*, March 8, 2004, p. 1.

panied by increase in stock prices.[18] They also found that outside directors at target firms suffer reputational damage. Overall, they concluded that "vote no" campaigns appear more effective in causing corporate change than are shareholder proposals, but these campaigns are still only indirect mechanisms for doing so and function only episodically.

A second important recent tactic is the bylaw amendment by majority vote. After the demise of the shareholder nomination rule, institutional investors began sponsoring proposals for a bylaw amendment by majority vote at major corporations. These proposals would eliminate the current plurality voting system, in which directors need only receive one vote in favor of their election, and would replace it with one that requires directors to receive a majority of the votes cast at the annual meeting, or in some cases a majority of votes of the total shares outstanding. In response to strong shareholder support for these proposals, some companies, including Disney, have unilaterally agreed that any director that does not receive a majority of the votes cast at a meeting will be deemed not (re)elected. There is a strong trend toward voluntary adoption of these bylaws, although their fine print often limits their impact.

Even if majority vote proposals are widely adopted, however, they offer little hope to proponents of strong institutional shareholder activism. At present, there are no instances at major public companies in which shareholders have withheld more than 50 percent of their votes from any director nominee. Even if this were to change, most boards will still retain the power to replace any director that was not elected by a sufficient percentage of the shareholders and could even choose to name the very same person to fill the vacant director position. There is, therefore, little reason to expect strong institutional shareholder activism to come out of the majority vote concept, at least for the foreseeable future.

THIRD-PARTY VOTING ADVISERS: HELPING IMPROVE CORPORATE GOVERNANCE OR CREATING UNREGULATED AGENTS? Activist institutional investors must address several problems in their quest to bring about favorable corporate governance at portfolio companies, which include the cost of informing themselves about the issues at these companies and the difficulty in communicating with other institutions about taking joint action on these issues. Cost-effective activism requires solutions to these problems. In addition, all institutional investors, activist or not, face fiduciary obligations to inform themselves about how to vote their shares at portfolio companies and need to find a way of doing so on a cost-effective basis.

18. Del Guerico, Wallis, and Woidtke (2006).

Against this backdrop, as early as the mid-1980s, a number of third-party vot-ing advisers began offering their services to institutional investors. Today, several companies, including most prominently Institutional Shareholder Services (ISS) and Glass, Lewis & Co., offer proxy advisory services to institutional investors to help them decide how to vote their shares. Institutions that subscribe to these ser-vices are given recommendations on how to vote on a broad range of issues, in-cluding shareholder proposals, corporate elections, mergers and acquisitions, auditor ratification, and a host of other topics.

The use of third-party advisers allows institutions to pool their resources to generate the research and analysis that they can use in their activism. It also helps to solve the free rider problem because the advisers' costs are prorated over all member institutions, thereby taxing otherwise free riding institutions to help facilitate shareholder action.[19] Not surprisingly, these third-party advisers have had a significant impact; their recommendations against management proposals have been found to be outcome determinative.[20]

Critics of the third-party advisory services claim that they are unregulated agents pursuing their own agenda, even at the expense of investors. One promi-nent commentator has charged that institutions delegate their voting decisions to third-party advisers because they "don't want to think."[21] If this is true, it raises the question of who is monitoring third-party advisers. Given their enormous power, if their clients are not paying close attention to why the third-party advis-ers are making their recommendations, there is the potential for the advisers' power to be abused. This might be particularly true for noneconomic issues where the returns to shareholders from activism are suspect. Furthermore, some third-party advisers, such as ISS, have been accused of selling their services to both institutions and their portfolio companies, thereby creating the potential for conflicts of interest in the advice that they offer.

LABOR UNION ACTIVISM AT THE BALLOT BOX: THE "TWO HATS" PROBLEM. Since the early 1990s, labor unions and labor-affiliated pension funds have been the most aggressive institutional shareholders, using their vast stockholdings and voting power to push for corporate governance changes at targeted companies.[22] Unions and their pension funds have been at the forefront of innovative methods of using corporate and securities laws to pressure companies to bring about the changes they desire. These methods include mandatory bylaw amendments to try to force companies to eliminate their takeover defenses and introducing share-

19. Coffee (1991, p. 1358).
20. Bethel and Gillan (2002).
21. Strine (2005).
22. Schwab and Thomas (1998).

holder proposals on the floor of the shareholder meeting.[23] They have also supported, or initiated, "vote no" campaigns at a number of other companies, such as the Disney Corporation.

Although unions frequently pitch their activism as pursuing traditional shareholder objectives, targeted companies have been quick to point out that unions' initiatives sometimes implicate labor's interests as workers' interests. Thus union activists have sometimes used shareholder activism to further corporate campaigns targeting companies engaged in collective bargaining negotiations.[24] In these cases, labor acts qua worker, rather than as an investor. This raises a potential for conflict between investors' interests in the maximization of the value of the firm and workers' interests in gaining a larger share of corporate income.

One example of the "two hats" problem is in labor's use of traditional shareholder activism techniques, such as Rule 14a-8, Proposals of Security Holders. In the 1990s, for example, unions were the most successful group in attracting high levels of investor support for their shareholder proposals. At that point in time, labor shareholder proposals largely targeted the removal of antitakeover defenses, a very popular idea with other shareholders that was generally viewed as value increasing for all investors.[25] In more recent years, unions have concentrated their shareholder proposals on topics related to executive compensation, which have attracted less shareholder support and seem less likely to raise firm value. Unions do, however, focus public attention on a topic that is embarrassing for corporate management. A possible explanation for this shift is that unions are more concerned with their roles as workers now.

Union activism's potential conflict of interest is undeniable but perhaps overstated in the heat of particular disputes. Like many institutional investors, labor unions and pension funds hold diversified portfolios, rarely holding more than a small percentage of a target company's stock. To win at the ballot box, labor therefore needs to convince other shareholders of its beliefs. If other investors are rational in voting in their own self-interest, this will limit labor's ability to engage in self-interested conduct in these dual role situations.[26]

Suing

When faced with suspected corporate wrongdoing or mismanagement, shareholders have the right to file suit against the firm's officers and directors. These suits commonly take one of three forms: class action lawsuits for federal securities

23. Schwab and Thomas (1998).
24. Schwab and Thomas (1998).
25. Thomas and Martin (1998).
26. Schwab and Thomas (1998).

fraud, state court derivative actions, and state court direct actions challenging the terms of mergers or acquisitions. As we discuss below, institutional investors have taken an active role in the federal litigation but have done very little in the state courts.

SECURITIES FRAUD LITIGATION: TAKING THE LEAD PLAINTIFF POSITION. The litigation role of institutional investors has been most apparent in federal securities class actions, largely after 1995 when Congress passed the Private Securities Litigation Reform Act (PSLRA). This statute was designed in part to encourage institutional investors to step forward as lead plaintiffs.[27] Before that time, agency costs were widely seen as pervasive in these class actions with entrepreneurial attorneys having free rein to file, prosecute, and settle suits with little regard to the interests of the shareholders they claimed to represent. PSLRA was intended to reduce these agency costs by insuring that the holder of the largest claim, usually an institutional investor, was named as the lead plaintiff and placed in control of the litigation by the court.

Although institutions were quite cautious at first about appearing as lead plaintiffs, in the past few years, institutions as lead plaintiffs have been appearing in steadily greater numbers. Some studies estimate that institutions are now lead plaintiffs in about 30 percent of all recently filed securities fraud class actions.[28] However, many institutional investors remain cautious about acting as lead plaintiff, preferring to pursue any legal claims that they have on an individual basis without bringing along smaller investors. Still others appear to completely ignore shareholder litigation, not even bothering to file claims to receive their portion of the settlement in many securities class actions.[29]

When institutions become lead plaintiffs, they appear to have a significant effect. Two recent studies have found that institutions when acting as lead plaintiffs were successful in winning larger settlements, controlling for other factors, than were other lead plaintiffs.[30] On the cost side of the equation, institutional lead plaintiffs have successfully negotiated lower awards of attorneys' fees in many cases.[31] Anecdotal evidence suggests institutional investors have also brought about corporate governance improvements and sharpened the deterrent effect of securities litigation by insisting that individual director defendants contribute personally to settlements in such high profile settlements as those at WorldCom and Enron.

---

27. Cox and Thomas (2005).
28. Cornerstone Research (2005).
29. Cox and Thomas (2002).
30. Cox and Thomas (2005); Choi, Fisch, and Pritchard (2005).
31. Perino (2006).

Yet, shareholder litigation is an episodic experience for most companies. One study estimated that only a small fraction of public companies experience a shareholder suit, although more recent reports by consulting firms claim that companies face a 10 percent chance of a federal securities class action lawsuit over a five-year period.[32] Out of this set of cases, institutional investors still only appear in about one-third of the cases. Therefore, even with greater institutional investor involvement in securities fraud litigation, the overall impact of these suits seems relatively small.

Moreover, there is a potential dark side to the drive toward institutional lead plaintiffs. Some plaintiffs' law firms have been accused of making campaign contributions to elected officials who are decisionmakers at certain public pension funds.[33] These "pay to play" allegations raise doubts over whether appointing institutions as lead plaintiffs will reduce the agency costs associated with securities fraud class actions.

STATE COURT CLASS ACTIONS: DERIVATIVE SUITS AND DIRECT CLASS ACTIONS. Historically, derivative lawsuits were one of the principal mechanisms by which shareholders attacked corporate mismanagement. Over time, their importance as a monitoring device has diminished both because of the increased importance of other corporate governance devices, such as independent directors, and because of procedural impediments created by state legislatures alarmed at the prospect of allegedly frivolous claims. Reflecting this change, a relatively small number of these derivative lawsuits are filed annually, about 45 a year in the Delaware Chancery Court, the most important corporate trial court in the country.[34] About one-third of these cases result in some form of recovery for shareholders, while the other two-thirds are dismissed without an award.[35] Institutional investors, however, do not appear as lead plaintiffs in these cases or otherwise take active roles in them.

The other important form of representative litigation in state court, class action litigation by shareholders, almost always involves challenges to the terms of proposed mergers and acquisitions.[36] These cases mainly attack acquisitions by control shareholders, (management buyout) MBO-type transactions, third-party

32. For the one study that estimated only a small fraction of companies experience a lawsuit, see Romano (2001); for more recent cases, see Miller, Foster, and Buckberg (2006).

33. Neil Weinberg and Daniel Fisher, "The Class Action Industrial Complex," *Forbes* 174, no. 5, September 20, 2004, pp. 150–57.

34. Thompson and Thomas (2004b).

35. Thompson and Thomas (2004b).

36. Thompson and Thomas (2004a).

friendly transactions, and hostile acquisitions. These cases result in substantive relief for shareholders in a substantial percentage of the cases that challenge transactions involving control shareholders, MBOs, and friendly third parties.[37] Only a handful of these cases are filed by institutional investors though.[38]

In sum, it does not appear that institutional investors have been very active in filing state court litigation challenging corporate managers' actions.

Change-of-Control Transactions: Buying and Selling

A third route that institutional investors could take in their activist efforts would be to engage in change-of-control transactions. As we noted earlier, there are significant barriers posed by corporate and securities law, such as the insider trading laws, facing institutional investors that wish to buy control positions in portfolio companies. However, institutions do not engage in these acquisitions for a variety of other reasons. For example, many institutional investors are subject to the prudent investor standard, a rule that mandates diversification of the institution's investments so that no one position puts at risk their returns to their beneficiaries.[39] This need for broad diversification and the relatively low cost of buying and holding long positions in stocks have led many institutions to index substantial portions of their portfolios, which effectively prohibits them from taking too large a position in any one company.

A number of other barriers exist to institutional control efforts. Some institutions, such as banks, are limited in how much of a company's stock they can own. Other institutions, such as mutual funds, face adverse tax consequences if they put more than 5 percent of their assets, or own more than a 10 percent stake, in any one company.[40] Poison pills and state antitakeover statutes also effectively limit institutional investments to well below control positions.

On the sell side, institutions are quite willing to facilitate change-of-control transactions by selling their stock. The Williams Act and subsequent SEC rules and regulations provide these institutional investors with time and information about takeover offers.[41] The one caveat is that because they are diversified investors, they frequently hold positions in the acquirer and target companies, and therefore, they evaluate a bid on the basis of the bid's overall impact on their portfolio. However, institutions are not the real agents for change when they are

37. Thompson and Thomas (2004a).
38. Thompson and Thomas (2004a), p. 187.
39. Black (1990, p. 553).
40. Black (1990, p. 552.
41. Thompson and Thomas (2004a, p. 1754).

selling into change-of-control transactions, but followers of other investors that instigate the transaction.

Institutions have also done little by themselves to thwart management-sponsored change-of-control transactions, such as leveraged buyouts. While sometimes grumbling over the terms of these deals, institutions in the 1980s and 1990s were unwilling to expose themselves to potential negative publicity and to spend the money necessary to organize unified opposition to these deals. However, with the rise of hedge funds, and to a lesser extent, this appears to be changing. As we will discuss further below, hedge fund event-risk arbitrageurs frequently target leveraged buyouts, or squeeze-out mergers, and use their positions in target companies to negotiate for better terms. Institutional investors have generally tagged along behind the hedge funds, free riding on their efforts to raise the prices paid in these transactions.

SUMMARY: INSTITUTIONAL INVESTORS HAVE HAD LIMITED SUCCESS AS ACTIVISTS. Two points emerge from this discussion: first, institutional investors can make a difference in corporate governance at targeted firms at the margins; and second, institutions have been unable, or unwilling, to get heavily involved in forcing more significant corporate changes, such as control changes at undervalued firms. In the third section of this paper, we look at the potential for hedge funds to fill in some of the gaps in institutional activism.

The Role of New Institutions and Instruments and the Rise of Hedge Funds

During recent years, hedge funds have emerged as a new and important player in financial markets. Although hedge funds have existed since the late 1940s, the industry has grown dramatically during the past decade. Hedge funds play numerous roles, and it is impossible to paint them with one brush. Nevertheless, it is apparent that hedge funds play an increasingly important role in corporate governance.

In this section, we discuss the unique background of hedge funds and assess the ways in which hedge funds can act to fill the gaps left by other institutional investors. This discussion requires us to take a step back and assess the different types of hedge fund approaches. Our analysis suggests that what has been described generically as hedge fund activism actually can be broken into four quite different strategies. We believe it is important to be analytically precise in describing these strategies, because the substance of the strategies is quite varied and because the policy implications of different types of hedge fund activism vary considerably.

First, hedge funds engage in what we call information asymmetry and convergence trades. Activism in this area is analogous to the typical arbitrage function in markets and is not particularly controversial. Although there are behavioral arguments about hedge funds engaging in parallel activities and related concerns about systemic risk, this first category of strategies is consistent with the general understanding of arbitrage-related trading.

Second, hedge funds engage in trades motivated by capital structure. These strategies are more controversial, although not entirely new in concept. Indeed, much trading motivated by capital structure is roughly similar to the strategies employed by private equity funds during the late 1970s and early 1980s. However, new elements of these strategies, and the recent literature on financial innovation, suggest that these strategies generate some difficult theoretical questions for scholars who maintain that the objectives of firms should be to maximize shareholder, rather than firm, value.

Third, hedge funds have been active in merger and risk arbitrage and in particular have used new financial techniques to take positions betting on whether deals will be completed. These forms of risk arbitrage are far more complex than the ones used even in the recent past. We consider how they might lead to some problems at the intersection of risk arbitrage and financial innovation.

Finally, and most controversial, hedge funds have become activist in governance and strategy. Hedge funds commonly take substantial long positions in a firm's shares and then demand changes in governance and strategy. They often use financial derivatives and private contracts, including options and swaps, to reduce costs, increase leverage, and control the release of information about these positions.

To present a more complete picture of hedge funds, we begin by offering some observations about the differences between hedge funds and traditional institutional investors. We then offer a detailed discussion of our four-pronged taxonomy of hedge fund strategies and discuss the role of financial innovation. In the following section, we look at how hedge funds fill the gaps left in the traditional institutional investors' activism.

Background on Hedge Funds versus Other Institutional Investors

There is no generally agreed-upon definition of a hedge fund. The term "hedge fund" does not appear in the federal securities laws. Indeed, when the Securities and Exchange Commission held a roundtable discussion on hedge funds in 2003, one participant cited fourteen different definitions found in government and industry publications.[42]

---

42. See SEC Roundtable on Hedge Funds, comments of David A. Vaughan, May 13, 2003 (www.sec.gov/spotlight/hedgefunds/hedge-vaughn.htm).

In our view, hedge funds generally have four characteristics: (1) they are pooled, privately organized investment vehicles; (2) they are administered by professional investment managers; (3) they are not widely available to the public; and (4) they operate outside of securities regulation and registration requirements.[43] Although many private equity or venture capital funds also have these characteristics, those funds are distinguished from hedge funds because of their focus on particular private markets. Mutual funds are heavily regulated compared with hedge funds, which manage to avoid those regulations by having a relatively small number of sophisticated or wealthy individual and institutional investors.[44]

Scholars attribute the development of the first hedge fund to Alfred Winslow Jones, a sociologist and journalist who in 1949 established a private investment partnership that reduced risk by buying one stock while shorting another in the same industry.[45] Winslow's approach had several advantages. First, the structure of the investment partnerships was flexible, and the partnerships could trade positions quickly, using leverage to make large bets on the movements of individual stocks. Second, the partnerships were not subject to regulation under the Investment Company Act of 1940 and thus could act outside of government scrutiny. Finally, and perhaps most important, instead of charging a fixed fee, Winslow set his compensation at 20 percent of profits, aligning his interests with those of his investors by giving him strong incentives to maximize fund value.[46]

During the following years, numerous investment partnerships were formed on the basis of Winslow's model. A 1968 survey by the Securities and Exchange Commission identified 140 funds operating at that time.[47] The number of hedge funds has grown rapidly since to roughly 3,000 by 1998 and to approximately 8,000 today. Total assets managed by hedge funds were roughly $300 billion in 1998 and are estimated to be well over $1 trillion today.[48] Although many hedge funds are quite small, the largest have several billion dollars under management.

43. See 15 U.S.C. § 77d(2), Securities Act of 1933 registration requirements; 15 U.S.C. § 80a-2(a)(51)(A), Investment Company Act of 1940 registration requirements; 15 U.S.C. § 80a-3(c)(7), Securities Exchange Act of 1934, reporting obligations; 15 U.S.C. § 80b-3(b), Investment Advisers Act of 1940 registration requirements.

44. Most hedge funds are exempt from the Investment Company Act of 1940, because either they have 100 or fewer beneficial owners and do not offer their securities to the public or all of their investors are "qualified" high net worth individuals or institutions. See 15 U.S.C. § 80a-3c(1), c(7).

45. Caldwell (1995).

46. Brown, Goetzmann, and Ibbotson (1999).

47. President's Working Group (1999).

48. Patrick M. Parkinson, deputy director, Division of Research and Statistics, Federal Reserve Board, "The Role of Hedge Funds in the Capital Market," testimony before the Subcommittee on Securities and Investment, Committee on Banking, Housing, and Urban Affairs, U.S. Senate, 109th Cong., 2nd.

In general, hedge funds are considered to be active market participants that use leverage aggressively, pursue short-term strategies, and take long and short positions. However, hedge funds vary considerably in their investment style and the types of financial instruments they trade. Global "macro" funds take positions based on economic forecasts and focus on government bonds and foreign exchange. Risk arbitrage, event-driven, or "special situation" funds take positions based on merger announcements, bankruptcies, reorganizations, and legal developments. Relative-value, convergence, or market-neutral funds take long positions in securities they believe are undervalued, while also taking countervailing short positions in securities they believe are overvalued.

Early studies of hedge fund performance suggested that hedge funds offered greater risk, but also greater expected return, than did other more common investment strategies, including index-based strategies.[49] However, more recent studies have reached more mixed conclusions. For example, a study in 2005 estimated the value added by hedge funds (alpha) as 3.7 percent, approximately the same amount as the average fees earned by hedge funds.[50] Other recent studies have suggested that once hedge fund data are corrected for various biases hedge funds do not outperform other investment strategies.[51] Moreover, at least some hedge funds generate an asymmetric risk-reward profile, with a substantial probability that the fund will outperform a particular index, but also with a higher probability of ruin. For example, although Long-Term Capital Management (LTCM) had a Sharpe ratio of 4.35 for its first three years, it lost more than 90 percent of its value during 1998.[52]

During the past several decades, hedge funds consistently have charged high fees: typically 2 percent of assets under management plus 20 percent of the fund's annual returns. As a result, hedge fund managers are among the most highly compensated people in the world, and annual compensation of more than $100 million per year is not uncommon for some individuals.[53] Hedge fund managers typically are compensated on the basis of absolute returns, not returns relative to an index, and therefore they have incentives to be more aggressive in their strate-

---

sess. (Washington: May 16, 2006) (www.federalreserve.gov/boarddocs/testimony/2006/20060516/default.htm).

49. Fung and Hsieh (1999); Brown, Goetzmann, and Ibbotson (1999).

50. Ibbotson and Chen (2006).

51. Kat and Palaro (2006); Malkiel and Saha (2006).

52. Partnoy (2004, p. 255).

53. In 2005 the top 25 hedge fund managers each made more than $130 million. See Jenny Anderson, "Atop Hedge Funds, Richest of Rich Get Even More So," *New York Times*, May 26, 2006, p. C1.

gies compared with managers at other institutional investors. As we will see in the next section, this has significant implications for their activism.

One purported advantage of hedge funds is that their returns are not highly correlated with other investment vehicles. To minimize correlation, hedge fund managers have incentives to follow strategies different from those of other institutions and other hedge funds. Indeed, sophisticated investors typically assess hedge fund managers on their ability to produce high absolute returns, above those they could achieve by simply investing in an index. However, many critics have suggested that the returns of hedge funds are more highly correlated than was previously believed with market indexes and other hedge funds.

Hedge funds differ from other institutions because they typically raise money through private offerings to a relatively small number of wealthy investors and large institutions that are not subject to the same regulations as those of other institutional investors. Moreover, hedge funds typically require that investors lock in their investments for a fixed period of time, ranging from six months to several years. By comparison, other institutional investors, particularly mutual funds, are subject to more-rapid investor redemptions. Because of these differences, hedge fund managers are more independent of their investors than are managers of other institutions.

Moreover, whereas mutual funds must have independent boards and permit shareholders to approve certain actions, hedge funds can more completely separate ownership and control, if they choose. The typical hedge fund is a partnership entity managed by a general partner; the investors are limited partners who are passive and have little or no say in the hedge fund's business.

In recent years, critics around the world, particularly in continental Europe, have called for more extensive regulation of hedge funds. In late 2004 the Securities and Exchange Commission responded to some of the criticism by adopting new rules that required hedge funds to register with the agency and imposed limited disclosure requirements.[54]

Whereas most institutional investment advisers had been required to register with the SEC, hedge fund advisers—the general partners—typically were exempt under a special private adviser exemption, because they advised fewer than fifteen "clients."[55] The SEC's new rule effectively required hedge funds to register by including in the definition of clients the limited partner investors in a fund. Following the

---

54. "Registration Under the Advisers Act of Certain Hedge Fund Advisers," 69 Fed. Reg. 72054, December 10, 2004.

55. The general partner's only client was the partnership entity itself.

SEC's new interpretation, if a fund had fifteen or more investors, it had to register. Most funds had more investors than that, and therefore the new SEC rule required that they register.

This regulation took effect in February 2006, and it was immediately challenged. It is worth noting that the new regulation was not particularly onerous. Essentially, it required that hedge fund advisers file a brief registration statement and make certain limited disclosures, including their names and addresses. It did not subject them to substantive SEC regulation. Nevertheless, many hedge fund managers, a highly private group, opposed the very notion that they would be required to reveal their existence, names, and addresses to regulators. They argued that the new regulation would have unduly leveled the informational playing field between hedge funds and other institutions in the United States and would have led many hedge funds to relocate abroad.

The legal dispute over the rule revolved around the definition of "client." The SEC's authority for the new rule stemmed from the language in the Advisers Act exempting "any investment adviser who during the course of the preceding twelve months has had fewer than fifteen clients."[56] But what is a client? Is it a *fund*, in which case the adviser is exempt, because it advises only one (or a few) funds? Or is it an *investor*, in which case the adviser is not exempt, because the typical hedge fund has fifteen or more investors?

The appeals court struck down the rule, siding with the hedge funds and against the SEC. In a nutshell, the court held that the rule was arbitrary because, for example, it would force hedge fund advisers with between 15 and 99 investors to register under the Investment Advisers Act, even though the fund itself would be exempt from the more demanding Investment Company Act since it had fewer than 100 investors.[57] The SEC chose not to appeal the case to the Supreme Court.

Hedge funds quickly responded to the case by withdrawing registrations they had filed since February 2006 when the rule took effect. They also requested and obtained from the SEC a no-action letter indicating that they could withdraw and maintain exempt status even if they had marketed themselves to the public while they were registered or even if they had taken on more than fourteen clients.[58]

At the moment, hedge funds remain subject only to the antifraud provisions of the securities laws, and the SEC has brought cases against hedge funds alleging securities fraud. Compared with other institutional investors, this is a relatively

56. 15 U.S.C. § 80b-3(b)(3).
57. *Goldstein* v. *SEC*, No. 04-1434 (D.C. Cir. June 23, 2006).
58. Paul E. Roth & Jeffrey E. Tabak, SEC No-Act Letter, August 10, 2006.

light burden. For example, hedge funds are not subject to the substantive disclosure requirements or governance-related regulations that impact mutual funds. Some regulators favor additional rules governing hedge funds, and countries outside the United States have imposed more onerous regulation. As of October 2006, Congress was considering additional hedge fund legislation.

One final regulatory distinction between hedge funds and other institutions is worth mentioning. Because hedge funds do not fall under Investment Company Act regulation, they are permitted to trade on margin and engage in short sales, strategies that are not available to other institutions, such as mutual and pension funds.[59] These two strategies—leverage and short selling—have become particularly important in recent years for several reasons.

First, although the largest mutual funds and pension funds have more assets under management than do hedge funds, hedge funds can and do use leverage and financial derivatives to acquire larger positions. For example, one prominent fund, Long-Term Capital Management, borrowed an amount equal to several times its capital—at one point it was leveraged 100 to 1—and it held approximately $1 trillion of derivatives positions before it collapsed in late 1998.[60] In 2006 numerous hedge funds had more capital under management than did LTCM, including several hedge fund families with more than $10 billion under management, although the degree of leverage had declined.

Leverage also enhances a hedge fund's ability to focus on particular companies. Because hedge funds are more focused on absolute returns, rather than on performance relative to an index, they are more likely to hold concentrated equity positions that are larger than the positions held by traditional institutional investors with substantially more capital under management. This enables them to capture a greater percentage of the value of any target firm created by their activism.

One final effect of heavier leverage is that hedge funds tend to trade more frequently than other institutional investors. As a result, hedge funds account for roughly half of trading on stock exchanges and are active participants in derivatives markets. Such active trading generates substantial fee income for investments banks. These banks compete for this business by offering prime brokerage accounts to hedge funds and giving them a first choice on any of their proprietary research on potential target companies. Some funds reward the banks that identify the most successful investment opportunities by directing their trading business to them.

---

59. See 15 U.S.C. § 80a-12(a)(1), a(3).
60. Partnoy (2004, p. 260).

Moreover, regulations prohibit many large institutional investors from taking short positions (or using many other derivative instruments); hedge funds are not restricted from shorting, however. Because hedge funds can short shares, they can engage in numerous strategies not available to other institutions. They also can obtain concentrated exposure to particular companies at relatively low cost. Recently, the SEC has loosened some restrictions on shorting, and it has proposed to liberalize this market even more. As the cost of shorting declines and the market expands, hedge funds acquire an even greater advantage over other institutions that cannot short.

In addition, hedge funds have shown great facility in using financial derivatives to acquire short positions. They frequently buy and sell exposure to individual stocks by using private options transactions to replicate share trades. They also are active in the share lending market and obtain favorable treatment on share lending transactions from the financial institutions where they hold prime brokerage accounts. It is easier and cheaper for a hedge fund to sell short a security than it is for virtually any other investor. (It is interesting that an alternative method of acquiring short positions in shares, the trading of security futures, was introduced in 2002, but this method never gained sufficient liquidity.)

A Taxonomy of Hedge Fund Activism and Financial Innovation

Hedge funds have played an important role in making markets more efficient, but in doing so, they have introduced new risks and costs. For example, hedge funds are more flexible than other institutional investors, and therefore they can more easily take positions in securities they believe are under- or overvalued. This is particularly important with respect to potentially overvalued securities, because traditional institutional investors—particularly those investors who follow an indexing or buy-and-hold strategy—will have neither adequate incentives nor the ability to make large short-term trades on the basis of perceptions about the relative value of securities.

In this section, we explore the impact of hedge funds on market efficiency. We begin by classifying hedge fund activism in equity markets into several different categories: information asymmetry and convergence trades, capital structure–motivated trades, merger and risk arbitrage, and governance and strategy. We go on to examine more closely the last category—governance and strategy—and find some parallels to the private equity activism during the 1980s. However, we also find some important differences from the earlier activism, particularly with respect to the increased usage of financial innovation.

INFORMATION ASYMMETRY AND CONVERGENCE TRADES. Many hedge funds engage in trading strategies to exploit information asymmetry between sellers and buyers of financial assets. In this sense, these hedge funds resemble any arbitrageur who seeks to profit from information not currently reflected in market prices. In general, this kind of arbitrage activity makes markets fairer and more efficient, because it causes market prices to reflect additional information as prices change in response to hedge fund trading.

The success of these trades rests on hedge funds capturing an informational advantage over other investors, and there is some evidence that such an advantage does in fact exist. First, as noted above, there is evidence of positive alpha returns to hedge funds, and investors continue to be willing to pay hedge fund managers high fees (even if returns have declined). This suggests that hedge funds actually are successful at exploiting information asymmetry. Second, because of their compensation structure, hedge funds attract top financial talent. If anyone can find and exploit informational advantages, it seems reasonable that these highly skilled individuals would be likely candidates. Third, because of their flexibility, hedge funds are able to move quickly to get into (and out of) large positions in markets, in which other institutional investors might not be able to move as quickly or to invest in such large amounts. Fourth, hedge funds are not subject to significant regulation. As a result, they are able to engage in investment strategies that might lead to scrutiny if these strategies were to be employed by other institutions.[61]

Hedge fund trading that is driven by information asymmetry might reduce market volatility as well. For example, the increase in hedge fund activity has been correlated with a decline in volatility. The average of the Chicago Board Options Exchange Volatility Index, VIX, from 1990 through 2003 was more than 20 percent, and during 2003 the VIX average was 21.99 percent. In 2004 and 2005, it was 15.48 percent and 12.81 percent, respectively.[62] Although this correlation does not establish a relationship between hedge funds and declining volatility, it is consistent with the argument that hedge funds, by reducing information asymmetry, have reduced the substantial swings in securities prices upon revelation of important information. If hedge funds are able to uncover information over time that otherwise would surprise investors all at once, their buying and selling activities would result in a smoothing of financial asset prices by reducing uncertainty.

In particular, hedge funds have been uniquely active in acquiring negative information about companies and then shorting those companies' securities. Several dozen hedge funds manage billions of dollars based on short strategies. In theory, informed shorting by hedge funds should lead to more accurate and less

61. Most recently, some critics have suggested that hedge funds are engaged in extensive insider trading because of their privileged access to information not available to the public.

62. (www.cboe.com/micro/vix/historical.aspx).

volatile financial asset pricing. To the extent informed hedge fund trading reduces risk, it should lead to higher equity values overall as well.

Regulators have been critical of hedge fund shorting and have investigated several high-profile hedge funds that have shorted a company's shares and subsequently generated and published negative information about that company. The New York state attorney general and the SEC have investigated short selling by hedge funds, such as Greenlight Capital, Aquamarine Fund, and Tilson Capital Partners. One hedge fund, Gotham Partners, that exhibited annualized returns of more than 40 percent for 20 years was targeted for such practices. Although Gotham typically took long positions, it sometimes had taken short positions in companies and soon thereafter published research with detailed information explaining the rationale for its short position. For example, in 2002 Gotham published a sixty-six-page report indicating that MBIA, the AAA-rated municipal insurance company, was engaging in dubious accounting practices. The report contributed useful information not previously available in the market, which led others to investigate MBIA. At the urging of MBIA, New York state attorney general Eliot Spitzer investigated Gotham's report and share trading, but he did not bring charges. MBIA's share price fell in response to the Gotham report and as of October 2006 was still at early 2002 levels.

Of course, trades driven by information asymmetry, long and short, are not always successful. Numerous hedge funds believed that Enron was overvalued and took short positions on the stock during 2000 and 2001 as the share price continued to increase. The literature on behavioral finance has shown that timing concerns and restrictions on shorting can also lead to inefficient pricing of securities in the short run.

Hedge funds often act in concert to take concentrated risk positions. Indeed, for decades, hedge funds have been active in so-called convergence trades in financial assets other than equities, in which the funds would take a long position in what they believed was a relatively undervalued financial asset and a short position in a relatively overvalued asset. Salomon Brothers and later LTCM engaged in such trades in the bond market. George Soros did such trades in foreign exchange.[63]

The risk concentration associated with parallel convergence trades has mixed effects. On the one hand, concerted action might be necessary to move prices. Hedge funds that are simply mimicking others are unlikely to generate above-average returns. On the other hand, concerted action can increase systemic risk and liquidity risk. The credit crisis during the fall of 1998 generated system-

---

63. Partnoy (2004).

wide worries, not only because of the collapse of LTCM but because so many hedge funds had made the same losing bets, although when some funds learned about LTCM's positions, they took opposite positions in anticipation of LTCM's difficulties.

In 2005 numerous hedge funds lost money on similar trades in synthetic collateralized debt obligations, renewing concerns about systemic risk. Although there were substantial losses among hedge funds from similar trades, most regulators and commentators believed the settlement processes associated with the trades were of greater concern than the systemic financial risks.

On balance, we find that information-driven activism by hedge funds is beneficial and should be encouraged. If there are concerns that hedge funds engage in market manipulation, publish false information, or engage in insider trading, regulators could address those concerns directly. Indeed, recent prosecutions suggest that regulators have the tools to do precisely that.

CAPITAL STRUCTURE–MOTIVATED TRADES. Hedge funds also engage in trading strategies directed at changing companies' capital structures. Essentially, hedge funds take equity positions and then try to persuade managers to change the capital structure of the company (typically to pay substantial dividends, repurchase shares, or take on additional debt) in ways that the hedge funds believe will maximize the value of shares. In certain respects, the recent increase in these kinds of strategies resembles the increase in pressure on public companies from private equity investors during the 1980s. Although hedge funds today do not typically seek to take companies private, their capital structure–driven strategies resemble a kind of early-stage leveraged buyout. In addition, at least in theory, hedge funds could take a range of positions, depending on a company's actual capital structure compared with its optimal one.

Unlike the private equity and leverage buyout approaches of the 1980s, the hedge funds' recent strategies have led some scholars to rethink the theory of the firm and capital structure. For example, whereas many 1980s deals were thought to be driven by the positive returns associated with the disciplining effect of debt, or perhaps tax advantages, more recent deals motivated by capital structure are viewed more skeptically, as perhaps being no more than a redistribution of corporate resources to debt holders or redistribution of other slices of the capital structure to shareholders.

Thus hedge fund activity raises an important theoretical question about the nature of the corporate enterprise. If managers owe duties to maximize share value, hedge funds that opportunistically induce the firm to breach contracts with nonshareholders might generate positive returns ex post that would lead to costly

Figure 4-1. *Example of Two Equivalent Firms with Differing Capital Structures*

	DebtCo		OptionsCo
Debt	$1,000	Equity	$1,000
Equity	$500	Options	$500

ex ante protections. But if managers owe duties to maximize firm value, rather than share value, they should be able to resist hedge fund efforts to redistribute value.

Some scholars have argued that, given the recent insights from financial innovation, from the perspective of theory shareholder maximization generates intractable contradictions.[64] For example, an approach for wealth maximization for shareholders leads to perverse results, depending on the capital structure. Consider the following thought experiment: suppose two firms, DebtCo and OptionsCo, are precisely equivalent in every way except capital structure (that is, they have the same assets and the same potential projects). Their capital structures are depicted in figure 4-1.

Note that both firms have the same market capitalization: $1,500, which is consistent with the assumption that their assets and future projects are equivalent. If each corporation seeks to maximize the value of shares, the corporate actors will have incentives to behave differently, even though the firms are equivalent in every other way. More concretely, suppose each firm faces two choices. The risky strategy pays $10,000 with a 10 percent probability and nothing with a 90 percent probability. The conservative strategy pays $1,500 with certainty. The firms, and society, are better off if each firm selects the conservative strategy.

Now suppose that activist hedge funds hold equity and seek to persuade managers to maximize shareholder value. Assuming risk neutrality, DebtCo will maximize the expected value of equity by choosing the risky strategy over the conservative strategy, and thus its board should select this option if its goal is to maximize shareholder value. However, OptionCo's board will maximize expected shareholder value by choosing the conservative strategy. Note that the conservative strategy should be dominant for both firms if their goals are to maximize expected firm value. Thus, to the extent hedge funds are successful in pushing for a goal of maximizing shareholder value only, they will encourage the misallocation of capital.[65]

64. Partnoy (2004).
65. Moreover, if hedge funds also held options positions, particularly options with short maturities, they would have incentives to pursue shorter-term strategies than would shareholders without such positions.

Jensen, Murphy, and Wruck have recognized the problems with the simple approach to the shareholder maximization norm, particularly in the context of executive compensation.[66] They have suggested that the corporate objective should be to maximize firm value. Other scholars have made compatible arguments. Our analysis of hedge fund activism provides a new area of support for these arguments.

Hedge funds also engage in other, more controversial trading strategies motivated by capital structure that some argue are designed to extract profits without generating benefits. Examples include convertible bond arbitrage and manipulation of so-called death spiral securities. Although these activities often are confined to smaller, less liquid stocks, public disputes have occurred surrounding attempts by hedge funds to extract value from these kinds of strategies. For example, a hedge fund might buy convertible bonds and simultaneously short shares. In these cases, it can be difficult to untangle the question of whether the hedge fund is simply trying to arbitrage an underpriced conversion option embedded in a convertible bond, or instead whether it is attempting to manipulate downward the price of shares so that it can profit from a cheap conversion.

On balance, we find hedge fund activism that is driven by capital structure is less likely to be beneficial to investors than is hedge fund activism driven by information. Although the hedge fund strategies of today might resemble the private equity deals of the 1980s, the technologies they use are more complex and can facilitate manipulative behavior. It can be difficult to ascertain whether a hedge fund is exploiting an arbitrage opportunity associated with a firm's suboptimal capital structure or whether the fund is using financial techniques to engage in short-term market manipulation.

MERGER AND RISK ARBITRAGE. Hedge funds, and numerous other investors, have engaged in merger and risk arbitrage for several decades. In perhaps the most common trade, a hedge fund takes a long position in a merger target and a short position in the acquirer and then simply waits for the merger to close. The hedge fund makes a spread upfront between the higher value of the short target position and the lower value of the long acquirer position. At the merger closing, the two positions offset.

In theory, such trading strategies should not earn positive risk-adjusted returns because they resemble selling options, in which the trader earns a small premium with high probability in exchange for a high magnitude loss with low probability. In fact, although many hedge funds have earned premium income from merger arbitrage over time, they also have experienced substantial losses when mergers are

66. Jensen, Murphy, and Wruck (2004).

not completed. Indeed, LTCM was a prominent example—it lost money on a risk arbitrage position when the merger was abandoned.

There is, however, a dark side to merger arbitrage. A hedge fund that purchases shares in the target is entitled to vote on the merger, but it is not a "pure" residual claimant of the target. Indeed, a hedge fund that owns target shares and is short acquirer shares has an incentive to vote in favor of the merger, even if the merger will result in a reduction in the aggregate value of the acquirer and target. This incentive arises from the fact that the hedge fund makes a small profit if the merger closes but loses a much larger amount if the merger does not close.

This particular problem has not been studied extensively, and we have not found data that would permit an industry-wide empirical analysis. However, there is at least anecdotal evidence suggesting that the problem is not merely theoretical and that hedge fund voting has led to suboptimal approval of mergers. Aggregate hedge fund long positions in share-exchange mergers are substantially higher than hedge fund positions in companies that have not announced mergers. Several merger votes have been close enough that hedge voting may have determined the outcome. Perhaps the most prominent case was the HP-Compaq merger, a transaction that many commentators regarded as value destroying, where even one hedge fund that faced the perverse incentives described above would have tipped the vote.

In addition, hedge fund incentives have suboptimal, second-order effects, such as leading companies to prefer share-exchange merger deals to cash deals. Indeed, managers considering a merger—or at least their investment bankers—understand that the voting polity is likely to turn over rapidly just before the merger record date, with longer-term holders selling out to hedge fund managers, who in turn will vote for even a value-reducing deal. Thus managers and their bankers have incentives to propose mergers even if they believe they would be opposed by current shareholders.

An opposite, and perhaps equally serious, problem is that hedge funds could engage in antimerger strategies, taking positions that would benefit if a merger collapsed and then strategically voting against the merger. Again, there is some evidence of such practices. For example, in the Cadbury acquisition of Adams, hedge funds voted against the merger, surprising Cadbury. Likewise, the Elliott Associates–Woolworth merger presented a battle between hedge funds with substantial (around 7 to 9 percent), but opposite, stakes.

Perhaps most important, hedge funds can use financial derivatives to acquire voting positions at a much lower cost than the cost of the shares. In the King-Mylan merger, Perry Corporation acquired shares at minimal cost by entering into an offsetting equity derivatives transaction with Goldman Sachs. Perry could then vote these "cheap" shares in favor of the deal, which other "pure" shareholders, including Carl Icahn, opposed. To the extent shareholders have hedged the economic risk of their share positions, they likely would vote in ways that are contrary to the interests of shareholders who do not hold any countervailing positions.

It is impossible to know how widespread these problems are at present. For more than a decade, hedge funds and other investors have been using equity derivatives to offset share positions for various purposes, including avoiding regulation. Because hedge funds are only lightly regulated, and the over-the-counter derivatives they use are almost entirely unregulated, there is no disclosure about how prevalent these strategies have become.[67]

Finally, merger arbitrage is unlikely to generate the same kinds of benefits as other information-driven trading by hedge funds. The pricing gaps due to expectations that a merger might not close are relatively small—leading some funds to abandon merger arbitrage, while others have found that it does not generate above-average returns. Moreover, a market for the risk of non-consummation of mergers could be created synthetically by having parties trade separate derivative instruments—which would not have a vote—on the basis of whether the merger closed.

Overall, we believe that the role of hedge funds in merger arbitrage is potentially problematic. The same technologies that generate benefits with respect to information arbitrage create perverse incentives for merger arbitrage. Moreover, at least in the case of strategies promoting merger activity, corporate managers have little incentive to defend against hedge fund efforts to engage in such activities. Indeed, if managers obtain private benefits from such activity, we might expect managers and hedge funds to be complicit in such strategies. Unlike the private equity deals of the 1980s, the more recent instances of merger arbitrage are more likely to be associated with value-destroying mergers.

GOVERNANCE AND STRATEGY. During recent years, hedge funds became much more active in strategies that involve buying shares of companies and seeking to profit by persuading the company to change its governance practices or to implement some new business strategy. This type of corporate governance–strategy activism has the potential to transform the internal structures of targeted companies and to lead other firms to change their corporate governance structures before they become targets.

As with institutional shareholder activism, the theoretical justifications behind corporate governance activism by hedge funds are easily understood—the agency

67. Likewise, there is little information to support or contradict claims that hedge funds have engaged in insider trading in advance of merger announcements.

costs associated with the separation of ownership and control in publicly held firms can be reduced by informed shareholder monitoring. Well-informed, large investors can pressure boards to remove underperforming managers and directors, to stop value-destroying conglomeration strategies, to force disgorgement of excess cash, and to reduce executive compensation. In contrast with institutional investor monitoring—which as discussed in the first section has been weakened by collective action problems, conflicts of interest, high information costs, regulatory constraints, inadequate management incentives to actively monitor, and political constraints—hedge fund activism for corporate governance is more robust. These largely unregulated funds are run by fund managers whose compensation rests on their success and who operate with few, if any, conflicts of interest with respect to their choice of targets. They are better potential monitors than are institutional investors.

Of course, many questions exist about the impact of these funds. For example, are they targeting underperforming companies? Do they create value for themselves or for all shareholders? Are they reducing long-term value when management responds to their demands for immediate short-term action? Corporate managers in particular have stressed the potential conflict between some of the short-term, value-creating activities that are recurrently stressed by hedge funds and their possible negative consequences for the long-term future of target firms.

In an effort to quantify the amount of this activity, we examined a small data set of Form 13D filings. Form 13D filings are useful because all investors, including hedge funds, must file a Form 13D when they purchase 5 percent or more of a company's shares. We note that not all hedge funds filing Form 13D's are engaged in activism based on corporate governance or strategy and, conversely, that not all attacks on corporate governance or strategy are by hedge funds that have accumulated a 5 percent stake and therefore were required to file a Form 13D. Nevertheless, the number of such filings should be indicative of the level of hedge fund activism in the area of corporate governance and strategy.[68]

To assess the extent of hedge fund activism in greater detail, we examined every Form 13D filed during a randomly chosen two-week period during the previous year (November 4–18, 2005). We found 319 Form 13D filings during this period and coded them by the category of filer, as shown in table 4-1.

The frequency of hedge fund filings during this two-week period is consistent with an overall increase in Form 13D filings from 2005 to 2006 and is significantly higher than the frequency in previous years. The hedge fund filers during

---

68. In a separate article (Brav and others 2007), we and others plan to examine in greater detail the Form 13D filings of activist hedge funds from 2001 to 2005. For our purposes here, we believe it is sufficient to make our argument with more-limited evidence.

Table 4-1. *Number and Share of Filings of Form 13D, by Category of Filer,*
November 4–18, 2005

Filer category	Filings	Percent
Hedge fund	68	21.3
Investment adviser or manager or pension fund	55	17.2
Corporate insider	53	16.6
Corporation or operating company	51	16.0
Bank	25	7.8
Individual investor or charity	24	7.5
Venture capital firm or private equity firm	16	5.0
REIT or real estate adviser	9	2.8
Consultant	2	0.6
Unclassifiable	16	5.0
Total	319	100[a]

Source: Authors' calculations using information taken from SEC filings on the EDGAR system.
REIT = real estate investment trust.
a. Percentages do not add up to 100 because of rounding.

this period included several of the most frequent filing funds during the previous two years, including Pride Capital Partners LLC, Carl Icahn, Steel Partners II, and Third Point LLC. We believe these data support the widely held view that hedge fund activism has increased and is led by a relatively small number of funds.

We also categorized the Form 13D filings during the period of study on the basis of the purpose of the investment. The regulations applicable to Form 13D require that each 5 percent holder include such a description in the filing. Although the non–hedge fund filings were for a variety of purposes, the hedge fund filings were overwhelming for the purpose of shareholder activism, including communicating with management or mounting a proxy contest. Hedge fund filings only rarely stated that they were for other purposes, such as investment purposes. A summary of the data is set forth below in table 4-2.

We are aware of anecdotal evidence that hedge funds have engaged in activism without crossing the 5 percent ownership threshold that triggers the Form 13D filing requirement. Hedge funds holding less than 5 percent stakes have sought governance or strategy changes at Time Warner, McDonald's, and Wendy's International, among others. Nevertheless, we believe the From 13D data described above are useful in drawing conclusions about recent hedge fund activism, much of which has involved hedge funds acquiring stakes of 5 percent or more, particularly in smaller and midsize companies.

Table 4-2. *Number and Share of Filings of Form 13D, by Non–Hedge Funds and Hedge Funds, by Purpose of Investment, November 4–18, 2005*

Purpose category	Non-HF	Percent	HF	Percent
Investment purposes	46	18.3	3	4.4
Shareholder activism, communication with management, or proxy contest	49	19.5	61	89.7
Mergers and acquisitions (including tender offers)	22	8.8	1	1.5
Intracorporate transaction or corporate partnership	23	9.2	0	0
Insider transaction, executive compensation	33	13.1	1	1.5
Financing transaction or loan	33	13.1	0	0
Self-tender, leveraged buyout, or corporate restructuring	12	4.8	0	0
Public offering	9	3.6	0	0
Sale of shares by filer	17	6.8	2	2.9
Estate administration or share distribution	7	2.8	0	0
Total	251	100	68	100

Source: Authors' calculations using information taken from SEC filings on the EDGAR system.
Non-HF = non–hedge funds; HF = hedge funds.

In general, we believe this increase in activism has the potential to accomplish many of the goals set out for institutional shareholder activism discussed earlier. As with hedge fund activism in the capital structure area, there is positive and negative potential for improving firm value. To the extent hedge fund managers succeed in acting as a new advocate for shareholders, the benefits will be substantial. But there also is the risk that hedge funds will increase the returns to shareholders by reducing returns to other firm claimants. As in the capital structure area, hedge funds might simply reallocate returns from nonequity slices of the capital structure to shares. Therefore, we believe that it is too early to draw firm conclusions about the normative effects of this increase in shareholder activism.

Many open questions remain, including the question of whether hedge funds will be able to generate profits from shareholder activism. Some recent commentators have expressed skepticism, and evidence from the performance of hedge funds in the past suggests support for a behavioral story about some of the recent hedge fund entrants mistakenly believing they can generate abnormal returns from shareholder activism.

Tentatively, we suggest that a combination of the stories is likely true. Some of the increase in hedge fund activism is likely due to increased activity among parties who have been successful in the past playing an activist role. But part of the increase may also be due to new entrants, who might not be as successful in the relatively complex role of shareholder advocate.

Hedge Fund Activism and Gap Filling: Policy Implications

What are the policy implications of the changes in hedge funds and financial innovation? In this section, we focus on the issues that activist hedge funds raise in the areas of voting, litigation, and change-of-control transactions. In particular, we are concerned about whether hedge fund activism is filling in the gaps left by institutional investors. We also look more closely at whether what hedge funds are doing is beneficial to other shareholders or just to themselves.

Voting

Hedge funds eschew the voting mechanisms used by institutional investors—Rule 14a-8, "vote no" campaigns, majority vote bylaws, and such—in favor of more aggressive uses of the ballot box. All hedge fund activism for corporate governance is backed up—implicitly or explicitly—by the threat of a proxy contest for corporate control, while merger arbitrage rests firmly on the threat of using the vote to block a proposed merger or acquisition. Voting, in hedge fund investors' eyes, is related to change-of-control transactions.

However, hedge fund voting raises several novel problems. For example, the canonical view of shareholder voting is that each common share receives one vote—known generally as "one share–one vote"—and that this allocation is appropriate because common shareholders are the residual claimants to a corporation's income.[69] State corporate law supports this view, because of the assumptions that "preferences of one class of participants are likely to be similar if not identical" and that "it is not possible to separate the voting right from the equity interest."[70]

Hedge fund activism illustrates that these assumptions are wrong. Financial innovation enables hedge funds (and other shareholders) to hold claims that do not resemble those of a typical residual claimant. The simplest case is of a shareholder who also holds a countervailing short interest, either through a short position, security futures, a long put–short call, or some other equity derivative. That shareholder has a residual claim on the corporation's income through the share, but a shareholder's incentives differ from those of a residual claimant because of

69. Easterbrook and Fischel (1983).
70. Easterbrook and Fischel (1983), pp. 405, 410.

the countervailing position. The shareholder is not a "pure" shareholder yet receives a vote. Put another way, the shareholder holds an economically encumbered share.[71]

This problem is not merely abstract. The Perry-Icahn transaction cited above is one example, and scholars have cited numerous others.[72] For example, parties also can engage in record date–capture trades: buying shares before the record date to capture a vote but selling (or selling forward) a few days later.

Conversely, nonshareholders can acquire residual-like claims through financial engineering. Imagine a corporation that has issued all 100 of its shares to an individual who enters into a derivative transaction with a counterparty to take a short position in all 100 shares. Now, the counterparty holds the residual interest, even though the corporation has no relationship with the counterparty and might not even know its existence or identity.[73]

In addition, the practice of voting shares in street name creates distortions in the voting markets. Shares held in a margin account typically are eligible to be loaned to other parties; indeed, brokers earn substantial returns from such share lending. Investors typically have no way of knowing whether particular shares have been loaned, to whom they were loaned, or on what terms they were loaned. Instead, most shareholders assume that because they own shares, they are entitled to vote them.

They are incorrect. Only the final holder of the share in the chain of lending has the legal right to vote the share. The earlier "owners" lose the right to vote by virtue of the loan. An obvious problem is presented when shareholders who have been divested of the right to vote give proxies to their brokers. What do the brokers do?

In the past, brokers quietly have voted the proxies of shareholders who had lost the right to vote because the broker had loaned out their shares, either by submitting more votes than they had the right to vote as record holders (overvoting) or by giving disenfranchised voters the voting rights of some other shareholder who did not submit a proxy (vote switching). Regulators recently have learned of these practices, and their investigations have revealed numerous instances of overvoting.[74]

71. One of us has argued in a previous article that such economically encumbered shares should not be entitled to a vote; see Martin and Partnoy (2005).

72. Martin and Partnoy (2005); Hu and Black (2006).

73. A similar problem arises in the bond and loan markets, where moral hazard is created when banks use credit derivatives to off-load credit risk to third parties with no relationship to the borrower.

74. See "NYSE Regulation, Inc. Fines UBS Securities, Goldman Sachs Execution & Clearing, and Credit Suisse Securities (USA) $1.35 Million for Proxy-Handling Violations in Corporate Elections," June 13, 2006, New York: NYSE Group (www.nyse.com/Frameset.html?nyseref=&displayPage=/press/1150107128723.html).

Traditional institutional investors may be unaware of these practices. If they wished to protect their right to vote, informed institutions could transfer shares from a margin account to a cash account or otherwise contractually protect their votes. To the extent institutions lock up shares, lending and overall liquidity will decline.

Although hedge funds have tipped regulators to some of the difficulties associated with voting practices, the central problem is not the behavior of hedge funds but rather the nature of the U.S. system of corporate voting. Indeed, institutions other than hedge funds appear to be exacerbating voting problems; hedge funds are merely reacting to the failures of other institutions to exercise their franchise for the benefit of all shareholders.

Consider, for example, the emergence of exchange traded funds (ETFs). To the extent non–hedge fund institutions have created a gap in governance because of their failure to exercise voting power in the interest of shareholders, ETFs have substantially widened that gap.

ETFs are investment funds that track financial instruments or indexes but are traded on exchanges. Because ETFs are exchange traded, they can be bought and sold during the day (unlike mutual funds). ETFs do not have sales loads and typically have lower transaction costs than do many other investments.

Not surprising, ETFs do not have the extensive time and resources to devote to corporate governance and voting decisions. Along the product-service continuum, they are more like a pure product—little or no service is provided. ETFs, like typical products, are tangible goods that can be inventoried or standardized, whereas services are intangible processes that can be simultaneously produced and consumed.[75] In many substantive areas, both economics and law depend on the product-services distinction, with good reason.[76] Products generally are subject to greater competition and less regulation than are services, in part because product markets have lower agency costs and transaction costs than service markets.

Given their product-like nature, one of the most interesting aspects of ETFs is how many of them approach voting. For example, the prospectuses for both Spiders and Diamonds, two prominent ETFs, state that "the Trustee votes the voting stocks of each issuer in the same proportionate relationship as all other shares of

75. See, for example, Rathmell (1966), discussing distinctions related to tangibility, inventorying, standardization, production, and consumption. For example, economists have noted that the marketing of services differs considerably from the marketing of products. See Bateson (1979).

76. Tax regulations are the most prominent example. See, for example, McLure (1997), which notes the differential tax treatment of products and services. The definition of a "security" also poses issues analogous to the product-service distinction.

each such issuer are voted to the extent permissible and, if not permitted, abstains from voting."[77] In other words, the trustee of the ETF votes the voting stocks of each issuer in the same proportionate relationship as all the other shares, which is essentially the ETF saying that its votes do not count and that it is taking itself out of the governance process.[78] This reaction would be rational for a product-like fund: the ETFs are explicitly saying that their involvement in corporate governance and voting is not worth the cost. Perhaps mutual fund and index funds should and would do the same—if they were not prevented from doing so by regulations that require them to be involved in voting and governance.

As ETFs and index funds become more popular, the policy argument for giving them voting and governance responsibility becomes weaker. Given the cost structure of ETFs, it is unlikely they will exercise independent and informed votes. One alternative is for them to follow a third party's recommendations; we discussed the disadvantages of such an approach in the first section. Another alternative is for hedge funds to fill the gap. Notwithstanding the temptation of hedge funds to manipulate the voting process, they are emerging as perhaps the sole constituency with incentives and resources to vote in the interests of shareholders.

Suing

Unlike institutional investors, hedge funds use litigation frequently against target companies. Their larger stakes and more aggressive investment approaches combine to make lawsuits a necessary tactic in some situations. For instance, if a hedge fund is seeking to address allegations of management wrongdoing or excessive executive compensation, it may need to file a books and records case to obtain internal corporate information or file a derivative suit to seek damages.

Differences in how hedge fund managers are compensated as contrasted with other institutional investors may impact on their willingness to engage in litigation. Suppose both a mutual fund and a hedge fund each lost $10 million from a share price decline allegedly caused by a fraud at a portfolio firm. The mutual fund managers, consistent with their fiduciary responsibilities to their clients, would want to collect any cost-justified recoveries for their funds. However, because hedge fund managers receive a percentage of the profits recognized by their portfolios, they have suffered actual out-of-pocket losses from the fraud. This gives them a stronger incentive to become active plaintiffs in shareholder litigation to recover from the company.

77. DIAMONDS Trust, Series 1, 2004 Prospectus, p. 61; SPDRS Trust, Series 1, 2004 Prospectus, p. 60.

78. It is unclear how the ETF managers know what the eventual vote will be when they submit their proxies or even what proxies that conformed with their policy might say.

Hedge fund litigation raises some novel issues for the courts. One important question concerns whether they should have the same right to bring suit as other shareholders when their long positions in a defendant company are offset by countervailing short positions. For example, in one recent Delaware case, the court found that a hedge fund was entitled to examine the books and records of a company simply by virtue of the size of its long position, even though the court was aware that the hedge fund held a larger countervailing short position.[79] In other words, the court not only granted legal rights to a "shareholder" without a residual interest, it granted those rights to an entity whose economic incentives were the opposite of those of typical shareholders.

Similar problems have arisen in the now-common battle for lead plaintiff status in securities class actions. Since the Private Securities Litigation Reform Act of 1995, courts have selected lead plaintiffs based in large part on evidence as to which party had the "largest financial stake" in the litigation. Because hedge funds do not file information about negative equity positions, they might appear at first to have a very substantial loss upon a decline in share price, when in reality they profited from the decline. For this reason, some courts have rejected hedge funds' applications to become lead plaintiffs on the grounds that their short selling activities render them inadequate class representatives, although other courts have permitted it.[80]

Financial innovation has other effects on shareholder litigation. Some of these problems are similar to those discussed above with respect to voting. For example, if share lending creates more shares than the company has issued, it also creates more claimants in securities class actions. In some cases, the parties appear to be aware of these challenges, and they address them through the use of damage studies that increase the aggregate amount of damages available to plaintiffs on the basis of estimates of the amount of short interest in the company's shares during particular time periods. In other cases, share lending is ignored. In settlement distributions, parties are not required to establish that they held legal title to the shares, as the last one in the lending chain. They merely must show that they owned the shares—in a cash or margin account—during the appropriate time. As a result, shareholder class action settlements may overcompensate some investors (those with encumbered holdings), while undercompensating other investors (those with unencumbered holdings).

Some funds could take advantage of financial innovation by creating a "litigation fund." A fund might simply buy a collection of shares and simultaneously

---

79. *Deephaven Risk Arb Trading, Ltd.* v. *UnitedGlobalCom, Inc.*, 2005 Del. Ch. LEXIS 107 (July 13, 2005).
80. Kahan and Rock (2006).

short those shares using whatever method it found most efficient. For a relatively small price, the fund could capture the right to participate in any recovery. Although we are unaware of any instances where this has occurred, it illustrates another potential challenge posed by corporate governance hedge fund activism.

Change-of-Control Transactions

Hedge funds can have a dramatically different impact from that of institutional investors in change-of-control transactions. Recall that institutional investors almost never attempt to initiate change-of-control transactions for portfolio companies. By contrast, there are several ways that hedge funds can be involved in change-of-control transactions. As we discussed above, merger arbitrage routinely targets mergers and acquisitions by companies. The fund may invest in the target firm and may seek to negotiate better terms for a sale of their interest. Alternatively, or sometimes simultaneously, the fund may take a position in an acquiring firm and take a position on the merger designed to maximize its profit.

Hedge funds may also identify undervalued target companies and push them to sell off underperforming divisions, to put themselves up for sale, or to get them to engage in other value-enhancing control-related transactions. If the target refuses to take the recommended action, hedge funds may be willing to launch a control contest themselves if their larger stakes in the target firm permit them to capture enough of the potential increase in the value of the target firm to justify the cost. Alternatively, hedge funds may succeed in attracting other bidders, such as private equity funds, who will ultimately buy the target and pay the target's shareholders a premium price in doing so. Furthermore, just the potential threat of hedge fund activism may stimulate corporate managers to engage in change-of-control transactions to maximize value before they become targets.

In most cases, one would anticipate that these types of transactions would have a positive effect on shareholder value, at least in the short term. Some academics have raised the question of whether hedge fund activism has long-term value for shareholders; however, there is no empirical evidence either for or against this proposition at present.[81]

Hedge funds also can act as a check on opportunistic transactions, such as leveraged buyouts at lowball prices, by using their voting power to block such deals or to force the buyer to pay a higher price. Other shareholders can benefit from these actions as their shares are also purchased at the higher price negotiated by the hedge fund. Hedge funds might be willing to file appraisal actions to obtain a fair price for their shares in transactions that they are unable to block.

81. Kahan and Rock (2006).

Other shareholders might be able to file parallel appraisal actions and piggyback on the work done by the hedge funds.

Financial innovation and hedge funds can distort the market for corporate control though.[82] Hedge funds with countervailing short positions might favor mergers that would destroy value.

Further, the presence of hedge funds and financial innovation could skew the market for corporate control away from cash-based transactions to share-based transactions. If a company buys another for cash, there is less opportunity for risk arbitrage: hedge funds cannot bet on a deal's completion by purchasing target shares, shorting acquirer shares, and waiting. Because the distortions from trading are not available for cash deals, arbitrageurs will prefer share deals. And if managers understand the difference, they also will prefer share deals. Put another way, fully informed managers would know that they could propose a value-destroying fixed share-exchange merger and stand a good chance of shareholder approval, even if the current shareholders would disapprove of the deal. Obviously, when managers expect hedge funds to oppose their proposals, they will have an incentive to take the opposite approach and structure it as a cash deal to reduce the arbitrage opportunities.

On balance, however, hedge funds are clearly more effective than other institutions in initiating and pressuring for changes of control. Nevertheless, there remains the risk that hedge funds will use financial innovation to distort the market for corporate control.

Conclusion

During the 1980s, private equity investors placed enormous pressure on corporate managers to maximize shareholder value. Managers responded with a combination of leveraged buyouts and defensive tactics designed to deter these investors. During the 1990s, many commentators imagined that institutional investors such as pension funds, mutual funds, and insurance companies would play the role of activist shareholder. However, those investors faced, and continue to face, numerous constraints, and it is likely that they will not play such a role in the future.

Many commentators see hedge funds as the new shareholder activist. We find substantial evidence of hedge funds acting to reduce information asymmetry and to pressure corporate managers to adopt value-maximizing strategies. Moreover, the fact that hedge fund managers are so highly paid and are compensated based

82. Martin and Partnoy (2005).

on absolute performance rather than relative performance versus an index is a sign that many investors believe hedge funds have a capacity to add enormous value.

Overall, we find that hedge funds play a positive role, filling the gaps left by other institutions, particularly in uncovering negative information about companies. However, we also find that hedge funds face perverse incentives in many of their investment strategies. We are particularly concerned that hedge funds have the ability and incentive to manipulate corporate voting.

References

Bainbridge, Stephen. 2005. "Shareholder Activism and Institutional Investors." UCLA School of Law Working Paper Series 05-20. Los Angeles, California (September).

Barber, Brad M. 2006. "Monitoring the Monitor: Evaluating CalPERS' Shareholder Activism." Working Paper (November) (papers.ssrn.com/sol3/papers.cfm?abstract_id=890321).

Bateson, John E. G. 1979. "Why We Need Service Marketing." In *Conceptual and Theoretical Developments in Marketing*, edited by O. C. Ferrell, S. W. Brown, and C. W. Lamab, pp. 131–46. Chicago: American Marketing Association Proceeding Series.

Bethel, Jennifer E., and Stuart L. Gillan. 2002. "The Impact of Institutional and Regulatory Environment on Shareholder Voting." *Financial Management Journal* 31, no. 4: 29–54.

Bizjak, John M., and Christopher J. Marquette. 1998. "Are Shareholders All Bark and No Bite? Evidence From Shareholder Resolutions to Rescind Poison Pills." *Journal of Financial and Quantitative Analysis* 33, no. 4: 499–521.

Black, Bernard S. 1990. "Shareholder Passivity Reexamined." *Michigan Law Review* 89: 520–608.

———. 1992. "Next Steps in Proxy Reform." *Journal of Corporation Law* 18: 1–55.

———. 1998. "Shareholder Activism and Corporate Governance in the United States." In *The New Palgrave Dictionary of Economics and the Law*, vol. 3, edited by Peter Newman, pp. 459–65. New York: Macmillan.

Brav, Alon, Wei Jiang, Frank Partnoy, and Randall Thomas. 2007. "Hedge Fund Activism, Corporate Governance, and Firm Performance." Working Paper.

Brown, Stephen J., William N. Goetzmann, and Roger G. Ibbotson. 1999. "Offshore Hedge Funds: Survival and Performance 1989–95." *Journal of Business* 72, no. 1: 91–117.

Caldwell, Ted. 1995. "Introduction: The Model for Superior Performance." In *Hedge Funds: Investment and Portfolio Strategies for the Institutional Investor*, edited by Jess Lederman and Robert A. Klein, pp. 1–17. New York: McGraw-Hill.

Carleton, Willard T., James M. Nelson, and Michael S. Weisbach. 1998. "The Influence of Institutions on Corporate Governance through Private Negotiations: Evidence From TIAA-CREF." *Journal of Finance* 53, no. 4: 1335–362.

Choi, Stephen J., Jill E. Fisch, and Adam C. Pritchard. 2005. "Do Institutions Matter? The Impact of the Lead Plaintiff Provision of the Private Securities Litigation Reform Act." NYU Law and Economics Research Paper 04-08. New York University School of Law (April).

Coffee, John C., Jr. 1991. "Liquidity versus Control: The Institutional Investor as Corporate Monitor." *Columbia Law Review* 91, no. 6: 1277–368.

Cornerstone Research. 2005. "Securities Class Action Case Filings: 2005—A Year in Review." Menlo Park, California.

Cotter, James F., and Randall S. Thomas. 2005. "Shareholder Proposals in the New Millenium: Shareholder Support, Board Response, and Market Reaction." Vanderbilt Law School Working Paper 05-30. Nashville, Tennessee.

Cox, James D., and Randall S. Thomas. 2002. "Leaving Money on the Table: Do Institutional Investors Fail to File Claims in Securities Class Actions?" *Washington Law Quarterly* 80, no. 3: 855–81.

———. 2005. "Empirically Reassessing The Lead Plaintiff Provision: Is the Experiment Paying Off?" Vanderbilt Law School Working Paper 05-21 (August).

Davis, Gerald F., and E. Han Kim. 2005. "Would Mutual Funds Bite the Hand That Feeds Them? Business Ties and Proxy Voting." Working Paper (February 15) (papers.ssrn.com/sol3/papers.cfm?abstract_id=667625).

Del Guerico, Diane, Laura Wallis, and Tracie Woidtke. 2006. "Do Boards Pay Attention When Institutional Investors 'Just Vote No': CEO and Director Turnover Associated with Shareholder Activism." Working Paper (June) (papers.ssrn.com/sol3/papers.cfm?abstract_id=575242).

Easterbrook, Frank H., and Daniel R. Fischel. 1983. "Voting in Corporate Law." *Journal of Law and Economics* 26, no. 2: 395–427.

Fung, William, and David A. Hsieh. 1999. "A Primer on Hedge Funds." *Journal of Empirical Finance* 6, issue 3: 309–31.

Hu, Henry T. C., and Bernard Black. 2006. "The New Vote Buying: Empty Voting and Hidden (Morphable) Ownership." *Southern California Law Review* 79: 811–908.

Ibbotson, Roger G., and Peng Chen. 2006. "The A,B,Cs of Hedge Funds: Alphas, Betas, and Costs." International Center for Finance Working Paper 6-10. New Haven, Conn.: Yale School of Management (September).

Jensen, Michael C., Kevin J. Murphy, and Eric G. Wruck. 2004. "Remuneration: Where We've Been, How We Got to Here, What are the Problems, and How to Fix Them." Harvard NOM Working Paper 04-28; ECGI–Finance Working Paper 44/200, Brussels: European Corporate Governance Institute (ssrn.com/abstract=561305).

Kahan, Marcel, and Edward B. Rock. 2006. "Hedge Funds in Corporate Governance and Corporate Control." University of Pennsylvania Institute for Law and Economic Research Paper 06-16. Philadelphia.

Karpoff, Jonathan M. 2001. "The Impact of Shareholder Activism on Target Companies: A Survey of Empirical Findings." University of Washington Working Paper (August) (papers.ssrn.com/sol3/papers.cfm?abstract_id=885365).

Kat, Harry M., and Helder P. Palaro. 2006. "Replication and Evaluation of Funds of Hedge Funds Returns." In *Funds of Hedge Funds: Performance, Assessment, Diversification, and Statistical Properties*, edited by Greg N. Gregoriou, pp. 45–56. Burlington, Mass.: Butterworth-Heinemann (Oxford, United Kingdom: Elsevier).

Malkiel, Burton G., and Atanu Saha. 2006. "Hedge Funds: Risk and Return." *Financial Analysts Journal* 61, no. 3: 80–88.

Martin, Shaun P., and Frank Partnoy. 2005. "Encumbered Shares." *University of Illinois Law Review* no. 3: 775–813.

McLure, Charles E. Jr. 1997. "Taxation of Electronic Commerce: Economic Objectives, Technological Constraints, and Tax Laws." *Tax Law Review* 52, no. 3 (Spring): 269–423.

Miller, Ronald I., Todd Foster, and Elaine Buckberg. 2006. "Recent Trends in Shareholder Class Action Litigation: Beyond the Mega-Settlements, is Stabilization Ahead?" White Plains, N.Y.: National Economic Research Associates, Inc. (April).

Partnoy, Frank. 2004. *Infectious Greed: How Deceit and Risk Corrupted the Financial Markets*, 2d ed. New York: Henry Holt.

Perino, Michael A. 2006. "Markets and Monitors: The Impact of Competition and Experience on Attorneys' Fees in Securities Class Actions." St. John's Legal Studies Research Paper 06-0034. Jamaica, N.Y.: St. John's University School of Law (January).

[President's Working Group] President's Working Group on Financial Markets. 1999. *Report on Hedge Funds, Leverage, and the Lessons of Long-Term Capital Management*. Washington: U.S. Treasury (April).

Rathmell, Joan M. 1966. "What is Meant by Services." *Journal of Marketing* 30 (October): 32–36.

Rock, Edward. 1991. "The Logic and (Uncertain) Significance of Institutional Shareholder Activism." *Georgetown Law Journal* 79 (February): 445–506.

Roe, Mark J. 1991. "A Political Theory of American Corporate Finance." *Columbia Law Review* 91, no. 1: 10–66.

Romano, Roberta. 1993. "Public Pension Fund Activism in Corporate Governance Reconsidered." *Columbia Law Review* 93, no. 4: 795–853.

———. 2001. "Less is More: Making Institutional Investor Activism a Valuable Mechanism of Corporate Governance." *Yale Journal on Regulation* 18, no. 2: 174–251.

Schwab, Stewart J., and Randall S. Thomas. 1998. "Realigning Corporate Governance: Shareholder Activism by Labor Unions." *Michigan Law Review* 96, no. 4: 1018–094.

Strine, Leo E. 2005. "The Delaware Way: How We Do Corporate Law and Some of the New Challenges We (and Europe) Face." *Delaware Journal of Corporate Law* 30, no. 3: 673–96.

Thomas, Randall S., and Kenneth J. Martin. 1998. "Should Labor be Allowed to Make Shareholder Proposals?" *Washington Law Review* 73, no. 1: 41–80.

Thompson, Robert B., and Randall S. Thomas. 2004a. "The New Look of Shareholder Litigation: Acquisition-Oriented Class Actions." *Vanderbilt Law Review* 57: 133–209.

———. 2004b. "The Public and Private Faces of Derivative Lawsuits." *Vanderbilt Law Review* 57: 1747–793.

THOMAS BOULTON
KENNETH LEHN
STEVEN SEGAL

5

The Rise of the U.S. Private Equity Market

I N A CLASSIC article titled "Eclipse of the Public Corporation," Michael Jensen wrote that "the publicly held corporation . . . has outlived its usefulness in many sectors of the economy and is being eclipsed."[1] Jensen's article, written at a time when dozens of large U.S. corporations, including RJR Nabisco, R. H. Macy, and Trans World Airlines, had "gone private" in leveraged buyouts, appears highly relevant today. After a lull during the 1990s, the value of "private equity" transactions generally, and "going private" transactions in particular, have resurged during the past few years.

A recent editorial in the *Wall Street Journal* summarizes the dramatic increase in recent private equity activity:

> Private equity is booming, and sweeping up U.S. business in the process. Fifteen years ago, a handful of private equity firms managed a few billion; today, more than 250 firms control some $800 billion in capital. *Buyouts* magazine, which tracks private equity deals, estimates that nearly $175 billion in new money flowed into U.S.-based private equity firms last year alone, including giants such as Blackstone, KKR, and the Carlyle Group."[2]

1. Jensen (1989), p. 61.
2. "Hot Topic: Going Private," *Wall Street Journal*, June 3, 2006, p. A7.

Dozens of public companies have gone private in recent years, including well-known companies such as Vermont Teddy Bear, Toys "R" Us, Neiman Marcus, and La Quinta Inns. During the past few months, HCA (Hospital Corporation of America), Kinder Morgan, and Cablevision have announced plans to go private in $33 billion, $22 billion, and $19 billion deals, respectively. After fifty years as a public corporation, Ford Motor Co. recently announced it is considering going private. Dozens of other large public companies in the United States are rumored to be considering the same.

This paper describes the evolution of the private equity market with particular emphasis on going private transactions. It empirically examines the recent increase in going private activity in the United States and compares it with the going private transactions of twenty years ago that inspired Jensen to discuss "the eclipse of the public corporation." Specifically, we empirically examine a sample of 245 U.S. companies that went private during the period of 1995 to 2005. The following results emerge from our analysis:

—The number and market value of companies going private have increased over time. From 1995 to 1999, 101 firms (an average of 20.2 per year) with an inflation-adjusted average market value of assets of $231 million went private. From 2000 to 2005, 144 firms (an average of 24.0 per year) with an average asset value of $431 million went private (see table 5-1).

—The industry distribution of firms going private has changed over time. Compared with twenty years ago when going private transactions were almost nonexistent in technology industries, during the period 1995–2005, 15 firms in high-technology industries went private. Manufacturing accounts for the highest number of going private transactions during this period (79, 32 percent of the sample), followed by services (40, 16 percent), retail (37, 15 percent), and financial (27, 11 percent) (see table 5-2).

—The announcements of going private transactions are associated with statistically significant increases in the stock prices of target firms. The average residual return on the announcement day for the entire sample is 17.2 percent. Over a three-day window ranging from one day before through one day after the announcement day, the residual return is 21.4 percent. These results are similar to earlier results found for going private transactions.[3]

—The average residual return on the announcement day for 13e-3 going private transactions (that is, management-led transactions) is 20.2 percent versus 13.6 percent for other going private transactions (that is, those led by private equity firms and other investors) (see table 5-3). This evidence is inconsistent

3. See, for example, DeAngelo, DeAngelo, and Rice (1984).

with the view that management buyouts create an inherent conflict of interest that deprives target shareholders of value. It is consistent with results found for earlier going private transactions.[4]

—The average return on assets (ROA) of going private targets is not significantly different from the corresponding ROA of their respective industry peers in the year immediately preceding the going private transactions, and it is significantly higher than the corresponding ROA of their industry peers two years before the transactions. This indicates that firms going private in recent years do not underperform their industry peers in terms of this profit measure.

—Targets of going private transactions use more working capital per dollar of sales than their corresponding industry peers in the two years before the transactions. This suggests that improvement of working capital may continue to be a source of value creation in going private transactions.

—Incremental audit fees associated with complying with the Sarbanes-Oxley Act of 2002 (henceforth referred to as Sarbanes-Oxley) appear to be a large proportion of the premiums paid in small going private transactions. We estimate that the present value of these costs is 18 percent to 36 percent of the premiums paid in going private transactions from 2004 to 2005 involving companies with market capitalizations of less than $100 million. For companies with market capitalizations of more than $1 billion, these costs represent only 0.8 percent to 1.5 percent of going private premiums.

The paper is organized as follows. In the next section we provide an overview of the evolution of the private equity market from the 1970s to the present. The third section provides an empirical analysis of going private transactions, which are a subset of private equity transactions, from 1995 through 2005. The fourth section provides evidence on whether the costs of compliance with Sarbanes-Oxley are an important consideration in going private transactions since 2002. Concluding comments are contained in the last section.

Evolution of the U.S. Private Equity Market

For an understanding of today's U.S. private equity market and the forces behind the data reported in this paper, it is constructive to consider the history of private equity generally and leveraged buyouts (LBOs) in particular.

For purposes of this paper, the authors define *private equity* to be a general investment class in the alternative sector (that is, non–publicly traded securities). Going private transactions and leveraged buyouts are subsets of that class. Alternative

---

4. See Davis and Lehn (1992).

investments might include real estate, timber, other commodities, hedge funds, and private equity. Private equity includes venture capital, meaning capital for early-stage companies, as well as leveraged buyouts, meaning capital generally devoted to the purchase of established companies using both debt and equity.

In the 1970s and early 1980s, public stocks were "cheap." The average S&P 500 firm had a price-to-earnings multiple of 15.9 at the beginning of the 1970s. By the end of the decade, the average price-to-earnings multiple was 7.3. On the basis of dividends and splits, the Dow Jones Industrial Average opened the 1970s at 800 and managed to rise to only 875 by the end of 1981.

A few financial entrepreneurs, such as Jerome Kohlberg, Henry Kravis, Martin Dubilier, Ted Forstmann, and Thomas Lee, operating in the mold of merchant bankers, determined that they could acquire stable companies for modest purchase prices financed in large part by borrowed funds. Equity value was created, as the cash flow from these companies amortized the debt and the company was later sold. Because the purchase prices were low, the debt could be paid off in a few short years despite the high interest rates of the time, so the sale price of a company did not need to exceed the purchase price for those entrepreneurs to earn a handsome profit and internal rate of return on their equity.

In those early years of the LBO "industry," these entrepreneurs operated out of offices resembling nothing more sophisticated than a small law or doctor's office, and their methods were equally straightforward. They were essentially bargain hunters, looking for companies whose public valuation did not reflect private information uncovered in the due diligence process and whose values could be improved by strengthening managerial incentives. Also, these companies usually had substantial borrowing capacity, and the buyers used strategies and capital structures that were simple. Their returns, however, were nothing short of spectacular—compounded annual rates of return of 60 to 100 percent were not uncommon. Competition for deals was modest, and most firms had genuinely robust proprietary deal flow.

By the early to mid-1980s, these LBO sponsors began to publicize their returns to institutional investors, drawing more equity capital to the buyout sector. In addition, the relaxation of laws that restricted corporate pension plans from investing in private unregulated partnerships drew more capital into the market place. The LBO sponsors began hiring more people and slowly began to become more sophisticated in their financial and business analysis, particularly with the advent of spreadsheet software in the early 1980s.[5] Also by the mid-1980s, oil prices, interest rates, and inflation abated, and the stock market began

5. Such as VisiCalc and Lotus 123.

to develop steam. This allowed firms that had bought companies earlier to sell them into a market willing to pay higher prices. In addition to leverage, the sponsors' returns were enhanced by this "buy low, sell high" phenomenon.

With the economic and stock market tailwind at their backs, the LBO firms steadily increased the number of deals they did and the amount of money they managed. Success has many fathers, and also many imitators. More firms entered the fray, sensing opportunities to replicate the high returns earned by the incumbent LBO firms. Lenders too enjoyed success during this period. LBO loans generated hefty upfront fees for the lenders compared with other more traditional lending activities, and the interest rates paid by the borrowers were high. Default rates were low despite the leverage, so leverage increased substantially, further enhancing the returns of the LBO sponsors. In addition to major U.S. banks serving as money centers, the LBO lending community was joined by foreign banks; savings and loans; mutual funds; pension funds; insurance companies; finance companies, such as GE and Westinghouse; investment banks; and the bond market. With all these new players in both the lending and equity markets for LBOs, lending and investment standards became inconsistent. Competition for deals among sponsors increased, but most high quality firms could still brag of a portfolio of deals in which a substantial portion was generated on a proprietary basis, because of the unique networks of contacts, industry specialization, and brand recognition.

Michael Milken almost single-handedly created a high-yield bond market that fueled much of the LBO market in the 1980s. Milken operated out of the Los Angeles office of what was previously a sleepy little investment bank called Drexel Burnham Lambert. Milken figured he could get institutions to lend money to LBO companies by buying bonds, both public and private, if the institutions were offered higher interest rates, a slice of the equity in the buyouts if the loan was far enough down the capital structure, and a liquid market. Drexel Burnham Lambert often bought loans back or traded existing loans for new issues, which created market liquidity. In essence, this became a self-fulfilling prophecy as more investors entered the high-yield market, drawn by the high returns available.

Problems developed in the late 1980s as some companies could not meet their projections, which in some cases were brought on by leverage that started out with no margin for error and the onset of the recession of 1990–91. The ratio of EBITDA (earnings before interest, taxes, depreciation, and amortization) to cash interest coverage got as low as 1.01 to 1, on the assumption that growth would eventually allow companies to grow out of their leveraged positions. As default rates increased, lenders recognized that the lending market had overheated and that they were not being compensated enough for the risk they were taking.[6] The slivers of equity being attached to the riskiest of loans, when successful, were not enough to compensate for the losses on the companies that defaulted.

Drexel Burnham Lambert and others used a variety of financial instruments to finance LBOs in the 1980s, such as senior notes, senior subordinated notes, subordinated notes with warrants, zero coupon bonds, pay-in-kind preferred stock, and holding company debt, which allowed sponsors to delicately segment the capital structure to create maximum leverage. Also during the 1980s, many LBOs were based on breakup values of conglomerates. Disaggregating the conglomerates for values where the sum of the sold parts was greater than the whole could create equity value. An excellent example of this was Kohlberg Kravis Roberts & Co.'s leveraged buyout of Safeway in 1986. KKR used one of the first issues of zero coupon bonds, underwritten by Drexel Burnham Lambert, and sold off for relatively high valuations domestic and foreign divisions considered noncore. Although returns in the 1980s were not quite as good as they were in the 1970s, sponsors were still targeting internal rates of return above 40 percent.

The collapse of Drexel Burnham Lambert in 1990, the decline of the high-yield bond market, and the exit of many of the lenders and equity sponsors who were new to the party in the latter half of the 1980s brought a sense of calm back to the LBO market during the 1990s. The rise in value of the stock market, combined with the still increasing equity capital flowing to the established and surviving LBO sponsors in the 1990s meant purchase prices, measured as a multiple of EBITDA, began to rise significantly. Higher prices and lower leverage necessarily meant lower returns for LBO equity investors—but there was plenty of room to fall and still provide returns well in excess of traditional investment alternatives. Although *target* returns were in the mid-30s percent range, by the late 1990s, targeted returns had fallen to the mid- to low 20s, and for the largest buyouts even the high teens. The higher prices, lower leverage ratios, and lower expected returns necessitated a back-to-basics approach for most LBO practitioners.

After the credit contraction in the early 1990s, the focus of LBOs moved to companies with good corporate strategies and strong (at least when compared with the peaks of the 1980s) balance sheets. Investors also refined and rewarded quality entrepreneurial management with more sophisticated and more liberal equity incentives. Boards represented by LBO sponsors paid closer attention to operations and efficient, growth-oriented capital spending rather than exclusively to financial engineering. Sponsors also adapted capital structures to allow for

6. See Kaplan and Stein (1993) for a further discussion of this.

growth by borrowing longer-term senior notes or structuring back-end weighted amortization schedules to allow for growth investment spending even in a leveraged environment.

The fact that more money was being managed by virtually all successful firms also drove returns lower because of the financial incentives of the LBO firms. The larger amount of money under management and larger deal sizes did not require a commensurate growth in the number of partners at the LBO firms. Consequently, they could make the same amount of, or more, money per partner with lower returns simply by having more dollars invested. Toward the end of the 1990s and into the first decade of the twenty-first century, this generally reduced incentive for higher returns for the LBO sponsor, coupled with ever more money under management, continued to drive purchase prices higher. This was also helped by lower interest rates and a renewed willingness by lenders to push the leverage multiples higher. In the second half of the 1990s, the leading so-called mega funds were considered large if a fund was $1 billion. Today, those same mega funds manage multibillion dollar funds.

Today's U.S. private equity market is well developed and highly competitive. The market is awash in liquidity, both in debt and equity. Debt multiples for LBO loans of companies with EBITDA greater than $50 million have gone from approximately four times in 2000 to five times in 2006. Stock prices are high, and LBO purchase prices are high. The average LBO has gone from approximately $350 million to more than $1.2 billion during the same period.[7] Sellers are also well informed, sophisticated, and loathe to sell without an expansive search for the highest bidder. It would be rare to find a deal that was not represented by an investment bank and that did not go through at least a limited auction. With high purchase prices and fierce competition for deals, coming from not only a bevy of LBO firms but also from hedge funds seeking new avenues of opportunity and activism, even great LBO investors struggle for expected returns in excess of the high teens in this environment.[8]

Most LBO firms today continue to have strategies to add value to the portfolio companies in which they invest. In some cases, these practitioners can be patient implementing these value-added strategies in part because of the tax law change in 2002 that allowed dividends to be taxed at a capital gain rate. This change in tax rates did not have an effect on many of the tax-exempt investors, such as pension plans, endowments, and foundations, in LBO funds, but the

7. Standard & Poor's. 2006. "1Q06 Leveraged Buyout Review." PowerPoint presentation by Standard & Poor's Leveraged Commentary and Data group.

8. See Kapland and Schoar (2005) for a discussion of returns to private equity firms during the period of 1980–2001.

general partners of those funds, for tax purposes, could now treat dividends from portfolio companies in the same way that they treated sales of those assets.

Further, lenders today are very comfortable funding such dividends. These dividends give capital back to the LBO sponsors and their investors who can then take more time before selling the underlying company or taking it public. From 1997 to 2002, loan volume for funding such dividend recapitalizations averaged less than $2 billion per annum. From 2004 through the first quarter of 2006, these dividend recaps funded with loans were averaging $4.7 billion *per quarter*.[9]

Another strategy espoused by some of the very large mega funds is to compete for deals where the air is thin. These mega funds are raising vast sums of money, in the $10 billion to $15 billion range, and then collaborating on very large going private transactions such as the announced deals for HCA and Kinder Morgan noted earlier. This is a stratosphere in which very few firms can compete. It is interesting that despite the fact that, as we note, the firms are bidding with premiums to current stock market values, these collaborative bidding partnerships are catching the eye of the U.S. Department of Justice.[10] Only time will tell if these inquiries will have an impact on the recent trends in going private transactions.

An Empirical Analysis of Recent Going Private Transactions

In this section, we empirically examine several topics related to going private transactions, a subset of private equity transactions. Among the topics we examine are (1) the number and value of going private transactions in recent years, (2) the distribution of recent going private transactions across industries, (3) the effects of recent going private transactions on stockholder value, (4) whether the effect of going private transactions on stockholder value is different in management buyouts versus other going private transactions, (5) the attributes of firms going private in recent years, and (6) the relation between Sarbanes-Oxley and recent going private activity.

The sample for this study consists of 245 firms that went private during the period of 1995 through 2005. The sample was drawn from an original sample of 508 transactions identified as leveraged buyouts in the Securities Data Corporation (SDC) database of mergers and acquisitions. We cross-referenced this sample with the Center for Research on Securities Prices (CRSP) database to provide stock price and delisting information. In addition, the sample was matched to accounting data from the Compustat Industrial Annual database. Finally, we

9. Standard & Poor's, "1Q06 Leveraged Buyout Review."
10. Dennis K. Berman and Henry Sender, "Private-Equity Firms Face Anticompetitive Probe," *Wall Street Journal*, October 10, 2006, p. A3.

Table 5-1. *Number of Going Private Transactions, 1995–2005*

Year	Number of going private transactions	Average market value of firms going private[a] (millions of dollars)
1995	6	339.03
1996	10	142.99
1997	26	231.83
1998	19	171.76
1999	40	238.85
2000	43	204.70
2001	19	303.58
2002	18	331.88
2003	15	138.64
2004	21	838.70
2005	28	740.96

Source: Authors' calculations on a sample of 245 firms drawn from an original sample of 508 transactions identified as leveraged buyouts in the Securities Data Corporation database of mergers and acquisitions.

a. Market value is computed as the sum of the book value of debt, the book value of preferred stock, and the market value of common stock.

searched news stories for all companies to confirm that they were acquired in a going private transaction, resulting in our final sample of going private transactions. Missing data affect the sample size in some of the subsequent analyses.

Number and Value of Firms Going Private

Table 5-1 lists the number and average market value of assets of firms going private in each year during the sample period. Average market value of assets is inflation adjusted using the consumer price index to reflect constant 2005 dollars. The number of going private transactions was highest in the year 2000 (43), followed by 1999 (40), and 2005 (28). The average market value of assets for firms going private was highest in 2004 ($839 million), followed by 2005 ($741 million), and 1995 ($339 million).[11]

The table reveals that the average market value has increased significantly since the passage of Sarbanes-Oxley in 2002, from an annual average of $233 million during the 1995–2001 period to an annual average of $572 million from 2003 to 2005, an increase of more than 146 percent. Of course, some of the increase in

11. The market value of assets is computed as the sum of the book value of debt, the book value of preferred stock, and the market value of common stock.

the average asset value of firms going private over time reflects a general appreci-ation in the value of public companies during this period. However, the general increases in the market values of firms going private account only for a relatively small portion of the increases in the asset value of firms going private since 2002. For example, the average year-end value of the S&P 500 increased by only 11 per-cent from the period of 1995–2001 to the period of 2003–05. Hence, it appears that since 2002 there has been a substantial increase in the size of firms going pri-vate, even after adjusting for changes in overall equity values.

Industry Distribution of Firms Going Private

Table 5-2 details the industry distribution of going private transactions in our sample. Firms going private are ordered by one of ten general industry classifica-tions based on the standard industrial classification (SIC) code provided in the CRSP database. For the full sample, the number of going private transactions is highest for firms classified as manufacturing (79), followed by services (40) and retail (37). Almost 64 percent of the going private transactions in the sample come from one of these three industries. Table 5-2 also reports the sample indus-try distribution for the two periods 1995–99 and 2000–05. The proportion of the deals targeting manufacturing firms declines significantly from the first period to the next (44.6 percent of the early period targets are classified as manufactur-ing versus 23.6 percent during the latter period). While going private activity in manufacturing decreases in the latter half of the sample period, the wholesale, retail, financial and high tech industries experience significant increases.

The Effect of Going Private Transactions on Shareholder Value

To examine the effect of going private transactions on shareholder value from 1995 to 2005, we conducted an event study of the announcement dates for the 245 going private transactions.[12] The event study was conducted with a 250-day estimation period, ranging from 270 trading days before the first announcement date through 21 trading days before the announcement date. An equal-weighted market index was used to estimate the parameter value. The announcement date identified by SDC was used as the announcement date in the event study.

Table 5-3 contains the residual returns from the event study for the entire sam-ple and various subsamples. The mean residual return on the announcement date for the full sample is 17.2 percent and is statistically significant at the 0.01 level. The cumulative residual returns over the window of one trading day before the

---

12. The software package used for conducting the event study was Eventus®, published by Cowan Research.

Table 5-2. *Number of Going Private Transactions, by Industry,*
1995–99 and 2000–05

Industry[a]	Full sample		1995–99		2000–05	
	Number	Percent	Number	Percent	Number	Percent
Agriculture	3	1.2	1	1.0	2	1.4
Mining	4	1.6	1	1.0	3	2.1
Construction	1	0.4	0	0	1	0.7
Manufacturing	79	32.2	45	44.6	34	23.6
Transportation	18	7.3	8	7.9	10	6.9
Wholesale	21	8.6	6	5.9	15	10.4
Retail	37	15.1	11	10.9	26	18.1
Financial	27	11.0	9	8.9	18	12.5
Services	40	16.3	16	15.8	24	16.7
High-Tech	15	6.1	4	4.0	11	7.6

Source: Authors' calculations (see table 5-1).

a. Broad industry definitions are based on the standard industrial classification provided in the database of the Center for Research on Securities Prices.

announcement date through one trading day after the announcement date (that is, the [–1, +1] window) is 21.4 percent and is also significant at the 0.01 level. The corresponding residual return over the [–5, +5] window is 23.5 percent. These results are similar to results previously documented in the academic literature on going private transactions.[13]

Effect of Management Buyouts versus Other Going Private Deals
on Shareholder Value

Table 5-3 also presents evidence on residual returns in management-led going private transactions as compared with going private transactions led by private equity firms or other, nonmanagement investors. Management-led going private transactions result in a so-called 13e-3 filing, named for Rule 13e-3, which the SEC adopted in 1979. The rule was adopted to address concerns by investors, legal commentators, and others of an alleged inherent conflict of interest in management buyouts versus buyouts led by third parties.[14] The basis for this concern was that managers allegedly wore two hats in management buyouts, one as the acquirer who would like to acquire the company at the lowest possible price and

13. See, for example, DeAngelo, DeAngelo, and Rice (1984); Lehn and Poulsen (1988).
14. See, for example, Brudney (1975); Solomon (1975).

Table 5-3. *Cumulative Residual Returns Associated with Announcements of Going Private Transactions, 1995–2005*[a]

	Mean returns (percent)				
Sample	[0]	[–1, +1]	[–5, +5]	[–20, –2]	[1, 20]
Full (N = 245)	17.2	21.4	23.5	4.0	2.4
	(0.01)	(0.01)	(0.00)	(0.00)	(0.02)
13e-3 (n = 134)	20.2	26.3	28.8	3.8	3.7
	(0.00)	(0.00)	(0.00)	(0.00)	(0.01)
Non-13e-3 (n = 111)	13.6	15.3	17.1	4.4	0.8
	(0.00)	(0.00)	(0.00)	(0.04)	(0.60)
1995–99 (n = 101)	13.6	15.7	17.9	4.4	0.9
	(0.00)	(0.00)	(0.00)	(0.05)	(0.58)
2000–05 (n = 144)	19.7	25.3	27.4	3.8	3.5
	(0.00)	(0.00)	(0.00)	(0.00)	(0.02)
1995–2002 (n = 181)[b]	17.2	21.1	23.7	5.4	1.9
	(0.00)	(0.00)	(0.00)	(0.00)	(0.10)
2003–05 (n = 64)[c]	17.2	22.0	22.8	0.2	4.0
	(0.00)	(0.00)	(0.00)	(0.92)	(0.10)

Source: Authors' calculations (see table 5-1).

a. Cumulative residual returns are estimated over various windows surrounding the first announcement of a going private offer. The [0] window denotes the relative return on the announcement day; [–1, +1] denotes the window of one trading day before the announcement through one trading day after the announcement and so forth. An estimation period of 270 trading days before the announcement date through 21 trading days before the announcement date is used to estimate parameter values for the event study. *P*-values are in parentheses.

b. Going private transactions completed before the passage of Sarbanes-Oxley in 2002.

c. Going private transactions post–Sarbanes-Oxley.

the other as an agent for shareholders who had a duty to maximize the price shareholders received for their shares.

The table reveals that residual returns associated with recent going private transactions are actually higher in 13e-3 transactions than they are in non-13e-3 transactions. The mean residual return on the announcement date for the 134 13e-3 transactions in the sample is 20.2 percent versus 13.6 percent for the 111 other transactions in the sample. Similar results hold for other windows surrounding the announcement dates—residual returns are consistently higher in 13e-3 versus non-13e-3 transactions. The results indicate that, as a general matter, shareholders have not been deprived of value in going private transactions led by managers as opposed to those led by third parties during the period of study 1995–2005.[15]

---

15. This result is consistent with evidence from going private transactions during the 1980s. See Davis and Lehn (1992).

Effects of Going Private Transactions on Shareholder Value over Time

Table 5-3 also shows that residual returns increased somewhat over the sample period. From 1995 to 1999, the mean residual return on the announcement date was 13.6 percent as compared with 19.7 percent during the period 2000–05. A similar pattern of differences in residual returns exists for other windows surrounding the announcement dates. To determine whether the increase is associated with the passage of Sarbanes-Oxley in 2002, the table reports the mean residual return during the 1995–2002 period with the corresponding return from 2003 to 2005. The results show that the two mean returns are essentially identical (17.2 percent in both periods), which suggests that Sarbanes-Oxley does not account for the higher residual returns in going private transactions.

Operating Performance of Firms Going Private

One popular explanation for why firms go private is that the firm is in need of operating improvements, which are more likely to be achieved under the governance structure of a private firm. Literature on going private transactions, and leveraged buyouts more generally, point to several features of private equity that create strong incentives for value creation. These features include greater equity ownership by managers, greater sensitivity about executive compensation tied to performance, greater decentralization of decision making, and high leverage.

Previous literature on leveraged buyouts and going private transactions finds evidence that going private transactions during the 1980s generally resulted in significant operating improvements. In a study of large management buyouts executed in the 1980s, Steven Kaplan documented larger operating income increases, capital expenditure decreases, and net cash flow increases for buyout firms relative to their industry peers in the three years following the buyout.[16] Kaplan concluded that operating improvements drove the increases in market value (which averaged 96 percent for his sample) during the buyout period for these firms. The following sections examine the stock price performance, operating performance, growth, and use of cash in the years preceding the going private transaction for our sample of deals.

Table 5-4 examines the return on assets and working capital management for the sample of going private firms relative to their industry peers during the two years preceding the deal announcement.[17] The table presents the mean difference

16. Kaplan (1989).
17. Return on assets and working capital management are two common measures of operating performance. Return on assets is calculated as net income divided by total assets. Working capital management is defined as accounts receivable plus inventory minus accounts payable, all divided by net sales.

Table 5-4. *Mean Differences between Target Firm and the Median Industry Firm, by ROA and Working Capital, 1995–2005*[a]

Sample	ROA_{-2} (percent)	ROA_{-1} (percent)	Working capital$_{-2}$ (percent)	Working capital$_{-1}$ (percent)
Full (*N* = 241)	1.4 (0.03)	0.2 (0.82)	1.4 (0.02)	1.8 (0.06)
13e-3 (*n* = 131)	2.2 (0.00)	2.3 (0.01)	2.1 (0.15)	2.3 (0.12)
Non-13e-3 (*n* = 110)	0.4 (0.77)	–2.3 (0.24)	0.6 (0.65)	1.2 (0.33)
1995–99 (*n* = 101)	0.5 (0.66)	–0.4 (0.85)	1.0 (0.38)	0.3 (0.81)
2000–05 (*n* = 140)	2.0 (0.01)	0.7 (0.50)	1.7 (0.24)	2.9 (0.05)
1995–2002 (*n* = 178)[b]	1.4 (0.07)	0.6 (0.63)	1.2 (0.22)	1.5 (0.12)
2003–05 (*n* = 63)[c]	1.4 (0.28)	–0.9 (0.52)	2.1 (0.43)	2.8 (0.31)

Source: Authors' calculations (see table 5-1).

a. Return on assets (ROA) and working capital are estimated for the target firm and the median industry firm for two years (–2) and one year (–1) before the going private announcement. The table presents the mean differences across all sample firms for which accounting data are available. *P*-values are in parentheses.

b. Going private transactions completed before the passage of Sarbanes-Oxley in 2002.

c. Going private transactions post–Sarbanes-Oxley.

between the average target firm's ROA (working capital) and that of the median industry firm.

The ROA results presented in table 5-4 do not show that targets of going private transactions significantly underperform other firms in their respective industries. On the contrary, the ROA results for the full sample two years before the announcement suggest that the average target firm actually outperforms its industry peers by 1.4 percentage points. However, the difference is not significant the next year. Finally, targets of management buyouts (13e-3) exhibit significantly higher average ROA than their corresponding industry peers both one (2.3 percentage points) and two years (2.2 percentage points) before a going private announcement.

The working capital management results in the final two columns of table 5-4 suggest that there may be room for improvement in this area for targets of going private transactions. The full sample results indicate that the average target firm uses approximately 1.8 percentage points more working capital per dollar of sales than does the average industry peer in the year before the announcement of the target firm going private. Additionally, the average target firm's measure of working capital management is 1.4 percentage points higher than the average industry firm two years before the deal announcement. Both results are statistically significant. Overall, these results suggest that operating improvements might still represent a source of value creation in going private transactions.

Growth Opportunities of Firms Going Private

Targets of going private transactions in the 1970s and 1980s typically were firms that operated in stable, low-growth industries that lent themselves to debt financing. To examine the growth opportunities of targets of recent going private transactions, we examine two proxies for growth opportunities—first, the ratio of property, plant, and equipment (PPE) to assets and, second, the ratio of market to book value of assets. Generally, growth opportunities are believed to vary inversely with the first proxy and directly with the second proxy.

Table 5-5 contains the results on growth opportunities, which present the mean difference between the average target firm's PPE to assets and that of the median industry firm. The results on the ratio of property, plant, and equipment to total assets indicate that a larger portion of the average going private firm's total assets are in the form of tangible assets relative to their industry peers. For the full sample period, in the year before the going private announcement, target firms tend to have 8.3 percentage points more of their asset base in the form of tangible assets. Two years before the deal announcement the difference is 6.6 percentage points on average. Both results are statistically significant. This relation holds for both management- and nonmanagement-led buyouts, in the later half of the sample, and both pre– and post–Sarbanes-Oxley. The only period for which this relation is not exhibited is the first half of the sample period (1995–99).

The PPE-to-total-assets results are consistent with Jensen's free cash flow hypothesis.[18] Free cash flow theory posits that firms with strong cash flows and low-growth opportunities are most likely to benefit from increased use of debt. Increased debt levels serve at least two functions in such firms. First, the servicing of debt consumes cash that might otherwise be used by management on value-destroying investments. Second, the increased use of debt strengthens the incentive for creditors to monitor the activities of management. Since going private transactions are generally financed through significant use of debt, such

18. Jensen (1986).

Table 5-5. *Mean Differences between Target Firm and the Median Industry Firm,
by Ratios PPE to Assets and Market-to-Book Ratio, 1995–2005*[a]

Sample	$PPE/Assets_{-2}$	$PPE/Assets_{-1}$	M/B_{-2}	M/B_{-1}
Full (N = 241)	6.6	8.3	0.1	0.6
	(0.00)	(0.00)	(0.92)	(0.67)
13e-3 (N = 131)	5.2	6.4	2.8	2.4
	(0.05)	(0.01)	(0.10)	(0.18)
Non-13e-3 (n = 110)	8.4	10.9	–3.1	–1.5
	(0.00)	(0.00)	(0.17)	(0.49)
1995–99 (n = 101)	3.1	1.1	–4.0	–2.1
	(0.22)	(0.68)	(0.05)	(0.32)
2000–05 (n = 140)	9.0	12.5	3.1	2.5
	(0.00)	(0.00)	(0.09)	(0.19)
1995–2002 (n = 178)[b]	4.9	6.0	–10.0	0
	(0.03)	(0.02)	(0.54)	(0.99)
2003–05 (n = 63)[c]	11.6	14.4	3.3	2.2
	(0.01)	(0.00)	(0.23)	(0.45)

Source: Authors' calculations (see table 5-1).

a. Property, plant, and equipment (PPE) as a percentage of total assets and the market-to-book ratio (M/B) are estimated for the target firm and the median industry firm for two years (–2) and one year (–1) before the going private announcement. The table presents the mean difference across all sample firms where accounting data are available. *P*-values are in parentheses.

b. Going private transactions completed before the passage of Sarbanes-Oxley in 2002.

c. Going private transactions post–Sarbanes-Oxley.

transactions may represent one manifestation of free cash flow theory in practice, as low-growth firms with strong income represent prime candidates for a buyout.

The final two columns of table 5-5 present comparisons of market-to-book ratio, another common proxy for growth opportunities. Unlike the results of the ratio PPE to total assets, the market-to-book results do not document a significant difference between going private targets and their industry peers.

Sarbanes-Oxley and Going Private Transactions

A common theme in some of the recent discussions about going private transactions is that some of these deals are being driven by the increased costs of being a public company. These costs presumably have increased for most public firms, at least in part due to the costs of complying with the Sarbanes-Oxley Act passed in 2002. Thomas Frist Jr., founder of HCA Inc., which recently announced one of the largest going private transactions in history, identified Sarbanes-Oxley as one factor in the decision to pursue a buyout.[19] Likewise, Georgia Pacific CEO Pete Corell cited Sarbanes-Oxley when discussing the buyout of his firm.[20]

The final three tables of this study are designed to explore the relation between Sarbanes-Oxley and recent going private transactions. One cost associated with Sarbanes-Oxley compliance is the increased audit fees that companies pay to comply with the act. This cost might be considered a direct cost of Sarbanes-Oxley compliance, but not the only direct compliance cost (for example, the cost of systems reengineering to comply with Sarbanes-Oxley would not be included in audit fees). Furthermore, the indirect costs of complying with Sarbanes-Oxley (for example, the value of management time) may swamp the increased audit fees associated with complying with the act. Hence, the incremental audit fees associated with Sarbanes-Oxley compliance, which is our proxy for the increased costs of being a public company after Sarbanes-Oxley, is likely a conservative estimate of these costs.

Audit Fees and Sarbanes-Oxley

We use regression analysis to examine the relation between audit fees and Sarbanes-Oxley. The sample consists of the 49 public companies that announced a successful going private transaction in 2004 and 2005. The dependent variable in the regressions is the natural log of the audit fees for a given firm-year of observation. We use two independent variables in the regression: the natural log of sales in the contemporaneous year, which is a proxy for variation in firm size over time, and a dummy variable that takes the value of 1 in years after 2002 (the year Sarbanes-Oxley was signed into law) and 0 otherwise. We estimate the model using both ordinary least squares (OLS) and fixed effects that control for individual firms. The results are reported in table 5-6.

As seen in table 5-6, the regression models do a good job of explaining the variation in audit fees. The adjusted R-squared is 0.353 in the OLS model and 0.885 in the fixed effects model. As expected, the coefficient on sales is positive and significant in both regressions, indicating that audit fees increase as the size of firms increases. The coefficients are 0.472 and 0.539 in the OLS and fixed effects models, respectively, indicating an elasticity of audit fees with respect to sales of approximately 0.5.

The main variable of interest in table 5-6 is the dummy variable, and its coefficient is 0.453 in the OLS model and 0.424 in the fixed effects model, respectively,

19. Dennis K. Berman, Gautaum Naik, and Ron Winslow, "Behind $21 Billion Buyout of HCA Lies a High-Stakes Bet on Growth," *Wall Street Journal*, July 25, 2006, p. A1.

20. Matt Morrow, "The SOX Appeal of Going Private," *BusinessWeek Online*, November 29, 2005.

Table 5-6. *Ordinary Least Squares and Fixed Effects Regressions of Audit Fees on Sales and a Post–Sarbanes-Oxley Dummy Variable*[a]

	OLS	Fixed effects
Intercept	3.232	3.033
	(0.00)	(0.27)
Sales	0.472	0.539
	(0.00)	(0.00)
Post–Sarbanes-Oxley	0.453	0.424
	(0.00)	(0.00)
N	49	49
Adjusted R squared	0.353	0.885

Source: Authors' calculations (see table 5-1).

a. This table reports results that take the value of 1 if the year is after the adoption of Sarbanes Oxley (that is, if the year is 2003, 2004, or 2005) and 0 otherwise. The sample consists of 49 public companies that went private in 2004 or 2005. The natural log of audit fees and sales is used in the regressions. *P*-values are in parentheses.

both of which are highly significant.[21] This indicates that audit fees are 42 to 45 percent higher after Sarbanes-Oxley, after controlling for changes in the sizes of firms. We use these coefficients to estimate the present value of increased audit fees after Sarbanes-Oxley for the targets of going private transactions in 2004 and 2005.

Present Value of Incremental Audit Fees Post–Sarbanes-Oxley

Table 5-7 further explores the relation between Sarbanes-Oxley and audit fees. Mean (and median) audit fees pre–Sarbanes-Oxley represent the average (and median) annual audit fees for firms during the two years leading up to the passage of the act (2000–01). This number is then multiplied by the coefficient on the post–Sarbanes-Oxley dummy variable from the fixed effects regression (0.424) in table 5-6 to estimate the mean (and median) incremental audit fees in the post–Sarbanes-Oxley years. Finally, the present value of the incremental audit fees is estimated using three multiples: 10, 15, and 20.

The results in table 5-7 paint an interesting picture. If one assumes that the present value of incremental audit fees is a product of a multiple of 10 and the audit fee at the base year (which is consistent with a discount rate of 10 percent and no expected growth in audit fees), the present value of incremental audit fees after Sarbanes-Oxley is $2.3 million, on average. A multiple of 20 (consistent with a discount rate of 10 percent and an expected growth rate in audit fees of

21. The dummy variable is equal to 1 if the year is after the adoption of Sarbanes-Oxley (2003–05) and 0 otherwise.

Table 5-7. *Estimate of the Present Value of Incremental Audit Fees Post–Sarbanes-Oxley*[a]

Mean audit fees, pre-Sarbox	Mean incremental audit fees, post-Sarbox	Mean present value (in millions of dollars) of incremental audit fees with multiples of		
		10	15	20
$536,942	$227,664	$2.3	$3.4	$4.6
$274,741	$116,490	$1.2	$1.7	$2.3

Source: Authors' calculations (see table 5-1).

a. The present value of incremental audit fees after Sarbanes-Oxley (post-Sarbox) for the sample of 49 firms that went private in 2004 and 2005 is estimated in the following way. Incremental audit fees after Sarbox are estimated as the average audit fee in 2000 and 2001, that is, mean pre-Sarbox audit fees multiplied by 0.424, the estimated coefficient on the post-Sarbox dummy variable in the fixed effect regression reported in table 5-6. The present value of the incremental audit fees is then estimated as a multiple of 10, 15, and 20 times the incremental audit fees.

5 percent) results in a present value estimate of $4.6 million. Overall, the results in table 5-7 suggest that one direct cost of being a public company has increased since the passage of Sarbanes-Oxley.

Present Value of Audit Fees as a Percentage of Market Capitalization and Premiums

Table 5-8 concludes the analysis of audit fees and Sarbanes-Oxley with an examination of the present value of the incremental audit fees after the adoption of the regulation as a percentage of the market capitalization of target firms and the premiums paid in going private transactions. Results are presented for the full sample and for subsamples on the basis of market capitalization. Small firms are defined as firms with market capitalizations of less than $100 million. Medium firms have market capitalizations between $100 million and $1 billion, and large firms are those with market capitalizations greater than $1 billion. It should be noted that this analysis is limited by the small sizes of the subsamples (that is, 10 small firms, 21 medium-size firms, and 13 large firms).

The results of table 5-8 indicate that the present value of the incremental audit fees after Sarbanes-Oxley represent between 1.3 and 2.6 percent (depending on the multiple used) of the average target firm's market capitalization when considered over the full sample. The percentage of market capitalization is greater for smaller firms, with the present value of incremental audit fees estimated at 3.6 to 7.2 percent for small firms and only 0.2 to 0.3 percent for large firms.

Table 5-8. *Present Value of Incremental Audit Fees Post–Sarbanes-Oxley as a Percentage of the Market Capitalization of Firms Going Private and Premiums Paid in Going Private Transactions*[a]

Sample	Market capitalization		Premium	
	Mean	Median	Mean	Median
Full (*N* = 44)	1.3–2.6	0.5–1.0	6.4–12.8	2.6–5.1
Small (*n* = 10)	3.6–7.2	2.4–2.9	18.1–36.2	12.1–24.3
Medium (*n* = 21)	0.9–1.7	0.6–1.2	4.4–8.7	3.0–6.0
Large (*n* = 13)	0.2–0.3	0.1– 0.2	0.8–1.5	0.5–1.0

Source: Authors' calculations (see table 5-1).

a. The present value of incremental audit fees after Sarbanes-Oxley (post-Sarbox) is expressed as a percentage of the market capitalization of 44 firms that went private in 2004 and 2005, as of 21 trading days before the first announcement of the offer, and the premium paid in the transaction, measured as the difference between the final price at which the company's public stock traded and its price 21 trading days before the first announcement of the offer times the number of shares outstanding. Small, medium, and large transactions are defined as those involving companies with market capitalizations of less than $100 million, between $100 million and $1 billion, and more than $1 billion, respectively.

The final two columns of table 5-8 examine the audit fees with respect to the deal premiums, which are measured as the difference between the target firm market capitalization as of the firm's final trading day and its capitalization 21 days before the deal announcement. The results suggest that the mean present value of the audit fees represents between 6.4 and 12.8 percent of the total deal premium over the full sample. It is interesting that the present value of incremental audit fees is 18.1 to 36.2 percent of the deal premium for small firms. This declines to 4.4 to 8.7 percent for medium-size firms and to 0.8 to 1.5 percent for larger firms.

Together, the results of tables 5-6 through 5-8 provide evidence, consistent with the costs of Sarbanes-Oxley compliance and more generally the costs of being a public company, as additional motivation for pursuing a going private transaction. Going private can reduce or even eliminate the costs associated with satisfying the regulations related to Sarbanes-Oxley and operating as a public firm. The results of this section suggest that one of these costs, the increased audit fees under Sarbanes-Oxley, may have been an important consideration for small firms that have gone private in recent years.

Conclusion

This paper examines the recent increase in private equity activity and going private activity in particular. We empirically examined a sample of 245 U.S. companies that went private during the period 1995 to 2005. We documented a number of results consistent with earlier studies of going private transactions.

We found that going private activity has increased during our sample period, both in terms of the number of deals and in the size of the average deal. Additionally, the industry distribution of firms going private has changed, with a shift away from targets in manufacturing and toward service and high-tech firms. Going private transactions continue to be associated with significant increases in shareholder value, with average returns of 17.2 percent on the days the deals are announced.

Targets of going private transactions do not underperform their corresponding industry peers in terms of return on assets, but they do underperform significantly in terms of working capital management. This suggests that working capital improvement remains a source of value creation in going private transactions. Consistent with the free cash flow theory, growth opportunities appear lower and cash levels higher for firms targeted in going private transactions. Finally, an examination of audit fees surrounding the passage of Sarbanes-Oxley suggests that one compliance cost associated with Sarbanes-Oxley may be an important consideration in some going private transactions, especially those involving relatively small firms.

References

Brudney, Victor. 1975. "A Note on Going Private." *Virginia Law Review* 61: 1019–056.

Davis, Jeffry, and Kenneth Lehn. 1992. "Information Asymmetries, Rule 13e-3, and Premiums in Going-Private Transactions." *Washington University Law Quarterly* 70: 587–611.

DeAngelo, Harry, Linda DeAngelo, and Edward Rice. 1984. "Going Private: Minority Freeze-outs and Stockholder Wealth." *Journal of Law and Economics* 27, no. 2 (October): 367–401.

Jensen, Michael C. 1986. "Agency Costs of Free Cash Flow, Corporate Finance, and Takeovers." *American Economic Review Papers and Proceedings* 76, no. 2 (May): 323–29.

———. 1989. "Eclipse of the Public Corporation." *Harvard Business Review* 89, no. 5 (September–October): 61–74.

Kaplan, Steven. 1989. "The Effects of Management Buyouts on Operating Performance and Value." *Journal of Financial Economics* 24, no. 2 (October): 217–54.

Kaplan, Steven N., and Antoinette Schoar. 2005. "Private Equity Performance: Returns, Persistence, and Capital Flows." *Journal of Finance* 60, no. 4 (August): 1791–823.

Kaplan, Steven N., and Jeremy C. Stein. 1993. "The Evolution of Buyout Pricing and Financial Structure in the 1980s." *Quarterly Journal of Economics* 108, no. 2 (May): 313–57.

Lehn, Kenneth, and Annette Poulsen. 1988. "Leveraged Buyouts: Wealth Created or Wealth Redistributed?" In *Public Policy Towards Corporate Takeovers*, edited by Murray L. Weidenbaum and Kenneth W. Chilton, pp. 46–62. New Brunswick, N.J.: Transaction Publishers.

Solomon, Lewis D. 1975. "Going Private: Business Practices, Legal Mechanics, Judicial Standards, and Proposals for Reform." *Buffalo Law Review* 25: 141–79.

Franklin R. Edwards

IT IS A pleasure to have the opportunity to comment on the papers by Frank Partnoy and Randall Thomas and Thomas Boulton, Kenneth Lehn, and Steven Segal. Both papers cover a wide range of recent developments in financial markets, and both raise provocative policy issues. The Partnoy and Thomas paper provides a comprehensive overview of the increasingly active role of hedge funds in corporate governance, with an assessment of whether increased hedge fund "activism" has, on net, enhanced welfare. The Boulton, Lehn, and Segal paper examines the rapid growth of private equity funds and the reasons for the increased incidence of public firms "going private" in the United States.

In this short comment I will not be able to discuss all aspects of these excellent papers but instead will focus on a few selected issues in each paper that I consider to be the most provocative.

A general conclusion of the Partnoy and Thomas paper is that hedge fund activism, on net, has enhanced the effectiveness of shareholders in the corporate governance process and, as such, has probably had a welfare-enhancing impact on corporate America. However, the paper raises potential concerns about hedge fund activism that may require regulatory consideration. In my view the two major concerns they raise are what I call the "vote-buying" tactics used by some hedge funds and the possibility that hedge funds might be motivated by short-run considerations at the cost of long-run firm value. In particular, it has been alleged that hedge funds may push firms to adopt strategies that while increasing the firm's stock prices in the short run may diminish the potential value of the firm in the long run.

The vote-buying issue typically arises in connection with change-of-control transactions, in which hedge funds have a strong interest in seeing a particular acquisition completed. A recent episode that received widespread press coverage, which the Partnoy and Thomas paper discusses, is the proposed acquisition of King Pharmaceuticals by Mylan Laboratories. Mylan made an offer, approved by its board, to buy King Pharmaceuticals at a significant premium. At the time, Perry Capital, a large hedge fund, possibly anticipating such an offer, held a large stock position (10 percent) in King and stood to make a handsome profit ($28 million) if the acquisition were completed.

The proposed deal, however, still had to be approved by a majority vote of Mylan shareholders, and such approval was uncertain. A major Mylan shareholder, Carl Icahn (who owned 10 percent of the Mylan shares), publicly announced that he would vote against the acquisition because he believed the acquisition would not be in the best interests of Mylan shareholders. Perry then bought 10 percent of Mylan shares so that it could vote those shares in favor of the acquisition, seeking to offset Icahn's "no" vote. The new wrinkle in this episode occurred when Perry used derivatives transactions to hedge all of its economic interest in its Mylan stock position via swap trades with Bear, Stearns and Company and Goldman Sachs.

The effect of the swap trades was to enable Perry to acquire the voting rights associated with Mylan stock while not having any economic interest in Mylan. Perry retained no rights to the cash flows (either benefits or costs) generated by Mylan. In effect, Perry was able to separate the voting rights and the economic rights associated with ownership of stock and "buy" only the votes attached to the Mylan stock. As a result, Perry's economic incentive was not aligned with that of the typical Mylan shareholder, who possessed an economic interest in Mylan. Indeed, in this case, Perry's economic interest was clearly to have Mylan pay as high a premium for King's stock as possible, notwithstanding the potential adverse effects on other Mylan shareholders. Of course, whatever the offer, the deal would still require the approval of the Mylan board and by a majority of Mylan shareholders, and Perry held only 10 percent of the Mylan shares.

But Perry's tactics nevertheless raise the prospect that more widespread use of the kind of vote-buying tactics used by Perry could possibly result in firms making decisions that were not in the interests of their shareholders generally. In particular, such tactics raise alarm bells because they could potentially undermine the widely accepted corporate governance principle of one share–one vote. This principle is founded on the belief that the best way to ensure that shareholder value is maximized is to align shareholders' voting rights with their economic interests in the firm.

The issue of the separation of voting rights from cash flow rights in the firm is not a new corporate governance issue. Super-voting (dual class) shares and pyramidal ownership structures, for example, are widely used mechanisms that enable voting rights and control rights to be disproportionate to economic interests of shareholders. These have long been controversial corporate governance issues. If activist hedge funds bring anything new to this controversy, it is that they are more willing and able to utilize recent financial innovations in derivatives markets to accomplish this separation and that these innovations have made it easier and less expensive to separate voting rights from cash flow rights for short periods of time.

Thus the potential problem raised by Partnoy and Thomas is whether a massive proliferation in the use of the kind of vote-buying tactics used by Perry Capital will occur, and, if this were to happen, whether this development would undermine the widely accepted corporate governance principle of one share–one vote. The paper does not reach a conclusion on whether there needs to be additional regulation to curb such vote-buying tactics, and does not discuss what appropriate regulatory responses might be. Indeed, it is not clear whether the vote-buying tactics used by Perry would generally result in worse corporate decisionmaking compared with what now occurs, nor is it clear whether regulation to prohibit the use of such tactics would be an improvement in corporate decisionmaking. Thus, although Partnoy and Thomas raise a provocative issue of shareholder voting associated with the recent voting tactics used by some activist hedge funds, there remains much to do to determine the likely economic effects of these tactics and whether such tactics call for a regulatory response.

The second issue raised by Partnoy and Thomas is whether hedge fund activism will result in firms adopting short-run (or "myopic") strategies to satisfy demands made by activist hedge funds. Again, corporate "short-termism" is not a new issue. In the 1980s there was a heated controversy about whether the short-termism (or "myopia") of U.S. corporations was the major reason for U.S. corporations losing market share to Japanese firms, which allegedly eschewed short-run strategies in favor of policies that furthered the long-run interests of the corporation. The focus of analysis at that time was on explaining the short-termism of U.S. corporate managers. A primary culprit was thought to be the short-termism of U.S. investors (stockholders) generally and the willingness of U.S. managers to acquiesce to shareholder pressures to maximize short-run stock value at the cost of the long-run welfare of the firm. This controversy slowly petered out as Japan fell into a sustained period of slow economic growth and U.S. corporations performed relatively better vis-à-vis their international competitors. Hedge funds were not part of this scenario. Few of any size even existed in the 1980s.

Hedge fund activism has revived this controversy of short-termism. Now the argument seems to be that the hedge funds are the culprit, as opposed to corporate managers or shareholders in general. If it were not for hedge funds, so the argument goes, corporate managers would want to maximize the long-run value of the firm, and shareholders would want managers to do this. Only hedge funds, which are small subsets of shareholders, seek to coerce managers to adopt myopic policies that increase share value in the short run at a cost of greater firm value in the long run.

I find this argument of dubious creditability. First, hedge funds typically hold a very small percentage of the stock of most U.S. companies—nothing like a majority or controlling position. Thus for hedge funds to be able to coerce corporate managers to adopt inefficient, myopic policies, they would need the support of many other shareholders. If the policies proposed by hedge funds were not in the interests of the other shareholders in the firm, it is difficult to see how hedge funds would be able to generate sufficient support for their proposals. Second, corporate law gives corporate managers substantial power to resist shareholder proposals, by hedge funds or others, that they believe are not in the long-run interests of the corporation or do not further the goal of maximizing long-run shareholder value. Thus I am dubious that hedge fund activism is capable of coercing managers to adopt polices that reduce value in the long run.

The more likely problem is that entrenched corporate managers will adopt strategies and policies that are not long-run value-enhancing and that passive shareholders will not be able to prevent this from happening. Hedge fund activism is a healthy counterweight to this problem and may result in greater rather than less corporate efficiency.

Turning now to Boulton, Lehn, and Segal, the primary focus of their paper is on explaining the growing incidence of going private transactions by U.S. firms. The authors examined a sample of 245 U.S. companies that went private during the period 1995 through 2005 and concluded that both the number and size (market value of assets) of companies going private increased significantly during this period. Specifically, comparing 1995–99 with 2000–05, the paper finds that the average number of firms going private increased from 20.2 per year to 24.0 per year, and the inflation-adjusted market value of assets of the firms going private jumped from $231 million to $431 million.

The most provocative finding of this paper is its conclusion that a major reason for the growing incidence of going private transactions is the enactment of the Sarbanes-Oxley Act in 2002. The authors find that the costs associated with being a public company have increased dramatically since the passage of Sarbanes-Oxley. In particular, they find that the costs of complying with Sarbenes-Oxley are between 1.3 and 2.6 percent of the market capitalization of firms that went private. Further, these costs are much higher for smaller firms than they are for large firms: 3.6 to 7.2 percent of market capitalization for firms with market capitalizations of less than $100 million compared with only 0.2 to 0.3 percent of market capitalization for firms with more that $1 billion in assets. Given these findings, the authors argue that a significant reason for the increased incidence of firms going private since Sarbanes-Oxley is the increased costs of compliance.

I am not convinced by their analysis. In fact, if their sample of going private transactions is broken into the three years immediately preceding the passage of Sarbanes-Oxley (1999 through 2001) and compared with the post–Sarbanes-Oxley years (either 2002 through 2005 or 2003 through 2005), one finds that the average number of firms going private each year *fell* appreciably after the passage of the Sarbanes-Oxley Act. Further, no matter how the data are analyzed, one thing that is indisputable is that after Sarbanes-Oxley the average size (market value) of firms going private increased significantly. If the cost of compliance with Sarbanes-Oxley was a major motivator for going private, I would have expected a much greater incidence of smaller firms than of large firms going private, since the relative cost of compliance for a small firm is much higher than that for larger firms (as the authors point out). This finding, therefore, seems inconsistent with the conclusion that higher compliance costs are a major explanation for the growing incidence of firms going private and suggests that there may be other, more important reasons why firms go private.

In conclusion, both papers examine important recent development in U.S. capital markets and raise provocative issues related to these trends. I have no doubt that the issues they explore will generate considerable controversy and research in the future.

JENNIFER E. BETHEL
ALLEN FERRELL

6

Policy Issues Raised by Structured Products

O NE OF THE most important changes in modern finance over the last three decades is the increased understanding and use of financial derivatives. These contracts, which include options, futures, and swaps, are created by financial firms for corporate issuers who seek to tailor their liability claims and lower their costs of capital. Derivatives can trade on organized exchanges, but most often they are created in unregistered form and traded in the over-the-counter markets.

These claims have become commonplace elements of many financial transactions. Within the domain of corporate finance, derivatives have allowed issuers' financing needs to be divorced from the requirements of the suppliers of capital. Today, issuers search for low-cost funds in whatever form that these financings take, and then they rely on the derivatives market to transform those claims to a risk profile that suits the financing needs of the firm. Sophisticated institutional investors have long used derivatives to obtain the risk exposures they desire and to dynamically manage their existing exposures in a cost-effective manner.

The authors thank Arete Consulting and StructuredRetailProducts.com for generously making their data available for this paper. The authors also thank Elizabeth Murphy, Frank Partnoy, Kenneth Scott, Erik Sirri, and the staff at the U.S. Securities and Exchange Commission (SEC) for helpful discussions. Allen Ferrell is grateful to the John M. Olin Center in Law, Economics, and Business at Harvard Law School for financial support.

As derivatives have become more accepted and commonplace in the financial markets, they have also become more competitively priced, and the margins earned by securities firms dealing in these claims have declined. To help protect their margins, dealers have begun to financially engineer more complex securities, one class of which is known as *structured products*. A structured product has no precise definition, either in a business or a regulatory context. We follow the broad definition used by regulators such as the SEC, National Association of Securities Dealers (NASD), and New York Stock Exchange (NYSE) that define a structured product as a security derived from or based on another security (including a bond), a basket of securities, an index, a commodity, or a foreign currency.[1] This definition encompasses a wide range of products, including equity-linked or commodity-linked debt, collateralized debt obligations, reverse convertibles, and credit default swaps. A typical structured product consists of a zero coupon or an interest-bearing note combined with a derivative whose value is typically realized at the maturity of the note. An example is a gold-linked note that makes periodic interest payments of a fixed amount and that pays at maturity the face value of the bond times the return of gold over the life of the note.

Dealers have further protected their margins by selling structured products to new classes of investors. They realized, for example, that investors with high net worth, classified as *accredited investors* under the securities laws, present an attractive market opportunity beyond their traditional client base of institutional investors. Accredited investors, a category that includes individuals with at least $1 million in net worth (including the equity in their real estate holdings) and $200,000 in individual income or $300,000 in joint income, can purchase unregistered structured products. Alternatively, products can be registered and sold to the mass retail market. Structured products are appealing to high net worth investors for a number of reasons. First, these investors often demand complex financial portfolios. Combinations of long positions in stocks and bonds may not provide the overall risk exposure they desire. Second, many of these investors use financial advisers who may be useful in navigating the significant intricacies of structured products. The payout patterns of these securities can be very complex, requiring sophisticated financial models for valuation and estimation of embedded fees. A sense of the substantial complexity of structured products can be seen from box 6-1, which summarizes the terms of PROPELS, a structured product marketed by Morgan Stanley. Finally, structured products can be tailored to offer

---

1. NASD Notice to Members 05-59; SEC Rule 434; Securities Act Release no. 42746 (May 2, 2000). It is important to note that this definition may be different from other usages. For instance, some commentators do not consider *synthetic assets*, defined as instruments that are created exclusively out of one or more derivatives, to be structured products.

> **Box 6-1.** *Morgan Stanley Protected Performance Equity Linked Securities*[SM] *(PROPELS*[SM]*)*
>
> - The principal amount and issue price of each PROPELS is $10.00.
> - The interest is 0.4 percent per year.
> - At maturity you will receive the principal amount of $10, plus a supplemental redemption amount, if any, based on the performance of the DJIA over the term of the PROPELS. The supplemental redemption amount equal to the product of (i) $10 times (ii) the percentage increase, if any, in the average protected index value over the initial index value:
>   — The initial index value will equal 10,619.03, the closing value of the DJIA on February 20, 2004, the day we offered the PROPELS for initial sale to the public.
>   — The average protected index value will equal the arithmetic average of the protected index closing values on eight specified determination dates during the life of the PROPELS.
>   — On each determination date, the protected index closing value will equal the greater of (i) the DJIA closing value on such determination date and (ii) the highest DJIA closing value on any previous determination date; provided that the protected index closing value on the first determination date will be the DJIA closing value on such determination date regardless of whether that DJIA closing value is higher or lower than the initial index value.
>   — The determination dates will be the 30th of each December, beginning December 30, 2004, to and including December 30, 2010, and December 27, 2011.
> - If the average protected index value of the DJIA is less than or equal to the initial index value, you will receive only the principal amount of the PROPELS at maturity and will not receive any supplemental redemption amount.
>
> Source: www.sec.gov/Archives/edgar/data/895421/000095010304000308/feb2404_424b3.txt.
> DJIA = Dow Jones Industrial Average.

highly nonlinear payout patterns that permit very specialized or state-contingent bets to be made on assets such as currencies, commodities, or various baskets of securities.

Recent evidence suggests that traditional retail investors in the United States increasingly are buying registered structured products. The American Stock Exchange (AMEX) reported an 18 percent increase in 2005 in the number of issues of structured products listed on the exchange compared with those listed in 2004 (136 in 2005 versus 115 in 2004), bringing the notional amount of structured products on the AMEX to over $13 billion.[2] The New York Stock Exchange reported $14 billion in new listings in corporate-issued structured products in 2005. According to Keith Strycula, chairman and founder of the Structured Products Association, about 40 percent of sales in structured products is retail,

2. "Despite Record $50 Billion in 2005, Structured Products Remain 'Wall Street's Best Kept Secret,'" SPA (Structured Products Association) chairman's letter, February 2006, p. 2 (www.structuredproducts.org/notes.shtml).

Figure 6-1. *Gross Sales of Structured Products in 2005 (in Billions of Dollars)*

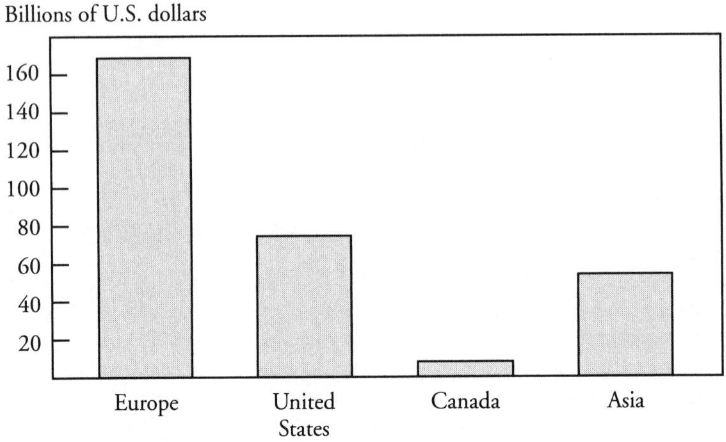

Billions of U.S. dollars

Source: Structured Retail Products (www.structuredretailproducts.com/module.php?moduleID=1).

which is the fastest growing area in the structured products market.[3] If experience with other financial products serves as a guide, the sale of structured products to the mass market of retail investors will increase. This outcome is by no means necessarily bad. In fact, relative to the United Kingdom and continental Europe, the United States is far behind in the penetration of the retail market by structured products. As shown in figure 6-1, the size of the U.S. market is roughly half that of Europe's.

This trend, however, does raise the interesting question about how well the disclosure-based system of securities regulation in the United States can cope with increasingly complex structured products being targeted to retail investors. Can the current securities disclosure regime that governs the offer and sale of structured products generate the type of information that can protect less-sophisticated investors? If not, how can these investors be protected? These questions are far from academic. The United Kingdom and continental Europe have experienced several financial mishaps related to the purchase of structured products by retail investors, a few of which are discussed below.

To answer these questions, we first look at changes in the market for structured products and evaluate the efficacy of the current regime for investor protection.

3. Dan Jamieson, "Regulators Eye Structured Products," *Investment News*, December 18, 2006, (www.investmentnews.com/apps/pbcs.dll/article?AID=/20061218/SUB/612180707/-1/INIssueAlert04).

Highlighting a few of its weaknesses, we then provide possible ways to enhance investor protection.

Structured Products

Structured products, as discussed here, are financial instruments designed to meet specific needs of investors and issuers by incorporating special, nonstandard features whose values are linked to, or derived from, such underlying assets as stocks, bonds, currencies, or commodities. The performance of a structured product is therefore based on the performance of this underlying asset and not on the discretion of the product provider. Often, but not always, the product relies on the use of derivatives to generate the return. Structured products typically come in two forms: growth products, which may provide an element of capital protection, and income products, which provide fixed high income but with a risk to the capital return.

If we were discussing structured products eight or ten years ago, the instruments would have been securities such as Reverse Convertible Basket Linked Notes, Adjustable Conversion-Rate Equity Security Units, Market Value Put Securities, and Reset Performance Equity-linked Redemption Quarterly-pay Securities. More recently designed structured products differ from and are more complex than structured products in the past. In addition to linking payments to new classes of assets, recent structured products are characterized by innovative combinations of underlying asset mixes. For example, issuers are combining credit derivative exposures with equity index underlyings and, as shown in box 6-2, combining interest rate and crude oil underlyings.[4] There has also been a shift in the protection of principal. Between 2000 and 2002, most U.S. products offered full principal protection, but since then a swing to nonprotected products has occurred.

Banks are continually innovating structured products to meet investor and issuer needs.[5] Structured products allow market participants who prefer a particular pattern of payments over time to access such a pattern, as well as to hedge certain risks. Structured products facilitate the transfer of risk, for a fee, from those who do not want to bear risk to those who are willing to bear it. This broader dispersion of risk across investors typically improves the effectiveness of risk transfer in the market, lowering the cost of capital. Structured products also allow investors to more fully

4. Keith Strycula, "Conference Report: An Industry in Transformation," *Structured Products*, April 2005, p. 28.
5. Investment banks focus in part on innovation to avoid commoditization of their products.

Box 6-2. *MACRO Securities Depositor, LLC, Light Sweet Crude Oil Up-MACRO Holding Trust and Light Sweet Crude Oil Up-MACRO Tradeable Trust*

On the closing date, Down-MACRO tradeable trust will issue Down-MACRO tradeable shares in the form of certificates representing undivided beneficial interests in the Down-MACRO tradeable trust. On the closing date, the proceeds from the sale of the Down-MACRO tradeable shares will be delivered to the trustee for the Down-MACRO tradeable trust, who in turn will deliver these proceeds to the trustee for the Down-MACRO holding trust. These proceeds, together with any proceeds from the sale of any Down-MACRO holding shares to holders other than the Down-MACRO tradeable trust, will be deposited into the Down-MACRO holding trust. The trustee for the Down-MACRO holding trust will then deliver the Down-MACRO holding shares to the Down-MACRO tradeable trust and the other investors in the Down-MACRO holding trust and the trustee for the Down-MACRO tradeable trust will deliver the Down-MACRO tradeable shares to investors in the Down-MACRO tradeable trust. The trustee for the Down-MACRO holding trust will use the net proceeds of the sale of its Down-MACRO holding shares to acquire bills, bonds, and notes issued and guaranteed by the United States Treasury and repurchase agreements collateralized by the United States Treasury securities, that are, in each case, scheduled to mature before the first quarterly distribution date.

Concurrently with the formation of the Down-MACRO holding trust, we have also formed the Up-MACRO holding trust to create "paired holding trusts." The paired holding trusts will enter into an income distribution agreement and multiple settlement contracts with each other. The Up-MACRO holding trust will issue the Up-MACRO holding shares that will be acquired by the Up-MACRO tradeable trust on the closing date. A portion of the Up-MACRO holding shares (representing less than 50 percent of the Up-MACRO holding shares) issued on the closing date may also be acquired by other investors who are not affiliated with the Up-MACRO tradeable trust. The Up-MACRO holding shares will be issued in the form of certificates, each representing an undivided beneficial interest in the Up-MACRO holding trust. The Down-MACRO holding shares and the Up-MACRO holding shares are "paired holding shares."

On each quarterly distribution date, the paired holding trusts will use income generated by their treasuries that remains available after each trust has paid its fees and expenses and the fees and expenses of the related tradeable trust to make payments under the income distribution agreement. On the final scheduled termination date or an early termination date, the paired holding trusts will make a final payment under each settlement contract using the maturity proceeds of the treasuries held by each trust. On any redemption date, one of the paired holding trusts will make a final payment under each settlement contract that is being settled by delivering to the other holding trust all or a portion of its cash or treasuries or both. Quarterly distributions and the final distributions on the holding shares or your tradeable shares will depend upon the underlying value of the Up-MACRO or Down-MACRO holding trusts. The underlying value of the holding trusts at any time will depend on the level of the light sweet crude oil price and the yield on the treasuries. If, for example, the level of the applicable reference price of crude oil on the relevant price determination day is above its starting level, the Down-MACRO holding trust will be required to make a final payment to the Up-MACRO holding trust in an amount proportional to the increase in the level of that price.

Source: www.sec.gov/Archives/edgar/data/1290059/000134100406000428/ny1073541-14.txt.

diversify their investment portfolios, because investors can access asset classes that would not otherwise be available through traditional investment vehicles. For example, structured offerings can take commodities, hedge funds, or foreign exchange markets as their underlying assets. The underlyings can include a mix of different asset classes, indexes, or baskets of individual equities. Such diversity within an overall investment strategy may reduce portfolio return volatility.

One result of this investor demand is a large and growing market for structured products in the United States. The Structured Products Association (SPA) estimates sales of structured products in the United States were $70 billion in 2006, up from $50 billion in 2005.[6] Both the registered and unregistered segments of the structured products market are experiencing growth. In 2004 issuers sold $12 billion in notional registered structured products in the United States, up more than 20 percent from 2003 when just under $10 billion was placed.[7] The market has grown 53 percent annually during the last four years. In terms of listed registered products, similar growth is reported. The NYSE, for example, reports that by June 2006 it had listed more than double the number of new products than it had listed during the same period in 2005.[8]

This growth in the unregistered and registered markets is arising in part from new distribution channels, including distributions to retail investors.[9] Investment banks are increasingly offering structured products in small denominations to retail investors through their broker networks. By 2004 and 2005, large retail institutions such as Raymond James, Deutsche Bank (DB) Alex. Brown, Credit Suisse First Boston (CSFB) Private Client Services, and Wells Fargo had expanded their staffs to include experts on structured products to educate brokers about the risks and rewards of these products.[10] In 2004 Citigroup's Private Bank, J. P. Morgan Private Bank, Mellon Financial, and UBS AG reported increased structured product sales to private investors.[11] Sales to retail investors were also higher in 2005. According to Keith Strycula, chairman and founder of the SPA, the growth of the structured products business in the United States resembles the growth of hedge funds in the 1990s. "Six, seven years ago, many

6. Dan Jamieson, "Regulators Eye Structured Products." These numbers do not include several smaller categories tracked by StructuredRetailProducts.com, which estimates sales in 2005 of approximately $75 billion.

7. *Structured Products Newsletter* 1, issue 4 (Winter 2004–05): p. 11.

8. Daniel Sheehan, "Slowed Down by the Watchdog," *Structured Products*, September 1, 2006, p. 35 (www.structuredproductsonline).

9. SPA Chairman's Letter, February 2006.

10. *Structured Products Newsletter* 1, issue 4 (Winter 2004–05): p. 11.

11. Jane Kim, "Wealthy Clients Add Options to Their Portfolios," *Wall Street Journal*, November 3, 2004, p. D2.

mainstream investors were just beginning to understand what a 'hedge fund' was. The same could be said for structured products at this point in time."[12] According to a managing director at J. P. Morgan Private Bank, twice as many private investors were holding options or similar investments in their portfolios in 2004 than in 2000.[13]

The Current State of Investor Protection

The sale of structured products to a wide range of investors, including retail investors, raises concerns about investor protection along several dimensions. At the most basic level, do investors have even a rudimentary understanding of the products they are purchasing? For example, the complexity of many of these structured products often entails embedded option features. On a related note, do investors understand the various fees, both embedded and explicit, they are being charged for the product? The answers to these questions turn on the quality of disclosures concerning structured products, the ability of investors to understand and analyze the disclosures that are made, and the responsibility of those facilitating the sale of structured products to ensure the suitability of a purchase for a given investor.

The extent of investor protection in the structured product area has been primarily set by four legal regimes: Regulation AB, the new regulations concerning offerings, suitability requirements, and the general antifraud provisions of the Securities Act of 1933 and the Securities Exchange Act of 1934.

Regulation AB

Asset-backed securities (ABSs) constitute a very important segment of the structured products market. ABSs are securities that are backed by, to use the words of the SEC, a "discrete pool of receivables or other financial assets," such as securities backed by mortgage loans or credit card receivables placed in a special purpose entity.[14] Although most investors in these securities tend to be institutional, there is nevertheless meaningful retail participation in some segments of the ABS market, such as securities backed by publicly traded debt.

---

12. Structured Products Association, "Chairman's Notebook," February 2006, quoting the speech of Keith A. Strycula, SPA chairman and founder, at the LaSalle Bank/ABN-Amro's 24th Annual Fixed-Income Symposium and Exposition, Boca Raton, Florida, January 19–21, 2006 (www.structured products.org/notes.shtml).

13. Jane Kim, "Wealthy Clients Add Options to Their Portfolios."

14. Item 1101(c)(1) of Regulation AB.

Regulation AB, promulgated by the SEC on December 15, 2004, is a comprehensive set of regulations governing the registration requirements for an ABS. In particular, there are four important components of Regulation AB that affect investor protection: the disclosure requirements, permissible communications during the offering process, potential liability, and the definition of asset-backed securities. Of course, one need worry about Regulation AB only if there is a public offering of an asset-backed security that hence must be registered, as Regulation AB deals with the registration process.

IMPROVED DISCLOSURE. Before the adoption of Regulation AB, disclosures specifically crafted with asset-backed securities in mind were not required in the registration process. This resulted in a mismatch between the disclosures required and the disclosures that would be relevant for purchasers of asset-backed securities. For instance, requirements to disclose information about an issuer's business are irrelevant given that the assets that back the securities are placed in a legally distinct entity. Beyond these assets, there simply is no business to report about. Moreover, requiring the release of an issuer's audited financial statements makes little sense as these financials focus on valuing the assets and liabilities of an ongoing business. Purchasers of ABS products, however, are typically focused on the cash flows generated by the assets backing the securities. This mismatch between the traditional disclosure regime and the needs of ABSs investors is not surprising given the recent vintage and growth of the ABS market.

To ameliorate this mismatch, which had been dealt with by the SEC on an ad hoc basis through the use of no-action letters, Regulation AB requires the disclosure of information that is of particular relevance to ABSs investors. Perhaps most important, sponsors of registered asset-backed securities must provide, to the extent material, "static pool" data consisting of the delinquency and loss experience of other pools of assets of the type to be securitized, which have also been established by the sponsor. The disclosure of data on delinquency and loss is required for as far back as the previous three years. It is an open question on how useful static pool information really is for ABSs purchasers, given that purchasers of ABSs before Regulation AB typically did not request this information informally from issuers.

In addition, Regulation AB requires increased disclosure concerning the composition and characteristics of the asset pool, including information such as capitalized accrued interest, whether the pool asset is secured or not, credit scores of obligors, and the interest rate being charged. Unlike static pool data, issuers typically provided this information before Regulation AB. Finally, prospectuses for registered ABS offerings will have to disclose far more detailed information on the fees that investors are being charged. Specifically, a separate table itemizing all the estimated fees and expenses to be paid out of the cash flows is now required.

Although disclosure can be quite useful, investor protection is enhanced only if it can be intelligently used either by investors themselves or broker-dealers acting on the investors' behalf. For instance, it is important that investors (or their broker-dealers) realize that credit scores of obligors that are now being disclosed speak only to the risk of default. Credit scores do not measure the riskiness of investing in the structured product. It is not uncommon for a structured product to be extremely risky but have little or no default risk.

COMMUNICATIONS DURING THE OFFERING PROCESS. Regulation AB largely limits the content of communications to investors during the registration process to factual information, referred to as "informational and computational material" (ICM), such as information about the structure of the various classes of the pool of assets. A communication generally cannot relay information that is not considered to be informational and computational material. Moreover, such communications are usually subject not only to section 12(a)(2) liability under the Securities Act of 1933, but section 11 liability as well. This liability exposure arguably helps ensure the accuracy and completeness of disclosures made in ICM communications.

DEFINITION OF "ISSUER." For purposes of the liability provisions of the Securities Act and the Securities Exchange Act, the *issuer* of an ABS is defined as the party that deposits the assets into the special purpose entity that holds the discrete pool of assets against which the securities are issued. The definition of issuer as the depositor in the context of an ABS raises a potential way to avoid liability by first depositing the assets into an intermediate depositor entity, which then deposits the assets into the issuing special purpose entity. The issuer of the ABS in that situation would appear to be the intermediate depositor entity. Structuring the transaction in this way would reduce the potential liability exposure of an entity wishing to place assets in a special purpose entity, thereby making the initial depositor more willing to offer registered structured products in the first place but with fewer consequences for misleading communications made during the registration process.

DEFINITION OF ABS AND SYNTHETIC STRUCTURED PRODUCTS. The definition of an asset-backed security in Regulation AB, and hence the scope of Regulation AB's provisions on disclosures and permissible communications, excludes synthetic securities. *Synthetic structured products* are securities whose payoffs do not depend primarily on the cash flows generated by a discrete pool of assets, but rather depend on assets, indexes, or securities that are not held in any specific pool. Synthetic structured products include a number of important products, such as credit default swaps, credit-linked notes, and most collateralized debt obligation securities. Of the $250 billion in issuances in the United States of collateralized debt obligation in 2002, approximately $187 billion were synthetic issuances.[15]

Many market commentators feared that the effect of not having the benefits and certainty of Regulation AB available to registered synthetic structured products would be to force these products into the private, nonregistered market. And, indeed, it appears that credit swaps and collateralized debt obligations are now overwhelmingly privately placed. However, most of these products undoubtedly would have been privately placed into the institutional market even if Regulation AB had included synthetic structured products in the definition of an ABS. In a private placement, or in any other exempt offering, there is simply no need to worry about the requirements (for which Regulation AB provides some relief and certainty) posed by a public offering. In any event, the SEC's comprehensive reform of the offering rules, in a set of regulations adopted on June 29, 2005, have gone a long way to alleviating the concern over the potentially negative effects of the differential treatment of ABSs and synthetic structured products.[16]

Private placements of structured products, whether they be synthetic products or not, with institutional investors would not seem to raise concerns about investor protection if one were to put aside the costs to the public (that is, reducing choice and diversification) of not having these products available through registered offerings. Purchasers of nonregistered securities may well have the resources and wherewithal to evaluate such investments, although even here concerns arise as a result of the modest requirements necessary to be deemed an accredited investor. This line of reasoning, however, ignores the fact that privately placed structured products can be sold to the public, typically after a two-year holding period (and even after one year if accompanied by certain disclosures), with little in the way of information, if the seller is not a control person, pursuant to Rule 144 of the Securities Act of 1933.

Not only are the disclosure requirements of the registration process not applicable with a Rule 144 sale to the public, but there will in all likelihood be no section 12(a)(2) liability for misleading or false statements made in connection with Rule 144 sales to the public. Most courts have interpreted the Supreme Court's opinion in *Gustafson* v. *Alloyd Co.* as limiting section 12(a)(2) liability to the original purchasers in a public offering.[17] The purchasers of a structured product in a

---

15. This is based on the estimates of the International Swaps and Derivatives Association.

16. SEC's reform of the offering rules was in a set of regulations that were adopted on June 29, 2005.

17. *Gustafson* v. *Alloyd Co.*, 513 U.S. 561 (1995). See, for example, *Rogers* v. *Sterling Foster & Co.*, 222 F. Supp. 2d 216 (E.D.N.Y. 2002).

Rule 144 sale are not purchasing securities in a public offering by the issuer but rather are purchasing in a secondary market transaction. They thus forgo the protections afforded by such liability provisions.

SEC's Securities Offering Reform

From the perspective of investor protection, there are two important changes resulting from the adoption of the new regulations on securities offerings: the deregulation of content restrictions for communications made during the offering process and changes in liability as delineated in section 11 and section 12(a)(2). These changes affect the process by which structured products are registered and offered to the public. Unlike Regulation AB, the new regulations concerning securities offerings apply to all registered securities, including structured products whether they are synthetic or not.

CONTENT RESTRICTION DEREGULATION. The new securities offering regulations dramatically deregulate the content of permissible communications during the offering process of a registered structured product. Structured products can now be promoted after the filing of a registration statement using a "free writing prospectus" so long as the issuer is a *seasoned issuer*. With some limited exceptions, an issuer of ABSs that is eligible to use Form S-3 (the form that is typically used to register asset-backed securities) is deemed to be a seasoned issuer. A free writing prospectus can be sent to a potential investor even if the issuer has not sent to the investor the most recent statutory prospectus on file with the SEC.

Although a free writing prospectus cannot be misleading or false on pain of facing section 12(a)(2) liability and the general antifraud provisions of the Securities Act and Securities Exchange Act, there is no requirement in the offering rules that it provide a balanced picture to investors. Nor is there a limit on the type of information that can be contained in the free writing prospectus, so long as it is not inconsistent with the registration statement. In other words, investor interest in a structured product offering can be solicited using a wide range of promotional materials, including information released to the media by the issuer.

For issuers of ABSs, the bottom line is that a seasoned issuer can send communications to potential investors pursuant to either the free writing prospectus rules or the ICM regulations under Regulation AB. In sharp contrast to the ICM offering rules for ABSs, there are no restrictions in the new offering rules on the content that may be included in the free writing prospectus. Information that cannot be included in an ICM communication, such as allotment and subscription information, can be included in a free writing prospectus, given its lack of content restrictions.

To some extent, the range of permissible communications is limited by the NASD regulations. NASD Rule 2210 requires that all sales materials and oral presentations by registered broker-dealers present a fair and balanced picture. This rule also prohibits an omission of material fact that renders the communication misleading. In September 2005 the NASD emphasized in a notice to members that prior or subsequent communications containing clarifying information will not cure an otherwise misleading or unbalanced communication.[18] This is consistent with several recent enforcement actions that rejected the claim that a prior or subsequent communication rendered a communication accurate and balanced.

LIABILITY FOR COMMUNICATIONS. There are several substantial changes in liability faced by issuers and underwriters of structured products resulting from the new offering rules that both reduce and expand potential liability in different ways.

The new offering regulations remove section 11 liability for omissions or misleading statements in the free writing prospectus, which is deemed not to be part of the registration statement. The lack of section 11 liability represents a significant reduction in liability exposure, as there is no due diligence defense for issuers under section 11, nor is there a scienter requirement as a prerequisite to section 11 liability. In contrast to free writing prospectuses, ICM communications on ABSs that are filed with the SEC are deemed to be part of the registration statement and, hence, create potential section 11 liability for issuer and underwriter. Thus using a free writing prospectus, rather than an ABS ICM communication, removes an important source of liability for issuer and underwriter.

In terms of section 12(a)(2) liability, an issuer will only be liable for misleading or false statements in the free writing prospectus if the communication was prepared by or on behalf of the issuer, the communication was referred to by the issuer, or material information in the communication about the issuer or the securities offered was provided by or on behalf of the issuer. As a result, an issuer is unlikely to face section 12(a)(2) liability when the communication was prepared and disseminated by other parties, such as an underwriter.

There is one change in the new securities offering regulations, however, that expands potential liability, at least relative to what much of the structured products community had believed was the law before the new securities offering regulations. Rule 159 of the Securities Act of 1933 explains that section 12(a)(2) liability will be based on information provided to an investor at the time of sale

18. NASD Notice to Members, 05-59 (September 2005).

without regard to information provided afterwards. Much of the structured products community had believed that misleading communications would not give rise to section 12(a)(2) liability if an accurate term sheet or final prospectus was subsequently given to the investor. "Rule 159 risk management" is now an important consideration for issuers who are publicly offering structured products.

Suitability Requirements

Suitability requirements have historically constituted an important source of investor protection in the markets. In its notice to members in September 2005, the NASD again emphasized the importance of broker-dealers fulfilling their suitability obligations when facilitating transactions in structured products involving retail investors, whether those products have been registered or not. There are three different sets of suitability requirements that attach to broker-dealers in this context.

First, broker-dealers must "make every effort to familiarize themselves with each customer's financial situation, trading experience, and ability to meet risks involved with such products and to make every effort to make customers aware of the pertinent information regarding [new financial] products."[19] It is important to note that this obligation applies to broker-dealers not only when making recommendations but also when accepting orders for *new* financial products. Second, a broker-dealer has the obligation before making a recommendation to ensure that a structured product is suitable for at least some investors. In addition, a broker-dealer itself has the obligation to understand the product. And third, broker-dealers must, pursuant to NASD Rule 2310, ensure that a recommendation is suitable for a given investor by examining the investor's specific situation.

With the exception of the first requirement dealing with new structured products, these obligations apply to a broker-dealer who makes a recommendation. If an investor places an unsolicited order for an established structured product, these suitability requirements do not provide any investor protection. It is telling that the NASD has suggested that it might be appropriate for broker-dealers to either limit purchasers of some structured products to those already approved for options trading or develop "comparable procedures" designed to ensure that investors purchasing structured products are taking appropriate risk. Such a requirement would represent a significant extension beyond that provided by traditional suitability obligations that is conditional on a recommendation being made. In particular, there is concern that a *reverse convertible*, a structured product in which an investor purchases a bond and writes a put option to the issuer

19. See NASD IM-2310-2(e).

with the exercise price being payable in shares, is the type of structured product that the NASD believes requires preapproved options trading as a prerequisite to purchase. This requirement could have the effect of confining reverse convertible products and perhaps other structured products with embedded options essentially to the institutional market.

General Antifraud Provisions

In assessing the current state of investor protection, it is important to realize that the general antifraud provisions of the Securities Act and the Securities Exchange Act apply to sales of structured products just as they do with the sale of any security. These antifraud provisions include section 17(a) of the Securities Act and Rule 10b-5, Rule 13b2-1, Rule 13b2-2, Section 13(b)(5), and Section 20(e) of the Securities Exchange Act.

Is Current Investor Protection Sufficient?

To date, there are few documented instances of retail investors in the United States suffering financial losses because they were not able to understand the disclosures made concerning the returns and risks of structured products. In Europe, however, where the structured products market is more extensively developed than in the United States and where retail investors actively buy structured products, concern has emerged as retail investors have experienced losses.

Several recent events have garnered international attention. In 2002–03, for example, investor losses from equity-linked reverse convertibles, a structured investment that came to be known as precipice bonds, made the news. The payments from these bonds were linked to the performance of a basket of stocks, offering relatively high coupon payments, but no capital protection.[20] They thus promised big returns in rising markets but at a cost of a downside penalty if the market fell. The market eventually dropped, and many bondholders found themselves losing 2 percent of their investment for every 1 percent the market fell.[21] Following these losses, the U.K. Financial Services Authority (FSA) reviewed 150 financial services firms, which resulted in payments to customers of £125 million.[22] The FSA banned or fined several companies for misselling, including Lloyds TSB. In its investigation, the FSA found that relatively few structured products were being sold as a result of consumers receiving personalized advice. In the case

20. *Structured Products Newsletter* 1, issue 2 (March-April 2004): p. 5.
21. "Structured Products Guide" (www.trustnet.com/help/sp/).
22. "FSA Bans IFA Following Precipice Complaints," *Structured Products*, October 1, 2005 (www.structuredproductsonline.com).

of Lloyds, for example, the FSA found that 44 percent of the total number of policies sold to investors were unsuitable either because investors lacked sufficient prior experience with equity-related investment products or because the investments made up too big a share of their portfolios.[23]

Another high-profile case involved a very wealthy investor with prior experience in the currency swap markets, who purchased a structured product, called PERLS, from Morgan Stanley International and suffered substantial losses. The payment due on maturity to the holder of PERLS was linked to the spot exchange rate of several foreign currencies. Given the complexity of the product, the product's illiquidity, and the sizable investment made by the investor, a court concluded that the structured product was not a suitable investment.[24]

The concern about the current regulatory regime includes, but is not limited to, the misselling and suitability issues described above. Concern has also arisen as to the transparency of the fees charged, which is considered in other areas of securities regulation to be very important. For example, the regulatory regime for investment products such as mutual funds emphasizes the cost of investments, which are often taken to include expenses, selling charges, and commissions. In the case of mutual funds, most of these costs are relatively easy to calculate and disclose, because they are taken as charges against the net assets of a fund.[25] Thus a fund may have an annual expense ratio of 0.8 percent and may be sold with a one-time front-end load charge of 3 percent, all of which must be clearly disclosed at the point of sale. So important is fee disclosure in this regime that there is pressure in some quarters to go still farther with fee regulation and required periodic disclosure of dollar fees paid per quarter.

Now consider the case of structured products. If a security is offered at a price of $10, there may be an underwriting discount of $0.40, meaning that only $9.60 of the initial $10 is invested in the product. Note, however, that this cost may be the only cost that is clearly disclosed and that investors may be charged other far more significant costs. So, for example, suppose that the product is a five-year equity-linked bond with an annual coupon of 1 percent, that it has a guarantee that the investor loses none of the face amount of principal invested, and that the terminal payment is equal to the greater of the face amount of the bond or the percentage increase in the level of the S&P 500, with a maximum of 10 percent per year over the life of the bond. Suppose the volatility of the market is 20 per-

---

23. "Final Notice" to Lloyds TSB Bank PLC from Julia M. R. Dunn, head of retail selling, FSA Enforcement Division, September 24, 2003.

24. See *Morgan Stanley UK Group* v. *Puglisi*, Queen's Bench (1998).

25. Soft dollars, or the payment of commission in excess of the minimum possible, and related practices are notable exceptions.

cent, the interest rate is 5 percent annually, and the bond is sold at par. The product appears attractive because the investor cannot lose the principal, can make up to 10 percent per year in appreciation, and can get a guaranteed 1 percent return. But is this an expensive or a cheap product? To know the answer to this question, one needs to price the embedded options in the structured note. In this case, from the investor's perspective the note includes a long put struck at par and a short call struck at $(1.10)^5$ or 161 percent above the current index level. The call is priced at $9.69 and the put at $7.02, implying an additional cost to the investor of $2.67 ($9.69 – $7.02) or 267 basis points at issue, far outstripping the underwriting charge. One might point out that this calculation neglects the 1 percent annual coupon paid to the investor. However, this calculation also does not include dividends paid on the S&P 500 that the investor forgos in making the investment, instead of investing in the underlying and buying the securities themselves. Because the forgone dividend yield of the index is above the 1 percent coupon on the bond, this represents an additional cost to the investor.

The point of the above example is threefold. First, it illustrates that even a simple structured product such as a plain-vanilla equity-linked bond can require considerable effort and knowledge to decompose it to its elements. Second, and more important, it shows that only through such decomposition can the true cost of a structured product be understood. If the goal is to compute a cost that is on a comparable basis to the expense ratio and selling costs of a mutual fund share, then such an exercise is required. It must be clear that very few investors would be capable of such an analysis. More interesting is the question of how many selling brokers are capable of providing the salient results of such an analysis at the point of sale. With certainty the underwriting broker would be capable of this analysis, but there is no requirement that such information be presented. Whether a typical introducing broker can or would present such information is, we believe, highly doubtful. There is probably room for the introduction of an examination that would be a prerequisite to being allowed to sell structured products, similar to the Series 3 examination that is a prerequisite for anyone applying for registration as a futures commission merchant or commodity trading adviser. Finally, the example demonstrates that a structured product's design can dramatically affect the magnitude of the embedded fees charged to investors and that even simple changes to a note's design can lower such fees to a more attractive and appropriate range.

One final concern about structured products is the difficulty of reselling products before maturity. The secondary market for most structured products is highly illiquid, which means that investors who want to resell their securities face high transactions costs. Although some dealers may be willing to buy securities back from investors, few guarantee that they will repurchase them or support a secondary market.

Such a concern is all the more important given the future demographics of the United States. The baby boomers of the 1950s and 1960s are now reaching retirement age. The U.S. Census Bureau estimates that the number of people who are 65 and older will increase from 36.7 million in 2005 to more than 63.5 million in 2025.[26] These people are likely to be disinvesting from homes and equity securities, exiting out of corporate retirement plans, and putting their funds to work in fixed-income-type investments. The investment and brokerage communities see this demographic shift as a bonanza and are trying to either retain or increase their share of these dollars. Structured finance products represent a likely place for these monies to be invested, and perhaps appropriately so given their flexibility. However, the regulatory concerns should be clear: elderly investors who need current income, who have a potentially diminished ability to understand new products, and whose risk behavior is likely to arise from a fear of running out of money before death may make easy prey for unscrupulous brokers.

At the same time, all of these concerns must be balanced against the clear benefits that can be conveyed by structured products. In the case of the equity-linked bond above, nowhere can a typical investor generate such a pattern of cash flows (no loss of principal, guaranteed income, and substantial potential for price appreciation) other than in a structured product. Even if investors know how to synthesize such a bond, it would be prohibitively expensive to do so in terms of transactions costs, given the size of a typical retail investment. As former commissioner of the Commodity Futures Trading Commission Sharon Brown-Hruska made clear in her address to the SPA, one has to be careful in restricting the ability of retail investors to take on and manage risk.[27] Even seemingly innocent reporting, registration, or disclosure solutions can substantially increase the costs of trading derivatives, whose chief benefit is low transactions costs. This increase in costs may in turn affect the supply or terms of the products offered in the market. Thus it is up to regulators to balance the costs and the benefits to the retail investor of the chosen investor protection regime.

26. U.S. Census Bureau, Population Division, Interim State Population Projections, 2005, "Interim Projections of the Population, by Selected Age Groups for the United States, Regions, and Divisions, April 1, 2000 to July 1, 2030" (www.census.gov/population/projections/SummaryTabC1.xls).

27. "Flexible Regulatory Approaches to Risk Innovation," keynote address by Sharon Brown-Hruska, former commissioner of the Commodity Futures Trading Commission, at the Structured Products Association America Conference, May 5, 2006.

Possible Solutions

Before one begins to suggest remedies, it is important to specify appropriate policy goals. In this case, we take the policy goal to be the design of a regulatory regime that prevents investors from unknowingly holding inappropriate structured products in their investment portfolios. This overall goal encompasses two subsidiary goals: ensuring that retail investors purchase products at reasonable fees, which includes those fees that are embedded, and that retail investors hold products with a risk profile that is appropriate for their investment needs. For the reasons discussed above, the particular regulatory pressure points for structured products differ from those of traditional retail investment vehicles, such as mutual funds. For one, these products are much more complicated to understand, often relying on complex mathematical formulas and models to determine cash payouts and fees. Second, these products can be linked to one or a few state variables, such as a commodity price, an index price, a currency price, or some combination of the above. These variables provide important hedging or investment opportunities to investors and allow investors to develop such exposures at much lower cost than they could if they packaged such products on their own. Hence the products can confer important benefits, but at the concomitant cost of complexity and potential opaqueness.

On the one hand, there may be little cause for concern about the protection of retail investors. Although structured products are likely to be too complex for the average investor to understand, as one commentator points out, "How many people understand the intricacies of insurance accounting?"[28] Yet they still are able to purchase insurance. On the other hand, the past two decades have witnessed a dramatic disintermediation of the financial markets, with retail investors increasingly holding financial assets directly or through mutual funds. In particular, structured products are typically not fungible, which makes it very difficult to comparison shop. To the extent this trend continues, the ability of investors either to rely on the advice of brokers or financial advisers or to discern the risks and rewards of investments directly is increasingly important. Here we discuss several possible avenues that might help mitigate the problem.

If one wants to reduce the risk of holding inappropriate structured products for those retail investors who do not rely on the advice of a broker or financial adviser, rethinking what it means to be an accredited investor might be one obvious way to go. Under the current regulatory regime, one can easily think of any

28. Tony Tassell, "On London: Retail Investors Join the City Revolution," FT.com, August 11, 2006.

number of occupations that might allow someone to meet the definition of an accredited investor but that might not prepare the person to appreciate the intricacies of the payments, fees, and risks of structured products. Different criteria could be crafted that would vary depending on the type of investment vehicle that an investor wants to purchase or whether the investor has a financial adviser providing advice. Indeed, as will be discussed in more detail later, the FSA's proposed regulatory regime depends on the type of product, more specifically its riskiness, that an individual is purchasing. To the extent that structured products are privately placed, tightening the definition of accredited investor would preclude certain retail investors who currently qualify as accredited investors from purchasing structured products (ignoring for the moment the possibility of Rule 144 resales). On the one hand, sales to these investors may be inappropriate. On the other hand, these investors would no longer have access to what are potentially important and desirable products. This outcome is a real cost that should not be underestimated. The FSA in crafting its regulatory regime has appropriately emphasized the legitimate and important role that structured products can play in investors' portfolios.

On a related note, the SEC in the past has required firms to issue securities in minimum denominations to be granted regulatory relief from the Securities Act of 1933 so as to increase the likelihood that securities remain in the hands of financially sophisticated investors. For example, firms selling securities pursuant to an offering based on Rule 144A/Exxon Capital were required to denominate securities in increments of $100,000. Similarly, the SEC permitted monthly income preferred securities (MIPS) to be eligible for Exxon Capital treatment if they were tailored for financially sophisticated investors:

—specifically, if the securities were to be issued in denominations of $1,000 (rather than $25 or $50, which was standard for retail products),

—if the securities paid interest semiannually (rather than quarterly, which again was standard for retail MIPS), and

—if the securities were not listed on an exchange.[29]

Before the *Ralston Purina* decision, one of the major facts, emphasized in a well-known opinion by the general counsel of the SEC, in deciding whether an issuance was a public offering and hence had to be registered was the denomination amount. Similar types of criteria might be appropriate for structured products.

For investors who are accredited and for brokers and financial advisers who offer assessments of whether particular structured products are appropriate for clients, enhanced access to information about private placements might enhance

---

29. SEC No-Action Letter 2/97.

investor protection. To this end, the SEC or an industry association might consider creating a web-based repository for offering memoranda of structured product deals to facilitate the transfer of information about offerings. Because this repository would contain documents relating to private placements, access to documents of restricted securities would need to be limited to accredited investors and qualified institutional buyers. Once securities were no longer restricted, access to those specific documents could be opened more broadly. The benefits of the system would hopefully mirror those provided by EDGAR (Electronic Data Gathering, Analysis, and Retrieval), the SEC's web-based system that automates the collection and dissemination of the financial data that public companies and their affiliated executives and officers are required to file with the SEC. By making information "available to investors via the Internet within 78 seconds of receipt, Edgar gives investors a foundation for making more informed decisions."[30] It would allow parties in both the primary and secondary markets to access detailed information on current and prior deals, information that is now largely in the domain of large investment companies and pension fund managers. Creating a repository of such documents would allow investors to compare the features and fees of products.

Improving the disclosure in both offering memoranda and prospectuses of structured product deals might also enhance investor protection. In particular, two types of disclosures seem particularly important in this regard. First, investors are likely to benefit from a clear presentation of the embedded as well as explicit fees being charged for products, much as is now required in Regulation AB offerings with respect to fees that come out of the cash flow generated by the underlying assets. Second, investors need to understand that a security's credit rating does not reflect the riskiness of its cash flows. Improved understanding of the true cost of a structured product and avoidance of the common confusion that a credit rating speaks to a product's risk would represent substantial progress. More generally, the SEC might consider establishing a fast-track review process for registered structured products for issuers committed to improving disclosure. The staff might then issue best practice guidelines to help other issuers improve their disclosure. In 1996 the SEC established a pilot program for public companies willing to file plain English documents under either the Securities Act of 1933 or the Securities Exchange Act of 1934. To compensate these issuers for being early adopters of plain English, the staff accelerated the review process. From those experiences, the industry was able to learn from the early adopters, who effectively created templates that lowered the

---

30. Megan Santosus, "Securities and Exchange Commission: Full Disclosure," CIO.com, February 1, 2003.

Box 6-3. *Performance of One Up-MACRO Holding or Tradeable Share under Various Scenarios*

The prospectus includes 15 tables that illustrate the performance of one Up-MACRO holding or tradeable share under various scenarios based on different assumptions about the level of the light sweet crude oil price and the yield on the treasuries in the paired holding trusts.

Scenarios:

1. Price increases and interest rates rise.
2. Price increases and interest rates fall.
3. Price increases and interest rates remain constant.
4. Price decreases and interest rates rise.
5. Price decreases and interest rates fall.
6. Price decreases and interest rates remain constant.
7. Price is volatile with no net approximate change and interest rates rise.
8. Price is volatile with no net approximate change and interest rates fall.
9. Price is volatile with no net approximate change and interest rates remain constant.
10. Price is volatile with a net decrease and interest rates increase.
11. Price is volatile with a net decrease and interest rates decrease.
12. Price is volatile with a net decrease and interest rates remain constant.
13. Price is volatile with a net increase and interest rates increase.
14. Price is volatile with a net increase and interest rates decrease.
15. Price is volatile with a net increase and interest rates remain constant.

Source: www.sec.gov/Archives/edgar/data/1290059/000134100406000428/ny1073541-14.txt.

cost for followers. To understand how the disclosure for structured products might be improved, one can look to the disclosure being developed for MACRO securities (MACROs) offered by MACRO Securities Depositor, a security designed for retail investors.[31] The payments to investors from these bonds are linked to two underlying assets, and the SEC's staff has worked to have the issuer incorporate scenario analyses into its disclosure. An example of some of the disclosures for MACROs is provided in box 6-3. As the box also demonstrates, however, enhanced disclosure is unlikely to be a substitute for honest financial advice for most retail investors, given the complexity of many structured products. As a result, there is much to be said for suitability requirements.

The above solutions are based on the notion of restricted access to structured products because of their registered or unregistered status and the classification of investors (private versus public market) and on enhancement of the quality of and access to information in the market. The hope is that if these mechanisms are implemented the securities that might dribble into the public market after their

31. See "MacroShares," MacroMarkets LLC (macromarkets.com/macro_securities/).

restricted period lapses, per Rule 144, would have a better chance of ending up in the hands of investors who understand and are suited to a particular product. An alternate regime, and one that is being considered by the FSA in London, is a protection regime aimed at the retail investor based instead on the characteristics of the product.[32] The core idea for the framework is that the level of regulatory protection for investors should be based on the product's risk more than on the regulatory classification of the security or its manner of sale. The FSA has created a designation called "wider range" products, a name that captures the notion that such a security is structured so that its range of possible payouts and terminal values is large relative to more conventional bonds. For example, a principal protected bond whose maturity is not too long is a good candidate for a structured product that may be broadly held. However, if the principal is not protected and the range of outcomes is very broad, the product is likely to be much more risky, and a higher level of investor protection may be required. Examples of such protection might include enhanced disclosure, special point-of-sale information, or the required participation of a registered financial adviser. Of course, such a determination of whether a product is wwider range, by definition, is a subjective judgment. This structure is also reflected in the European Union's new Markets in Financial Instruments Directive (MIFID) due to come into effect in Europe in April 2007.

Notable in the FSA's regulatory framework is the recognition up front of two risks: misselling by sellers and misbuying by investors on the one hand and the opportunity cost suffered by investors who do not get access to such products because of regulatory restrictions on the other. These two risks are weighted nearly equally in the FSA's discussion paper. This approach contrasts sharply with the SEC's approach, which usually weights investor protection far more heavily that it does opportunity costs.

It is appropriate to make two final closing comments. First, we should address the role of efficient markets with respect to complex financial products. Efficient markets will guarantee that structured product securities are appropriately priced, given all available public information. To the extent that the characteristics of a security in question are public information and are accurately and completely described and that markets are liquid, then the price at which the securities are traded will be "fair." One problem with the secondary markets for structured products is that liquidity is often limited even for listed products. In addition, this mechanism solves only a portion of the problem we discussed above. The concern is not just fair pricing, though that is important, but it is also the appropriateness of the fees and the riskiness of investments for retail investors. An unwitting

---

32. "Wider-Range Retail Investment Products," FSA Discussion Paper 05/3, June 2005.

investor may buy and hold a fairly priced risky security and suffer harm in the process. Efficient pricing does not ameliorate the problems of high fees or unsuitability of the riskiness of the investment for particular investors.

Second, a number of commentators have argued that one need not be too concerned about investor protection, because financial services firms have incentives to adequately advise investors so as to protect their own reputations. Although we believe a number of firms do take the protection of their reputations seriously, anecdotal evidence strongly suggests that it is not a panacea. Herding behavior on the part of banks to supply structured products combined with the demand for such products by retail investors can lead to situations that may endanger the regulatory goal we stated in the beginning. We continue to believe that investors are unlikely to fully understand the cost of structured products and their cash flow risk. The challenge remains in finding an investor protection regime in which investors can accrue the benefits afforded by structured products without their protection being compromised.

Conclusions

Several possible regulatory approaches are possible to ensure investor protection:
   —rethinking requirements as to who is eligible to purchase structured products, such as tightening the definition of which individuals will be deemed to be accredited investors;
   —structuring the distribution of these products, such as selling in large denominations or enhanced suitability requirements, to reduce the probability that investors hold inappropriate structured products; and
   —improving disclosure of and access to information by requiring the disclosure of embedded and explicit fees, developing a web-based repository of offering memoranda, and encouraging the adoption of best practices in the disclosure arena.

As discussed earlier, any regulatory approach must consider the costs of restricting investor access, perhaps even inadvertently, to structured products, which can be valuable. Caution also needs to be exercised if disclosure standards are raised—increasing mandated disclosure may drive securities into the private markets. Although only financially sophisticated buyers will then be able to purchase the securities in initial placements, these securities will become available for purchase by less financially sophisticated buyers once they are no longer restricted. At that point in time, there will be little or no disclosure available.

It is promising that the Structured Products Association has created an informal working group to focus on developing best practices for the industry. The group is considering two projects: developing a program to further investor education on structured products and simplifying product categories for individual purchasers of structured products. As part of this effort, the group might also consider creating guidelines for the marketing and distribution of structured products. Industry self-regulation can serve as a valuable complement to other initiatives.

In short, these issues are likely to become only more important as the structured products industry grows, innovation continues, and retail investors become increasingly interested in this asset class. The key is to try to find solutions to the challenges presented by structured products before investors learn the hard way.

TODD J. BROMS
GARY L. GASTINEAU

7

The Development of Improved Exchange-Traded Funds in the United States

MANY OF MANKIND'S great ideas owe at least some of their success to serendipity. A popular legend suggests how serendipity helped mankind learn the usefulness of fire. When one of our ancestors came upon the site of a fire that had been started by lightning, this early human discovered that an animal's carcass had been burned by the fire. The "cooked" meat tasted better than raw meat. This kind of serendipity has been a common theme in many of mankind's innovations.

The Introduction of ETFs—Something to Trade on the American Stock Exchange

One of the best examples of serendipity in the financial markets—from several angles—is the early development of exchange-traded funds (ETFs). In attributing some features of exchange-traded funds to serendipity, we certainly do not mean to minimize the role of the developers of the early versions of these funds. They deserve full credit for the wisdom they displayed in designing the ETFs introduced in Canada and the United States. Our focus is on the interaction of serendipity and financial engineering in the development of some important elements of the structure of exchange-traded funds. Some key features became part of the ETF almost by accident, but they are so important that they serve as the basis for revolutionary financial engineering to reshape the U.S. fund industry.

We have described the early history of ETFs elsewhere, so this description will be brief.[1] The first viable open-end exchange-traded fund was developed in Canada and began trading in 1989 as the Toronto Stock Exchange Index Participations (TIPs). It took four more years for the American Stock Exchange to launch the SPDR, the first open-end ETF in the United States.

The American Stock Exchange (AMEX) has always operated in the shadow of other markets, principally the New York Stock Exchange. The original name for the American Stock Exchange was the New York Curb Exchange. The name comes from the fact that the exchange's early traders made informal markets standing on the sidewalk and in the street at the corner of Broad Street and Exchange Place outside the New York Stock Exchange. That corner is now occupied by a security guard's station for the New York Stock Exchange, a very different kind of security activity. "The curbstone brokers were always the have-nots, excluded from the privileges and information of the formal exchanges, but instrumental in forcing the evolution of efficient markets as the system moved from auction to pits to specialist to computers and continuous markets."[2]

After it moved indoors in 1921, the AMEX grew and sometimes prospered by developing and embracing new products to trade. By far, the most significant and most successful of the products introduced to U.S. investors by the AMEX is the exchange-traded fund.

The labels *exchange-traded fund* and *ETF* are applied to a number of financial instruments. The fact that investors can trade most of the products called ETFs throughout the day at market-determined prices that are very close to the intraday value of an underlying portfolio or index is one common feature of these securities. To the best of our knowledge, the term exchange-traded fund was first used by Nuveen Investments to refer to its closed-end funds a number of years before the S&P 500 SPDR appeared in the United States in 1993. Many so-called ETFs are not funds or even investment companies—as defined by the Investment Company Act of 1940. The ETF label has been attached to some open-end structured notes and to a number of trust products including HOLDRs and various instruments based on currencies and commodities. Vanguard offers classes of exchange-traded shares of a number of its mutual funds. Vanguard calls these shares ETFs, but these share classes do not have some important features that characterize the ETFs descended from the original SPDR.

The open-end ETFs based on the SPDR model have a number of specific features that will be fundamental characteristics of a new generation of funds. These

---

1. See Gastineau (2001, 2002c, pp. 31–54).
2. See the chapter "The Kerb (1921)" in Sharp (1989, pp. 193–96).

open-end ETFs do not have shareholder accounting expenses at the fund level, and they have few embedded marketing expenses. These expense-saving features and the fact that the fund shares are traded like stocks often make ETFs more costly to buy and sell but nearly always less costly to hold than comparable mutual funds. Some early investors in ETFs were attracted by the fact that the ETFs were low-cost index funds. However, today's index funds—ETFs and mutual funds—are not always the low-cost portfolios their owners expect.[3] It is also noteworthy that investors and the financial advisers who serve them have developed a number of ways to use ETFs with customized fee structures that meet both the investor's and the adviser's needs.

We want to focus on two important characteristics of the SPDR-style ETF that were, in some respects, serendipitous. These characteristics have helped attract investors, and they have been important in the early success of ETFs. These characteristics also provide a basis for growth in the SPDR-style ETF model well beyond its impressive beginnings. Not everyone attaches as much significance as we do to these two features, but we are convinced that they hold the key to development of better funds. The two features of existing ETFs that we emphasize are shareholder protection and tax efficiency.

Shareholder Protection

To illustrate the value of shareholder protection, we call your attention to two figures. Figure 7-1 shows how mutual funds were priced for sales and redemptions before 1968. The figure shows the pattern of fund intraday values during market trading hours for three consecutive trading days. At the end of each day, a mutual fund calculates its net asset value (NAV) per share. Before 1968, the price at which investors invested in the shares of a fund or redeemed their shares was the net asset value *as of the previous day's close.*[4] In figure 7-1, the fund publishes its net asset value at the end of Day 1. Before 1968, that net asset value was the basis for fund share transactions until the following day's market close—and the calculation of a new net asset value. Clearly, buying shares of the fund at Day 1's net asset value as the market rose on Day 2 was a great opportunity for trading profit—and for abuse of the fund's established shareholders by opportunistic investors. Correspondingly, if someone wanted to redeem shares in the fund, they would know from the intraday behavior of market indexes on Day 2 that they could redeem at a higher fund share

3. We will have more to say about index fund problems later.

4. The material described in this and the next few paragraphs is widely known but is not frequently discussed. A recent comprehensive description of mutual fund pricing over the years is available in Swensen (2005, chapter 9, pp. 270–94).

Figure 7-1. *Pre-1968 Buying and Selling of Mutual Fund Shares at Yesterday's Net Asset Value*

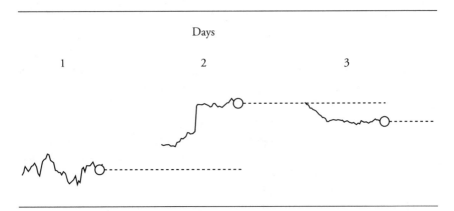

price by waiting until after the determination of net asset value on Day 2. As it became clear that the market was going to close lower on Day 3, redeeming fund shares at the net asset value from Day 2 would have seemed like a better idea than waiting for calculation of Day 3's lower net asset value. It would also be clear on Day 3 that the price of buying shares would be lower if the purchase was deferred until Day 4. Backward pricing led to a lot of abuses by dealers and by traders who could avoid the fund sales charges that were common in that period.

In 1968 the rules changed. The Securities and Exchange Commission (SEC) implemented Rule 22(c)(1), which required fund share transactions to be priced at the net asset value *next determined* by the fund. This meant that anyone entering an order after the close of business on Day 1 would purchase or sell fund shares at the net asset value determined at the close on Day 2. Correspondingly, someone entering an order to purchase or sell shares after the close on Day 2 would be accommodated at the net asset value determined at the close on Day 3. This process is illustrated in figure 7-2.

Although any mutual fund share *trader* might have preferred the pre-1968 system, most *investors* would agree that the basic idea behind Rule 22(c)(1) was a sound one. Allowing traders to decide today to buy or sell shares at yesterday's price is unfair to long-term investors in the fund's shares. However, there is still a transaction fairness problem for fund investors with Rule 22(c)(1) in place. That problem is illustrated in figure 7-3.[5]

---

5. Figures 7-3 and 7-4 and parts of the text are based on Broms and Gastineau (2006).

Figure 7-2. *Post-1968 Buying and Selling of Mutual Fund Shares at the Net Asset Value Next Determined*

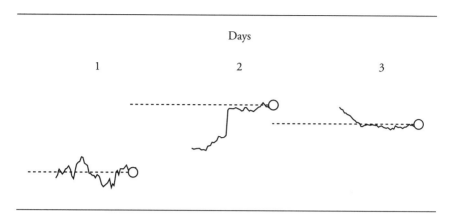

By pricing all transactions in the mutual fund's shares *at the net asset value next determined,* as required by Rule 22(c)1, the fund still provides free liquidity to investors entering and leaving the fund. All the shareholders in the fund pay the cost of providing this liquidity. As figure 7-3 shows, anyone purchasing mutual fund shares for cash gets a share of the securities positions already held by the fund and priced at net asset value. The new investor typically pays no transaction costs. Furthermore, all the shareholders of the fund share the transaction costs associated with investing the new investor's cash in portfolio securities. Similarly, when an investor departs the mutual fund, that investor receives cash equal to the net asset value of the shares when the NAV is next calculated. All the shareholders in the

Figure 7-3. *Cash Moves In and Out of a Mutual Fund: The Fund Trades Securities to Invest Incoming Cash or to Raise Cash for Redemptions*[a]

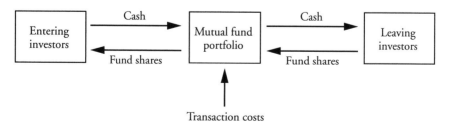

a. Share purchases and redemptions are priced at the next net asset value calculated by the fund.

Figure 7-4. *ETF Creation and Redemption is In-Kind: Transaction Costs
Are Paid by Entering and Leaving Investors*[a]

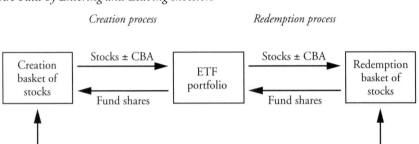

CBA = cash balancing amount; ETF = exchange-traded fund.
a. All securities transfers are priced at net asset value.

fund bear the cost of selling portfolio securities to provide this liquidity. To the
entering or leaving shareholder, liquidity is essentially free. To the ongoing shareholders of the fund, the liquidity given transacting shareholders is costly. Over
time, the cost of providing this free liquidity to entering and leaving shareholders
is a perennial drag on the fund's performance. We will discuss the size of this long-
term drag on performance in a few moments.

Figure 7-4 shows that exchange-traded funds work differently than mutual
funds. For exchange-traded funds, creations and redemptions of ETF shares are
typically made *in kind*. Baskets of portfolio securities are deposited with the fund
in exchange for fund shares in a creation. In a redemption, fund shares are turned
into the fund in exchange for a basket of portfolio securities. The creating or
redeeming investor—in most cases, a market maker in the ETF shares—is
responsible for the costs of investing in the portfolio securities for deposit and the
cost of disposing of portfolio securities received in the redemption of outstanding
fund shares.[6] The market maker expects to pass these transaction costs on to
investors when trading fund shares on the exchange. The cost of entering and
leaving a fund varies, depending on the level of trading activity of fund shares and
the nature of the securities in the fund's portfolio. For example, the cost of trading in small-cap stocks can be much greater than the cost of trading in large-cap
stocks.

6. The market makers even pay a modest fee for creation or redemption transactions to cover the
fund's administrative expenses.

ETFs are different from mutual funds in the way they accommodate shareholder entry and exit in at least two ways. The trading costs associated with ETF shareholder entry and exit are ultimately borne by the entering and exiting investors, not by the fund. Furthermore, unlike a mutual fund, an exchange-traded fund does not have to hold cash balances to provide for cash redemptions. An ETF can stay fully invested at all times. As a result of these differences, the performance experienced by ongoing shareholders in an ETF should, over time, handily surpass the performance experienced by ongoing shareholders of a conventional mutual fund using the same investment process. Ironically, even though the exchange-traded fund was designed to be traded throughout the trading day on an exchange, it is a much better product than a conventional fund for the shareholder *who does not want to trade*. As any market timer will tell you, a mutual fund is a better product to trade than an ETF because the mutual fund pays the timer's trading costs.

The conventional mutual fund structure that provides this free liquidity to investors who enter and leave the fund is behind the problems of late trading and market timing, which provoked the mutual fund scandals of 2003 and 2004. The SEC has spent a great deal of time and effort trying to deal with the problem of market timing trades in mutual funds without eliminating the free liquidity that ongoing shareholders in mutual funds give entering and leaving shareholders. A variety of operational patches have been made by some fund companies as they attempt to restrict market timing trades. The SEC is in the middle of implementing a complex and costly reporting structure with nearly mandatory redemption fees on mutual fund purchases that are closed out within a week. In the final analysis, the elimination of free liquidity—most easily through the in-kind creation and redemption process of the exchange-traded fund—is the only way to eliminate market timing without imposing unnecessary costs on all fund investors. Even if there is no such thing as a market timer in the future, long-term investors will fare better in funds that protect them from the costs of other investors entering and leaving the fund.

Tax Efficiency

One of the most frequently discussed advantages of exchange-traded funds is tax efficiency. Tax efficiency benefits some taxable investors profoundly, but it has value to tax-exempt investors as well. The tax efficiency of ETFs is essentially tax-deferral until the investor chooses to sell the fund shares. This deferral is a natural result of Subchapter M of the Internal Revenue Code that permits fund share in-kind redemptions (delivering portfolio securities to departing fund shareholders) without tax impact inside the fund. An in-kind redemption does not give rise to a distributable capital gain for shareholders of the fund.[7]

This kind of tax efficiency benefits tax-exempt investors because it prevents the buildup of unrealized gains inside an ETF. The buildup of unrealized gains in a mutual fund portfolio can lead to portfolio management decisions that adversely affect tax-exempt shareholders. When the choice facing a portfolio manager is to realize gains on appreciated portfolio securities and distribute taxable capital gains to the fund's shareholders or to hold overvalued securities and avoid realizing capital gains, the portfolio manager faces a conflict between the interests of tax-exempt and taxable investors.

The back story on the change of managers at Fidelity's Magellan Fund on October 31, 2005, and the results of that change illustrate the problems a mutual fund can have in dealing with the conflicting interests of tax-exempt and taxable investors. The change of Magellan managers led to the realization of substantial embedded capital gains that had given the fund a very large capital gains "overhang." The new Magellan manager realized capital gains, dramatically changed the composition of the portfolio, achieved good near-term performance, and distributed a mammoth capital gain that will be taxable to Magellan's taxable shareholders in 2006.[8] Although this policy change was certainly the best choice open to the new manager of Magellan, the situation illustrates the inherent portfolio management conflict between taxable and tax-exempt investors in mutual funds.

Magellan had performed poorly for a number of years before 2005, partly because its managers had been reluctant to sell low-cost portfolio securities. Portfolio managers of conventional mutual funds often defer transactions that would improve pretax performance because they do not want to trigger the distribution of taxable capital gains. The conflict of interest between taxable and tax-exempt investors—inevitable in a conventional mutual fund—disappears in an ETF.

---

7. For more details on ETF tax efficiency, see Gastineau (2005, chapter 3, pp. 39–66).

8. The Halloween date of the change in Magellan's manager was no coincidence. The timing of the manager change announcement made it clear to anyone familiar with mutual fund tax rules that dramatic portfolio changes were coming. Under mutual fund tax rules, gains realized in the last two months of the calendar year do not affect investors' tax returns for that year. The tax impact of portfolio changes made at Magellan during the last two months of 2005 would not affect investors' tax returns until 2006. Rather than wait until the end of 2006, Magellan distributed capital gains equal to about 19 percent of the fund's assets to its shareholders in May. Some aspects of the impact of this distribution are described in Eleanor Laise, "A Surprise Hit for Small Investors," *Wall Street Journal*, August 24, 2006, pp. D1, D5.

With exchange-traded funds, the decision to change the portfolio can be based solely on investment considerations, not on the tax basis of portfolio securities.

The conflict between taxable and tax-exempt shareholders disappears because the achievement of tax efficiency in ETFs is largely a matter of careful designation of tax lots so that the lowest cost lots of a security are distributed in kind in redemptions and high cost lots are sold to realize losses in the fund when a sale is necessary or appropriate.

Exchange-traded funds grow by exchanging new fund shares for portfolio securities deposited with the fund. Redemptions are also largely in-kind. Investors sell their fund shares on the exchange. Dealers buy the fund shares and turn them in to the fund in exchange for portfolio securities. This process serendipitously lets ETF managers take full advantage of the redemption in-kind provision of the Internal Revenue Code. The early developers of exchange-traded funds were aware of this tax treatment, but the tax efficiency it gives ETFs was by no means a significant objective in the early development of exchange-traded funds. It is largely serendipitous that most well-managed exchange-traded funds will never distribute taxable capital gains to their shareholders. In-kind creation and redemption not only transfers the cost of entering and leaving the fund to the entering and leaving shareholders. It also defers capital gains taxes until a shareholder chooses to sell the fund shares.[9]

The in-kind creation and redemption of exchange-traded fund shares is a simple, nondiscriminatory way to allocate the costs of entry and exit of fund shareholders appropriately and to solve the portfolio manager's conflict of interest between taxable and tax-exempt shareholders. This in-kind ETF creation-redemption process is an efficient, even elegant, solution to several of the obvious problems that continue to plague the mutual fund industry. A growing number of fund industry experts believe that the exchange-traded fund structure should replace conventional mutual funds. To make that happen, however, the serendipity of early ETF development needs to be harnessed through creative financial engineering to overcome weaknesses in the index ETF structure and to extend the best ETF features to a wider range of portfolios.

---

9. It is interesting that tax efficiency helps encourage shareholder loyalty to an ETF. An investor in a mutual fund will usually receive taxable gains distributions that increase the investor's basis as the value of his or her fund shares increases over time. When the investor sells the mutual fund shares, the higher basis reduces the capital gains tax on the sale. An investor in an ETF should never get a capital gains distribution. Consequently, the basis of the fund shares will stay at the investor's original cost. The tax due on sale of the ETF shares will tend to be greater than the tax due on an otherwise comparable mutual fund position. An investor with both mutual funds and ETFs will defer taxes by selling the mutual fund shares first when the investor needs money for living expenses. Hence, the ETF shareholder will be a more loyal shareholder simply because the shareholder wants to minimize and continue to defer his tax liability.

Improving ETFs

Understanding how effective and efficient ETFs can be requires us to examine a few features of an improved ETF model that builds on the strengths and overcomes the weaknesses of today's ETFs. ETF weaknesses are less egregious and more easily overcome than are some of the weaknesses of today's mutual funds. ETF weaknesses are weaknesses that can be eliminated. With SEC approval of a few modifications, a new breed of ETF can deliver marked improvements over the current model—and even more dramatic improvements over mutual funds. The 2003–04 scandals of mutual fund market timing mandate that all fund share transactions be consistent with the ETF model, wherein entering and departing shareholders pay the costs of their entry and exit. The great shareholder protection advantage that ETFs have over conventional mutual funds can provide more robust shareholder protection than is possible with the mutual fund model after any possible reform of mutual funds.

It is time to look at some new ETF features that will improve performance. If any fund is going to serve the interests of its shareholders, the portfolio manager needs to implement portfolio changes without revealing the fund's ongoing trading plans. Whether a fund is attempting to replicate an index or to follow an active portfolio selection or allocation process, portfolio composition changes cannot be made efficiently if the market knows what changes a fund will make in its portfolio before the fund completes its trades. A number of recent studies have highlighted a problem with changing an index composition that many of indexing's strong supporters have been aware of for some time: Benchmark indexes like the S&P 500 and the Russell 2000 do not make efficient portfolio templates. Investors in index funds based on popular, transparent indexes are disadvantaged by the fact that anyone who cares will know what changes the fund must make before the fund's portfolio manager can make them.[10] When transparency means that someone can earn an arbitrage profit by front running a fund's trades, transparency is not desirable.

The cost to ongoing shareholders of preannounced composition changes in the portfolios of index ETFs must be eliminated. The best way to improve index fund performance is to use *Silent Indexes*, indexes that keep portfolio composition changes confidential until after the fund has traded. This requires radically new procedures for the management of indexes and the management of some index

---

10. This problem is discussed at length in Chen, Noronha, and Singal (2006) and Gastineau (2002a; 2002b; 2002c, pp. 127–76; 2005, pp. 115–52).

funds. A similar procedure will be used for actively managed exchange-traded funds. Everyone seems to agree that actively managed funds require confidential treatment of portfolio composition changes until after the fund has traded. Only recently have investors begun to understand the costs that index transparency imposes on index fund investors. Making portfolio changes confidential and efficient requires changes in the ETF structure and the portfolio trading process.

Intraday trading in ETFs is useful to some investors. However, market makers and other large traders may have an intraday trading advantage over individual investors who are less able to monitor market activity and intraday fund price and value relationships. To state this problem in another way, there is asymmetry in the amount and kind of information available to large traders on the one hand and small investors on the other hand.

Many individual investors have a stake in being able to make small, periodic purchases or sales in their fund share accounts. The prototypical investor of this type is the 401(k) investor who invests a small amount in his defined contribution retirement plan every payroll period. The mutual fund industry has developed an elaborate framework that permits small orders for a large number of investors to be aggregated and for cash to enter or leave the fund to accommodate a large number of small investors at net asset value. There are ways to modify ETF procedures so that these investors, while paying a little more than they have paid in the past to cover the transaction costs of their entry and exit, will still be accommodated at low cost. The snowballing rush to greater transparency in the economics of defined contribution accounts like 401(k) plans will make fund cost and performance comparisons easier—to the advantage of ETFs.

ETF and Mutual Fund Economics

Table 7-1 provides an economic comparison of ETFs and mutual funds with the advantages of the ETF cost structure measured in terms of improved investment performance for fund shareholders. In the first column, the particular ETF advantage is shown first. The information in parentheses in that column is our estimate of the range of improved annual investment performance a long-term shareholder will enjoy, using an ETF rather than a mutual fund. As these numbers indicate, the advantage of an ETF over a comparable mutual fund can vary over a wide range in some instances.

In column two we list some problems with today's ETF structure, and column three notes the solutions that we propose for implementation in a new generation of ETFs. In a few cases (such as the need for more efficient indexes), the Silent

Table 7-1. *Using Exchange-Traded Funds to Deliver Better Investor Performance*

ETF advantages	Possible ETF problems	Solutions
Shareholder protection: (less than 0.1 to greater than 5.0 percent)	Uncertain transaction costs fairness of execution	New trading process improves on basic ETF shareholder protection
Lower operating costs and cost transparency: (0 to 0.35 percent)	Under the alternative minimum tax (AMT) embedded costs cover fees	New fund delivery structures
Capital gains tax efficiency: (0 to 2.5 percent)	None	None needed
Taxable–tax-exempt conflict: (0 to 1.0 percent)	None	None needed
Indexing: (Equal)	Inefficient indexes: The more popular the index, the greater the performance drag from index transparency	Silent indexes as portfolio templates
Active management: (Equal)	Confidentiality in portfolio changes is essential	Same portfolio disclosure as mutual funds

Index solution is equally applicable to conventional mutual funds that follow an indexing strategy. It is not in any fund investor's interest to pay significant transaction costs that the fund incurs because changes in its index are transparent.

Each of the features we propose for new ETFs merits at least a brief discussion. The first ETF advantage reflects the value of shareholder protection from the cost of investors entering and leaving a fund as we discussed in connection with figures 7-3 and 7-4. The return comparison in parentheses reflects the allocation of all entry and exit costs to entering and leaving shareholders. In an ETF transaction, a shareholder pays only the cost of his own entry into and exit from the fund. The mutual fund shareholder pays a pro rata share of the entry and exit costs of all fund buyers and sellers for as long as the shareholder owns the fund.

There has been only one appropriately designed study of the shareholder performance cost of the flow of cash into and out of mutual funds. In a study published in 1999, Roger Edelen, then a professor at the Wharton School of the University of Pennsylvania, measured the cost of flow for a sample of 166 equity and hybrid mutual funds using data from 1985 through 1990.[11] He calculated the

11. Edelen (1999). For a more detailed discussion of this paper, see Gastineau (2004).

cost of flow in terms of its adverse effect on fund shareholder performance at 143 basis points per year in the average fund in his sample. The shareholder turnover in the sampled funds was low enough that it is clear that market timing and late trading was not a significant factor in the cost of flow to these funds' shareholders. Shareholder turnover in most large mutual funds is lower today than it was in Edelen's sample from fifteen to twenty years ago. Some transaction costs associated with accommodating flow are also probably lower today. If the cost of flow for the average mutual fund investor (not the average mutual fund) is 1 percent per year for the $5 trillion equity fund market in the United States, this represents a performance loss to investors of $50 billion per year. If the cost is as low as 0.5 percent per year, the cost to investors is still $25 billion per year. This lost performance dwarfs the costs attributable to mutual fund market timing on any reasonable assumption.

Note the wide range we use for the cost of flow (less than 0.1 percent to more than 5.0 percent per year) in table 7-1. The less than one-tenth of 1 percent number is probably representative of some very large mutual funds with very low shareholder turnover. The more than 5 percent annual cost figure applies to some small and small-cap funds with high shareholder turnover. Clearly, the cost of accommodating market timers and late traders in some funds implicated in the 2003–04 scandals was well in excess of 5 percent per year.[12] There is at least some cost disadvantage to a mutual fund's ongoing shareholders relative to an ETF when there is *any* flow.

The only "problem" that limits the ability of ETFs to deliver this degree of shareholder protection is that the true transaction costs associated with buying and selling shares of an ETF can be difficult for an investor to determine in advance of trading. The information available to investors on intraday values of an ETF is not as good or as readily available as it should be. Calculations of intraday fund portfolio values are made and disseminated, but many investors—including some institutional and semi-institutional investors—do not have easy access to the every fifteen-second proxy calculations of net asset value for existing

---

12. The analyses made in connection with financial settlements paid by parties associated with the 2003–04 market timing scandals reveal that market timing was practiced by many fund share traders who did not have formal or informal arrangements with fund managers or distributors. In at least one case, "non-arrangement timing" accounted for more shareholder costs than arrangement timing. Furthermore, these analyses document some of the trading and dilution costs Edelen found in connection with ordinary fund share purchases and redemption transactions. See Shefali Anand, "Little Guys Were Market-Timing Funds, Too," *Wall Street Journal*, August 25, 2006, pp. C1, C9; U.S. Securities and Exchange Commission (2005), especially sections III–V. One of the most comprehensive discussions of the impact any purchase or sale of mutual fund shares has on the broadly defined transaction costs, opportunity costs, and dilution experienced by ongoing fund shareholders is in Green and Ciccotello (2004).

ETFs. Furthermore, these NAV proxy calculations, particularly those for funds that hold a significant number of illiquid or foreign securities, do not always give a meaningful intraday value for the fund. Although the ETF structure eliminates the need for fair value pricing, the limited availability and methodology for calculating intraday NAV proxy values can make ETF execution costs uncertain and, in some instances, can increase these costs.

Our proposed solution to this problem is a new trading process that increases the transparency of ETF transaction costs and, consequently, improves the ETF structural shareholder protection without compromising the ETF gold standard whereby investors entering and leaving the fund pay the costs of their entry and exit.

The second advantage of exchange-traded funds is that they frequently offer lower operating costs and greater cost transparency than conventional mutual funds. Some of the reduction in operating costs and increase in cost transparency are associated with the elimination of costs associated with shareholder accounting at the fund level. Some of these shareholder accounting costs still have to be borne by someone. They may be charged to investors by the financial intermediary that provides fund share transaction and custody services to the investor. In addition, sales and advisory charges are paid outside the fund by ETF investors who use those services.

Unbundling costs can create a problem for taxable investors—particularly for investors subject to the alternative minimum tax (AMT). The embedded costs of mutual funds, because they are taken out before the fund's income distributions are made, are deducted from the income that taxable investors receive. A separately billed advisory fee is usually not fully deductible and may not be deductible at all to an investor who falls under the alternative minimum tax regime. There can be significant advantages for many taxable investors to embed advisory and administrative costs and sales charges into the financial instrument rather than to have them billed as separate fees. The solution is a variety of new fund delivery structures that provide tax efficiency by reembedding some of the costs that have been taken out of exchange-traded funds.

Capital gains tax deferral and elimination of the taxable–tax-exempt conflict of interest are unmitigated gains for all ETF investors. There are no problems that we are aware of in realizing these advantages, so no solution is necessary. These important gains flow to ETF investors automatically.

With respect to the last two issues listed in table 7-1, performance penalties associated with transparency in indexing and the need for confidentiality of an active manager's trading activity, the solutions for the two fund structures are essentially identical: eliminate portfolio trading transparency. All index funds should be based on efficient indexes. There are some very efficient published indexes available today. An outstanding example of an efficient broad market index is the Dow Jones Wilshire 5000.[13] Some inherently inefficient indexes are used for such a small asset pool that scalpers who know what the ETF has to do to match the published composition changes in its index are not likely to increase the fund's transaction costs materially by front running the fund's portfolio manager.[14] Nonetheless, there is no reason why the index templates for most index funds should not be Silent Indexes. All investors should have the opportunity to buy index funds based on Silent Indexes to protect themselves from the cost of index composition front running trades.

In most discussions of actively managed ETFs, there has been appropriate concern expressed for the cost of achieving enough portfolio transparency to facilitate trading in ETFs without subjecting the fund's trades to the front running risk that all of today's index funds experience. The SEC's Concept Release on actively managed ETFs stressed the importance of finding a solution to this problem.[15] We believe—and we can document this—that the manager of an actively managed ETF needs to offer no more information on his portfolio composition and portfolio changes than the manager of a conventional mutual fund must publish today. Funds that do not require the full measure of confidentiality available under today's rules for fund asset disclosure can reduce transaction costs for their entering and leaving shareholders and market makers by providing more frequent disclosure.[16] But more frequent disclosure is not essential. An investment process that requires the maximum permitted portfolio confidentiality can work well inside an actively managed ETF.

Conclusion

Fund issuers can build on the compelling advantages of exchange-traded funds to offer better and more varied portfolios. New actively managed and Silent Index funds can offer the shareholder the protection from the cost of entry and exit by other fund shareholders and the tax efficiency that are inherent in the initial generation of SPDR-style exchange-traded funds. We propose a new ETF structure and an improved trading mechanism for investors who buy and sell

13. See Gastineau (2006).

14. If one of these funds grows in response to a spate of fortuitous index changes, the manager may face the same front running problems that S&P 500 and Russell 2000 index fund managers experience regularly.

15. U.S. Securities and Exchange Commission (2001).

16. Many funds already publish their portfolios more frequently or with a shorter lag than required by the SEC or both.

ETF shares. The new ETFs will offer alternative fund delivery structures and systems. Transparent index funds will be challenged by Silent Index funds, which will provide improved performance as a result of lower transaction costs in the fund. Actively managed ETFs will feature flexibility in portfolio disclosure to permit the fund manager to determine the degree of transparency that is appropriate for a specific fund.

In expressing confidence in the desirability—and the inevitability—of the improved exchange-traded funds we describe, we are well aware of the obstacles facing innovators in the financial services industry. John Y. Campbell, in his presidential address to the American Finance Association earlier this year, addressed this issue:

> I suggest that retail financial innovation is slowed by the cost of advertising and educating households, together with the weakness of patent protection for financial products. . . . I . . . speculate that the existence of naive households permits an equilibrium . . . in which confusing financial products generate a cross-subsidy from naive to sophisticated households, and in which no market participant has an incentive to eliminate this cross-subsidy. . . . It may be difficult for new investment products to gain acceptance if sophisticated households, who are the natural early adopters, must give up the benefit of a cross-subsidy when they move from an existing product to a new one.[17]

Campbell raises some important concerns, but there is every reason to believe that this innovation will succeed. Mutual funds subsidize the *fund share trading costs* of short-term investors (market timers and all other mutual fund share traders), small investors (young investors and others with few assets), and investors who invest small amounts periodically (largely owners of 401(k) plans and similar defined contribution retirement accounts). These trading cost subsidies come at the expense of some of the most "sophisticated households" that hold mutual fund shares as long-term investments. The regulatory interest in thwarting mutual fund timers and traders is well known. Small investors and 401(k) contributors tend to be long-term investors. They will pay a transaction cost to buy and sell ETF shares, but new delivery mechanisms should minimize this cost and clarify the total ETF cost and performance advantage. We believe the incentives for all long-term investors and regulators to embrace this new ETF fund structure are compelling.

17. Campbell (2006).

References

Broms, Todd J., and Gary L. Gastineau. 2006. "Exchange-Traded Funds: A Market-Based Solution to Mutual Fund Regulation." Paper presented at the conference "Competition for Mutual Funds from New Collective Investment Vehicles" at the American Enterprise Institute, Washington, April 26.

Campbell, John Y. 2006. "Household Finance." *Journal of Finance* 61, no. 4 (August): 1553–604.

Chen, Honghui, Gregory Noronha, and Vijay Singal. 2006. "Index Changes and Losses to Index Fund Investors." *Financial Analysts Journal* 62, no. 4 (July–August): 31–47.

Edelen, Roger M. 1999. "Investor Flows and the Assessed Performance of Open-End Mutual Funds. "*Journal of Financial Economics* 53, no. 3 (September): 439–66.

Gastineau, Gary L. 2001. "ETFs: An Introduction." *Journal of Portfolio Management* (Spring): 88–96.

———. 2002a. "Equity Index Funds Have Lost Their Way." *Journal of Portfolio Management* (Winter): 55–64.

———. 2002b. "Silence is Golden." *Journal of Indexes* (Second Quarter): 8–13.

———. 2002c. *The Exchange-Traded Funds Manual*. New York: John Wiley & Sons.

———. 2004. "Protecting Fund Shareholders from Costly Share Trading." *Financial Analysts Journal* 60, no. 3 (May-June): 22–32.

———. 2005. *Someone Will Make Money on Your Funds, Why Not You? A Better Way to Select Mutual and Exchange-Traded Funds*. New York: John Wiley & Sons.

———. 2006. "The Best Index for the Thoughtful Indexer." In *A Guide to Exchange-Traded Funds and Indexing Innovations*, edited by Brian R. Bruce, pp. 99–104. New York: Institutional Investor.

Green, Jason T., and Conrad S. Ciccotello. 2004. "Mutual Fund Dilution from Market Timing Trades." Social Science Research Network (September 27) (http://ssrn.com/abstract= 596482).

Sharp, Robert M. 1989. *The Lore and Legends of Wall Street*. Homewood, Ill.: Dow Jones–Irwin.

Swensen, David F. 2005. *Unconventional Success: A Fundamental Approach to Personal Investment*. New York: Free Press.

U.S. Securities and Exchange Commission. 2001. "SEC Concept Release: Actively Managed Exchange-Traded Funds Concept Release." Release no. IC-25258, File no. S7-20-01 (Washington: SEC, 17 CFR Part 270, November 8) (www.sec.gov/rules/concept/ic-25258.htm).

———. 2005. "Columbia Management Advisors, Inc. and Columbia Funds Distributor, Inc." File no. 3-11814 (February 9) (www.sec.gov/divisions/enforce/claims/columbia manage.htm).

COMMENT ON CHAPTERS 6 AND 7 BY

Kenneth E. Scott

Sᴉɴᴄᴇ ɪ ᴀᴍ addressing two papers with distinct concerns, I will take them up in the order presented. Fortunately, my brief does not extend to the Japanese securities market experience, about which I learned a great deal, indeed all I know, during this conference.

Structured Products

The paper by Jennifer E. Bethel and Allen Ferrell opens with a critique of the current SEC and NASD investor protection rules as they apply to structured products, by which they mean basically complex derivatives, with limited or no secondary markets. Typically, these products have a set level of income or growth over a certain period, with a range of outcomes for return of capital. The authors view many of these products as too complex for most retail investors to understand, even if the investor is "well-to-do" (or accredited), but these products are increasingly being marketed to the retail market.

The relevant SEC rules for registered offerings of structured products are a set of specialized rules in Regulation AB (17 CFR §229.1100-1123) for required disclosures relating to certain securities backed by an asset pool (asset-backed securities or ABSs) and the general rules under the Securities Act of 1933 for public offerings, which now permit greater use of free writing communications in addition to (but not inconsistent with) the statutory prospectus to sell the products. The main objection that Bethel and Ferrell raise to this regime is that the required disclosures, while useful, are far from sufficient to apprise retail investors of the risks involved, and the free writing prospectus is not constrained to give an overall "balanced" picture of the advantages and disadvantages of the particular product.

Perhaps these shortcomings are remedied by the NASD rules to which selling brokers are subject? Rule 2210(d) requires that all public communications must be "fair and balanced," without misleading material omissions; defects are not cured by information found in some other communication. And Rule 2310 provides that the broker, before recommending a security, must have reasonable grounds to believe that it is "suitable" for the customer in light of the customer's financial situation and other security holdings. In addition, to accept even an unsolicited order for "new financial products," the broker must "make every effort to make customers aware of the pertinent information regarding the products."[1]

Putting it all together:

—The selling broker is supposed to understand the payoff structure of the products; however, the products are sufficiently complex that, while the issuer or underwriter may have that understanding, few registered reps are likely to possess such an understanding.

—The purchaser is supposed to get all the necessary information but probably is incapable of understanding it, since the analysis may require advanced mathematical skills.

—There is legal liability for known material misstatements or omissions in the required disclosures, but not for their incomprehensibility.

That is a powerful and persuasive indictment of our current small investor protection regime, at least on the legal level. But it could also be applied to securities markets in general. Stocks are no doubt much more familiar instruments than the new high-tech structured products. But does the retail investor really understand the operations and business risks of the firms—many of them complex combinations of many inputs to produce a variety of goods and services—in which he or she invests? As provided by the Securities Act of 1933, the prospectus, if the investor gets one, provides a lot of descriptive and historical financial information. But does that enable the investor to become a securities analyst, project future cash flows, choose the appropriate risk discount, and determine an approximate present value for the company and its shares?

---

1. NASD Rule IM-2310-2(e): "Fair Dealing with Customers with Regard to Derivative Products or New Financial Products."

The primary protection for small investors is found in an efficient market. All the SEC disclosure apparatus is of value to, and processed by, professionals—analysts at investment banks and institutional investors—and those are the ones for whom the SEC disclosure rules and reporting requirements should be designed. As the structured products business grows with retiring baby boomers, in my view an important part of the question is to what extent there will or can be an active secondary market for at least some core products. Is there an analogy to the distinction between listed and OTC derivatives, and is that a valid analogy?

Assuming, I hope pessimistically, the absence of a significant active market, what is to be done? Bethel and Ferrell state that their policy goal is "the design of a regulatory regime that *prevents* investors from unknowingly holding inappropriate structured products in their investment portfolios" [emphasis added], and would leave it "up to regulators to balance the costs and the benefits" of the chosen scheme. That is a most demanding policy goal, to begin with, and I would fear that leaving it to regulators to strike the balance contains a strong bias toward risk avoidance over retirement benefits. Regulators, after all, share through criticism the risks that are realized but do not share in benefits achieved.

Bethel and Ferrell give us essentially two types of approaches to the problem: screen eligible investors, and screen eligible investments. Concerning investors, the authors urge rethinking of a "financial sophistication" test. They point out that the current standard of a net worth over $1 million for someone to be considered an accredited investor is hardly a good way to measure financial sophistication.[2] Neither is raising it. Net worth is relevant to capability to bear downside risk, which varies across instruments, and therefore is one part of a "suitability" determination. Financial sophistication per se is probably impractical as a screening criterion, and many of the investors who could benefit most from structured retirement products are almost certainly unsophisticated by any measure.

The second approach is to screen investments eligible for sale to retail investors. There are several ways to do that. One would be to look at the risk characteristics of the security. Bethel and Ferrell offer the proposal of the U.K. Financial Services Authority to impose different restrictions on "wider range investments"—products exhibiting a high degree of volatility, illiquidity, or complexity. The proposal itself recognized that the definitional difficulty would be severe, and the FSA has now abandoned it.[3]

Another approach to screening investments would be to look at the manner of sale and distinguish between registered and unregistered offerings, since only the

2. See the definition of an *accredited investor* under Rule 501(a) of the Securities Act of 1933.
3. "Wider-Range Retail Investment Products: Consumer Protection in a Rapidly Changing World—Feedback on DP05/3," Feedback Statement 06/3 (FSA, March 2006).

former can be widely sold to the public. But that brings us back to the limitations of the SEC prospectus model, on the one hand, and the limitations of the accredited investor model on the other. Bethel and Ferrell also suggest possibly requiring certain securities (the definitional problem again) to be sold only in high minimum denominations, which is a round-about way of imposing an imprecise net worth test.

Yet another approach would be to recognize that there is of necessity an interaction among the investor's characteristics (sophistication, if any, and loss-bearing capacity) and those of the security (volatility—both downside risk and upside return, illiquidity) in a (one would hope) diversified portfolio. No bright line rule can capture all the permutations. Basically, this is a suitability determination, and if the security is too complex for the investor to make that judgment, where does one go? One can try to educate the investor to be better able to make the analysis (which I view as worthy but not overly promising), or one can rely more on a professional gatekeeper (registered broker, registered financial analyst, certified financial planner) to make the recommendation or decision.

The suitability standard for broker recommendations now found in NASD Rule 2310 could be made clearer and more demanding. It is at present only a high-level standard, partially implemented by only a few more specific rules. Admittedly, it would be hard to write detailed rules to cover such a wide variety of circumstances as are posed by ever-evolving products and different customers. But in the common law world, very general terms and standards are refined over time through case-by-case adjudications. In the securities world, however, customer contracts call for disputes to go to arbitration, and the arbitration rules do not provide for reasoned written opinions explaining the award outcomes.[4] The NASD could change this, and in my view it would be helpful to investor protection if it did.

Exchange-Traded Funds

The paper by Todd J. Broms and Gary L. Gastineau has two components: the case for index ETFs being superior to index mutual funds, and thoughts for further improvement of ETFs. My comments will be brief, since I agree with most of what they have to say—which is a bad position for a commentator to find himself in.

The source for the claims of ETF superiority lies in the distinction between portfolio trades and shareholder investment trades. In mutual funds, the shareholder deals with the fund, so purchases and redemptions result in cash flows (and portfolio transactions) in and out of the fund itself. In ETFs, the shareholder deals

---

4. For disclosure in arbitration awards, see NASD Rules 10214 and 10330.

with market makers who manage their inventory by in-kind basket transactions with the fund. This process transfers portfolio trading costs and shareholder accounting costs out of the fund and to the market makers or account brokers. Those costs do not disappear, but they are ultimately borne by the shareholders who occasion them, rather than by all shareholders through the fund. In general, eliminating cross-subsidization promotes efficiency, but of course, those who no longer receive the subsidy (for example, market timers or day traders) will complain. They do not have my sympathy.

ETFs can claim some additional advantages. Index tracking requires less management time and talent, and thus management fees are lower. Lower portfolio turnover means less realization of capital gains, promoting tax efficiency (though not to the extent achievable by separately managed accounts). Market timing in the sense of information arbitrage could be reduced by the trading in ETF shares throughout the day, thereby sending a signal to the sponsor that its net asset value (NAV) calculation is inaccurate, but I am unclear as to how effectively that in fact takes place. A better solution to the stale price arbitrage encountered by mutual funds, which was brought to the public's attention by New York state attorney general Spitzer in 2003, would be to amend SEC Rule 22(c)(1) to provide for $T+1$ pricing, but the SEC seems enamored of the more cumbersome and costly apparatus of redemption fees, fair values, and intermediary account reporting.[5]

So on balance, I think Broms and Gastineau make their case that index ETFs have the edge over index mutual funds. An open question remains as to the role of all index vehicles when it comes to corporate governance. In the United States, at least, index mutual funds (and pension fund equivalents) have started to play a more active, and potentially constructive, role, but I am not aware that the ETFs have begun to follow suit.

The second part of the Broms and Gastineau paper deals with extending and improving the ETF model. In particular, they point out that tracking publicly published indexes, which are changed or rebalanced periodically by notice in advance, creates an opportunity for profitable front running of fund purchases and sales. To counteract this, they urge the adoption (by mutual funds as well as ETFs) of what they not too descriptively call a *Silent Index*—that is, an unpublicized fund rule or algorithm that it will reconstitute its portfolio at some distance from the index change date. That would of course also create a period of tracking error, together with a possible mechanism for fund managers to indulge in mar-

5. A transaction entered on day T would be executed at the net asset value (NAV) determined on day $T + 1$.

ket bets during the window. But Broms and Gastineau suggest it could add 100 basis points or more to annual returns, which is quite substantial.

And for a really improved model, they offer the actively managed ETF. (I think what that would improve the most would be the management fee, but that shows my bias in favor of true index funds.) To avoid front running, the manager's portfolio shifts (which could be numerous) would not be announced in advance. How this significant diminution in portfolio transparency would interact with the basket creation–redemption mechanism, which keeps the share trading price in line with fund NAV, is an important question that the paper does not undertake to discuss. But if we stop with true index funds, I find their arguments quite persuasive.

Contributors

Jennifer E. Bethel
Babson College

Thomas Boulton
Indiana University
 Kelley School of Business

Todd J. Broms
Managed ETFs

Franklin R. Edwards
Columbia Business School

Allen Ferrell
Harvard Law School

Yasuyuki Fuchita
Nomura Institute of Capital
 Markets Research, Tokyo

Gary L. Gastineau
Managed ETFs

Kenneth Lehn
University of Pittsburgh
 Katz Graduate School of Business

Robert E. Litan
Kauffman Foundation
 and Brookings Institution

Frank Partnoy
University of San Diego School of Law

Adam S. Posen
Peterson Institute for International
 Economics

Kenneth E. Scott
Stanford Law School

Steven Segal
Boston University
 School of Management

Yuta Seki
Nomura Institute of Capital
 Markets Research, New York

Randall Thomas
Vanderbilt University Law School

Index

Brookings Institution

The Brookings Institution is a private nonprofit organization devoted to research, education, and publication on important issues of domestic and foreign policy. Its principal purpose is to bring the highest quality independent research and analysis to bear on current and emerging policy problems. The Institution was founded on December 8, 1927, to merge the activities of the Institute for Government Research, founded in 1916, the Institute of Economics, founded in 1922, and the Robert Brookings Graduate School of Economics and Government, founded in 1924. Interpretations or conclusions in Brookings publications should be understood to be solely those of the authors.

Nomura Institute of Capital Markets Research

Established in April 2004 as a subsidiary of Nomura Holdings, Nomura Institute of Capital Markets Research (NICMR) offers original, neutral studies of Japanese and Western financial markets and policy proposals aimed at establishing a market-structured financial system in Japan and contributing to the healthy development of capital markets in China and other emerging markets. NICMR disseminates its research among Nomura Group companies and to a wider audience through regular publications in English and Japanese.

Tokyo Club Foundation for Global Studies

The Tokyo Club Foundation for Global Studies was established by Nomura Securities Co., Ltd., in 1987 as a nonprofit organization for promoting studies in the management of the global economy. It sponsors research, symposiums, and publications on global economic issues. The Tokyo Club has developed a network of institutions from Europe, the United States, and Asia that assists in organizing specific research programs and identifying appropriate expertise. In recent years, the research agenda has strongly focused on emerging trends in global capital markets as well as current issues in macro-economic stability and growth. Information about past and future programs may be viewed on the Foundation's website, www.tcf.or.jp/.